3.99

DICK CROSSMAN

A Portrait

DICK CROSSMAN

A Portrait

Tam Dalyell

Weidenfeld and Nicolson
LONDON

Contents

CONTENTS

Preface

I would like to thank Anne Crossman for many kindnesses during the ten years I stayed at 9 Vincent Square while the House of Commons was sitting.

Many people have been generous with their time in giving me information on points of fact and recollections. But I would particularly like to thank Sir Isaiah Berlin and Mrs Mary Bennett for giving me insights into Crossman's life before I knew him. The scholarly staff at the House of Commons Library have been unfailingly helpful.

I would also like to thank David Roberts, publisher at Weidenfeld, and Dan Millar, editor.

Finally, without my wife Kathleen's clear memories and judgements, this book would not have been possible.

T.D.

Illustration Acknowledgements

The photographs in this book have been reproduced by kind permission of the following:

Coventry Evening Telegraph 7 above, 8; *Hulton-Deutsch* 1 above, 2 below right, 3 above: *Mansell Collection* 2 below left; *The Warden and Scholars of New College, Oxford* 2 above; *Sport and General Press Agency* 3 below, 5, 6, 7, below; *Syndication International* 4; *The Warden and Scholars of Winchester College* 1 below.

Chronology

1907	Born
1919	Winchester College
1925	New College, Oxford
1930–37	Fellow and Tutor, New College, Oxford
1932	Married Erika Landau (divorced circa 1938)
1934–40	Leader, Labour Group, Oxford City Council
1937	Labour candidate, West Birmingham by-election (lost) Published *Plato Today* (2nd ed. 1959)
1938–40	Lecturer for Oxford Delegacy for Extra-Mural Studies and Workers' Educational Association
1938–55	Assistant Editor, *New Statesman*
1939	Married Inezita ('Zita') Davis (ex Mrs John Baker) (died 1952)
1941	Head of German Section, Political Warfare Executive (PWE)
1943	Deputy Director, Psychological Warfare, Allied Forces Headquarters (AFH), Algiers
1944–5	Assistant Chief, Psychological Warfare, Supreme Headquarters Allied Expeditionary Force (SHAEF), based in London
1945–74	Labour MP, Coventry East
1946	Anglo-American Palestine Commission
1952–67	Member, National Executive Committee (NEC), Labour Party

1954   Married Anne McDougall (children: Patrick, 1957–75; Virginia, born 1959)
1955–9   Columnist, *Daily Mirror*
1964 (Oct)–1966 (Aug)   Minister of Housing and Local Government
1966 (Aug)–1968 (Oct)   Lord President of the Council
1966 (Aug)–1968 (Apr)   Leader of the House of Commons
1968 (Apr–Oct)   Organized merger of Dept of Health and Dept of Social Security
1968 (Nov)–1970 (June)   Secretary of State, Dept of Health and Social Security (DHSS)
1970–72   Editor, *New Statesman*
1972–4   Engaged in preparing first two volumes of Diaries for publication
1974   Died 5 April
1975   *Diaries of a Cabinet Minister*, vol. 1
1976   *Diaries of a Cabinet Minister*, vol. 2
1977   *Diaries of a Cabinet Minister*, vol. 3
1981   *Backbench Diaries 1951–64*

As the table above indicates, Dick Crossman in the course of a turbulent life had some rather contrasting incarnations: Crossman, the precocious and iconoclastic Wykehamist; Crossman, New College undergraduate and don, whose lectures attracted the largest audiences in the Oxford of the early 1930s; Crossman the apostate, 1937–40, who left Oxford for WEA lecturing, journalism, and Labour candidatures; Crossman, the local government Opposition Leader in Oxford of the late 1930s; Crossman, the psychological warrior 1940–45; Crossman, the rebellious MP, 1945–52; Crossman, combining the uneasy persona of the National Executive Committee member of the Labour Party and popular journalism, 1952–64; Crossman, the Cabinet Minister who most commentators thought would be the first to resign or be sacked, lasting six years, 1964–70, as a senior Minister of the Crown; Crossman, the most informative political diarist since Samuel Pepys or John Evelyn; Crossman, unsuccessful editor, 1970–72, of the *New Statesman*, at the fag-end of his life; Crossman, farmer; Crossman, family man; and Crossman, enhancer of the lives of all around him.

Introduction

In April 1988, George Weidenfeld asked me to do a book on Dick Crossman. Rather peremptorily I declined. An active Member of Parliament has a busy enough life; besides I had just written for Hamish Hamilton a serious book about the misbehaviour to Parliament of Mrs Thatcher. I was also reluctant at this stage to resurrect in print a highly personal relationship. And, to be truthful, I was and am nervous about what certain people, above all Anne and Virginia Crossman, and such as James Callaghan, Michael Foot, Denis Healey, Elwyn Jones, Ian Mikardo, who worked with him, and who knew Crossman extremely well, might think. I cannot disguise that the opinion of the cognoscenti matters to me.

In June 1988, George Weidenfeld asked me and I declined. But he is a persistent peer and at the third time of asking I succumbed. It was partly that George Weidenfeld himself was one of Crossman's few real personal friends and a man he deeply admired.

I confess something else happened in July 1988 to make me change my mind. I got round to reading an account of a seminar held some twelve months earlier on Crossman and his *Diaries*. I had myself been invited to the seminar, but was unable to participate because it took place when my mind was focused entirely on the 1987 general election. Many of the criticisms made were justified and perceptive; but others, in my view, were not. I was stung by several criticisms which I consider quite unjust, emanating from men who had not cared for what they saw in print about themselves in the posthumously published Crossman *Diaries*. I believe the dead have rights; and one of these rights is, where

1

possible, the right of fair treatment by posterity and certainly by their friends. Those of us who remain have obligations to the dead. I was annoyed by derogatory, denigratory and in my view unjustified comment, coming close to a genteel and sophisticated slur. I admit there is an element of tit-for-tat in the genesis of this book.

I do not claim this is a rounded portrait of Crossman. Anthony Howard is doing that, and if his book on R. A. Butler is anything to go by, he will do it very well indeed. Rather, it represents the retrospective thoughts and perceptions of an eye-witness to the last eleven years of Crossman's life.

There was another self-evident consideration. If I were to talk to major persons or influences in Crossman's life, I'd better not procrastinate. Though I have copious notes of my own about what contemporaries such as George Brown, Ray Gunter, Frank Cousins, J. D. Bernal and Patrick Blackett have said about Crossman to me, it would have been helpful to have been able to talk to them again. And one vital witness and chief of dramatis personae, who is alive, is medically no longer in a position to reiterate his side of the story.

But others in their seventh, eighth or ninth decade are blessed with undiminished vigour. If I were to write about Crossman, and get the advantage of their view of him and of events, I had to beware of the proverb One of these days is none of these days!

The condition for talking to me imposed by several of my friends and senior colleagues was couched in these general terms: 'I will talk to you, Tam, provided you write about Dick warts and all. I liked Dick very much, the world was a more interesting place with him around, but for pity's sake I will not help a hagiographer. Dick Crossman was no angel.' It is necessary to explain to the reader why parliamentary friends of a quarter of a century might have suspected me of hagiographic tendencies.

In the 1960s, things were rather different from the present time, when Shadow Ministers have offices and the so-called 'Short' money pays for their advisers. Shadow Ministers were then pretty naked and had to do their own delving. When Crossman was appointed a Shadow Minister in 1963, he wanted a friend and sidekick, as James Callaghan, the Shadow Chancellor, had the young Merlyn Rees, and George Brown had Bill Rodgers. Crossman alighted on me, the wags had it, because an Old Wykehamist would bloody well choose an Old Etonian, but actually because I had very unusually at that time been putting down parliamentary questions on science policy, and science was in his port-folio. Briefly, I was potentially useful to him in the area he least knew about. I became secretary of the Labour Party Standing Conference on the Sciences, and my wife Kathleen and I did a lot of the sheer day-to-day work in organizing the thirty-four Two-Way-Traffic in Ideas Conferences, which helped create the climate for the 'White Heat of the Technological Revolution' and Labour victory in 1964. For reasons of his convenience and mine, I stayed with him and Anne Crossman in Vincent Square when I was in London during the parliamentary week, until after he died.

How on earth did you stick him? Or, more comradely, how on earth did you two stick each other for eleven years? (Or, most comradely of all, how the hell did Crossman stick you for eleven years?) These are questions which have been put to me, time and again, by parliamentary colleagues well disposed to us.

For Isaiah Berlin, the Oxford philosopher, who owed his first post at New College to Crossman, and was friendly towards him, lasting eleven years was a matter of 'wonderment'.

How then did the relationship survive so long? I was totally loyal to him. He knew that I worked hard and diligently, though he thought I could be politically reckless. On various occasions I embarrassed him with his Cabinet colleagues and the Prime Minister. For example, Harold Wilson was very angry indeed that I got myself in front of the Commons Privileges Committee for giving unpublished printed minutes of the select committee on Science and Technology visit to the Chemical and Biological Warfare (CBW) Research Centre at Porton to the *Observer* in 1967. Crossman pointed out that I knew from my own knowledge that there were no technical secrets in what had been said to the select committee, and though I was in the wrong, the House of Commons had made a meal of it, because they did not like my awkward questions on the Borneo War, East-of-Suez costs, and Anglo-French variable geometry aircraft, the proposed staging-post at Aldabra Atoll, and much else. Crossman gave me an almighty rocket in private, but told the Prime Minister that he should calm down, and that he would not sack me. (Possibly another element in the situation was that Michael Foot, Eric Heffer, Ian Mikardo and other members of the Left thought that in substance my anxieties about chemical weapons and Porton were correct, and said so. But the fact is that in the face of the Prime Minister, Crossman was loyal to me, and refused to get rid of me.)

3

My and his problem was that a number of extremely important personages in the Government, like James Callaghan and Denis Healey, thought that my endless parliamentary activity in the most controversial areas of defence and foreign policy represented what Crossman really believed. Yet, truth to tell, however sympathetic, he was not the instigator and could truthfully excuse himself by saying, 'I can't and don't control Tam Dalyell in these matters.' Come to think of it, my behaviour for a thirty- to thirty-five-year-old backbencher was a bit *de trop*. I wonder that would happen to a junior Tory who told Mrs Thatcher, as I told Harold Wilson, that he had been taken for a ride by Lee Kuan Yew, when in the Prime Minister's room in the House he asked me if I thought I was a better democratic socialist than 'the most gifted alumnus of your university [Cambridge]'. Or had shouting matches with the Foreign Secretary (George Brown, who in his day could be incomparable). Or was told by James Callaghan as Chancellor in his room that I was a 'chump' for going round every one of Harold Wilson's Cabinet by appointment, complaining about the Borneo War. No one was more spitting with rage at me than Barbara Castle or more embarrassed than Tony Greenwood when I sailed along to them as ministers, told them how they had influenced my generation from the platform of the Movement for Colonial Freedom, and quizzed them about their acquiescence in East-of-Suez policy. The only Cabinet minister who was not annoyed was Frank Cousins; and he was the one Cabinet minister who was not brought up in the etiquette, hierarchies and niceties of Parliament. (After an outburst against some campaigning activity of mine by Willie Ross, the dour Scottish Secretary, Crossman said, 'Well, I hand it to you, your capacity to annoy your colleagues surpasses my own.')

Annoy his colleagues, Crossman certainly did – and often mightily. And yet forgiveness was almost always forthcoming, and instantly. The reason? Simply that he was fascinating company. I saw – and the *Diaries* reveal – that James Callaghan, who had every reason to be offended when he was Chancellor and when he was Home Secretary, would sidle over to Crossman with some sardonic, half-humorous, wholly barbed remark, and enjoy a ten-minute chat, as a result of which he looked as if he felt cheered up. Crossman not only looked as if he was but actually was interested in the problems of other ministers, and expressed his views on those problems. That the view might have changed a few hours later was immaterial to the honesty with which it was expressed at the time. Lady Spearman told me that Crossman's pair, the distinguished Conservative MP, Sir Alec Spearman, senior partner of Griegson/Grant (now Kleinwort Benson), used to defend Crossman by saying his mind worked seventeen times quicker than anyone else's that he had met.

He was also a bringer-out of the cleverest of his colleagues. Never will I forget an evening when Anne Crossman, Kathleen and I were invited by Susan and Tony Crosland to their house. Crosland wanted to pick Crossman's brains on education, when he had just been made Secretary of State. As a clarifier of other clever men's thought, Crossman was a unique, if relentless and uncomfortable interrogator. Scrutiny for its own sake may sometimes have been carried to excess. Like a character from Shakespeare, he had an experiencing nature.

I suppose that the relationship lasted so long because we were both, in our own rather different ways, and could afford to be, issue politicians.

ONE
Father and Son

In the spring of 1963, Harold Wilson appointed Dick Crossman as the Labour party spokesman for science. The previous spokesman was Dick Mitchison, QC, MP, the brother-in-law of ex-Communist geneticist J.B.S. Haldane, and father of two Fellows of the Royal Society. Mitchison invited me to be the main speaker at the Corby May Day rally in his constituency. As we were travelling up in the car together, Mitchison repeated, 'To begin to understand Dick Crossman, you have got to understand his bizarre relationship with his father. I knew Mr Justice Crossman well. He was a considerable person.' From his obituary in *The Times*, from my lawyer colleagues in Parliament like the late Lord Silkin, who appeared before him, I do not doubt that Mr Justice Crossman was formidable. The picture drawn for me, however, of Charles Stafford Crossman by his younger son was altogether different and it is Dick Crossman's own perception of his father rather than the reality which matters.

His earliest memory of his father was at the assembly of the household at 7.55 a.m. precisely, for morning prayers. Mr Justice Crossman sat at one end of the breakfast table and Mrs Crossman at the other. The children were ranged on their special little chairs in front of the fire. At this point the bell was rung and, Crossman recollected, the maids and nurses solemnly filed into their places with their backs to the windows. Attending morning prayers before breakfast and changing into evening dress for dinner were practices Mr Justice Crossman required of his family until the day he died.

Crossman used to reflect that he and his father were deeply incompatible. It was the best, not the worst, in each of them which the other found unbearable. C. S. Crossman, through the eyes of his younger son, lived a life within the confines of the law, which turned a natural caution into a conformity so intense that he was scared in the end of any kind of moral or intellectual innovation. In his own case the turbulent rough-house of academic politics, parliamentary politics, political journalism had enlarged the priceless bump of irreverence inherited from his mother. Probably it was his father's style of life that nurtured the conditions for rebellion. 'In a country,' he used to say, 'where free thought and free action are almost smothered under sheer respectability, is not my most useful contribution to public life to expose the cowardice of conformity, wherever I find it, and challenge the organised hypocrisy of the Establishment?' This accounted for much of the Don-Quixote – not quite quixotic, for there is a distinction – behaviour of his academic, didactic and political life. Don Quixote was a description which he himself first assumed, not one initially ascribed to him by others.

On one occasion, I told him I was shocked at how spiteful Crossman was towards his father's memory. As a doting father himself, did he begin to understand the simple pain that he must have inflicted on the wretched Mr Justice Crossman? The reply was uncharacteristically gentle and subdued. Now, that he could see him more clearly, and look more dispassionately on the values that divided them, he no longer felt any remorse about the pain he had inflicted on his father. In his own fifties, Crossman surmised that for his father, no less than himself, the conflict between them was a fight that simply had to be fought out. He used to tell me that neither his father nor himself could have maintained their self-respect or lived life to the full without the break that severed the ties of father and son, and turned them into amicable strangers.

C. S. Crossman was a judge of the Court of Chancery, a dry calling among dry callings. Crossman's mental picture of him was in his heavy robes, leaning forward and looking at him apprehensively from under his wig. He confessed this was a fictitious memory. The reality was that shortly before his father became a judge, Crossman had broken with his family. Not once did he ever bother to visit his father's court during the sixteen years that he served on the bench. Curiously, it was the official court photograph of Mr Justice Crossman, peering at him with eyes uncannily akin to his own, that he remembered. He claimed never to have seen his father in full court wig and robes.

Neither the camera nor the fictitious memory was deceptive. As an overworked and underpaid junior counsel, Crossman believed, his father had become the very paradigm (a favourite word) of the judicial mind long before he earned the place on the bench accorded, by custom, to any Attorney-General's 'devil' who is not killed by the job. Crossman used to say, with a tinge of pity, that in contrast to so many other King's Counsels of the day, his father did not require consciously to put advocacy aside and assume judicial detachment when he sat down on the bench to try his first case. For the status and outward forms which C.S. Crossman acquired on that day pefectly expressed the attitude of the inner man. The chemistry of this attitude was scrupulous attention to precedent, the learning of an arid scholar, the passion of a pedant for precision, the strange mixture of unworldly innocence and worldly wisdom, of gentleness and harshness that distinguishes a mind dedicated for a lifetime to the English law of property.

In the very week in 1964 that I became his Parliamentary Private Secretary in the Ministry of Housing, I vividly recollect Crossman's disdain for a draft letter I had submitted for despatch on his behalf to a Party colleague. 'Whoever taught you any Classics?' Stung to reply, I referred to Sir Frank (F. E.) Adcock, editor of the *Cambridge Ancient History* and by repute the most intuitively gifted of all wartime code decrypters at Bletchley. Adcock! A man in my father's mould. He was a lawyer who loved the law as an ancient historian loves his period of Roman history, or an archaeologist his site. Proposals to reform the law of property in England seemed as vulgarian to his father as the notion of pulling down Westminster Abbey in order to put a more practical church in its place. One of the many arcane difficulties between Cross-man and his father was that the man who was to write *Plato Today* (and was in later life to tell James Callaghan all about Aristides the Just) was a Greekist by temperament and nature. Mr Justice Crossman belonged to Imperial Rome.

Despite this veneration for the law, Mr Justice Crossman was haunted by the fear that one of his children could get trapped into a legal action. Here his caution became an obsession. Crossman recalled how when he and one of his sisters, Mary or Bridget, returned from a party in their teens, the Judge would lie awake half the night, fearful lest he or his brother Geoffrey might be involved in a breach of promise action, or that a sister might become pregnant. His attitude was just as suspicious whenever one of the outer family came – as they not infrequently did – for free legal advice. C.S. Crossman would always help in the drafting of documents, and then warn against legal action. To his children Mr Justice Crossman issued a frequent warning: 'No one should go to law because he thinks that justice is on his side. We leave it to politicians and preachers to expound what is just: we are simply concerned to interpret what is the law. And anyone who fails to understand this distinction should keep clear of the courts.' My own father-in-law, Crossman's friend John Wheatley, who sat for thirty years on the Scottish bench and Appeal court, concurred. So did Crossman, other than when he thought he was certain of obtaining damages!

Crossman sensed that it was his father's fondest hope that one of his three sons would follow in his footsteps into the law. However, his older brother, Geoffrey, opted to work in the City of London. His younger brother, who was set for a legal career, joined the RAF and crashed to his death in 1940. (This was a loss about which Crossman spoke to me only once, and in the context of his philosophy of making the most of things, of going while the galloping was good, since he lived on borrowed time.)

In terms of natural gifts, as well as education at Winchester and Oxford, Crossman was almost ideally qualified to bestow on his father the blessing which he so much desired. Yet among Crossman's indelible childhood meories were the visits to, and waiting in, his father's dusty and dark chambers in Lincoln's Inn, which he came to hate. An even more potent cause for childhood resentment was the dreary drudgery and grinding work which brought his father home to Essex each night to consume his dinner in agonized silence, while he had to endure his children shouting at each other across the table. Most terrible of all, the teenage Crossman thought the law was spoiling his father as a man. No youngster can be more cruel to his parents than the Wykehamist (or Etonian) returning to the family home for the school holidays. He is often insufferable.

Mr Justice Crossman was not only a dedicated lawyer but a dedicated Old Wykehamist. Crossman, possibly on hearsay from his mother, attributed his father's entry in 1883 to College at Winchester to fiendish cramming at his prep school. The Crossmans were Founder's Kin – those who could trace their ancestry back to William of Wykeham, through the Danvers family, who coincidentally and astonishingly had connections with Prescote Manor, Cropredy, near Banbury, Crossman's beloved home of his later years. In 1695, two splendid rooms were built on to Prescote by John Danvers, who had married the rich lady of

Dauntsey in Wiltshire, from whose wool-merchant inheritance the Crossmans were to benefit. John Danvers himself was connected to William of Wykeham not only on the paternal side, but also through Ann Stradling, whom an ancestor-namesake had married in the fifteenth century.

Only those who themselves have been identified as Founder's Kin in an ancient organization can begin to know the embarrassment that such a position can cause in a youth. (I myself did national service in a regiment, the Royal Scots Greys, which an ancestor of the same name had raised in 1679.) The ability to survive embarrassments which would have daunted most men and caused them to cringe inwardly, may have originated partially in Crossman's time at Winchester, where son, like father, had the tag of Founder's Kin.

Crossman told me that he could not remember a time when he did not know that, through the Danvers connection, he was Founder's Kin at Winchester. I heard him tell John Danvers, then a BBC lobby correspondent, about his earliest Danvers memory: at the rear of the airing-cupboard in his southwest Essex childhood home at Buckhurst Hill* near Loughton, behind the kitchen there stood two ancient black boxes; one Saturday morning, when he was a seven-year-old, he was solemnly taken by his father to see these boxes. 'In these are the documents,' intoned C. S. Crossman, 'which prove you are Founder's Kin. But that is all you will ever get from the Danvers family. You will have to win a scholarship, just as I did, and that means starting early.'

In Crossman's earliest years, apart from the link with Winchester – of which he was quite inordinately proud – Mr Justice Crossman never showed much interest in the Danvers connection. Yet without it, Crossman thought, his father might well have remained all his life an unsuccessful schoolmaster. Though C.S. Crossman was one of the finest classical scholars of his year, first at Winchester, and then at New College, Oxford, his son opined that he lacked the self-confidence to enter for the All Souls fellowship which would have enabled him to fulfil his real ambition and read for the Bar. Instead, C.S. Crossman, in the disdainful phrase of his son 'sought safety' by accepting an invitation to return to Winchester and teach classics. Once there, he realized that he had difficulty with irreverent schoolboys, and that his heart was not in the job.

*Now in the northeast London borough of Waltham Forest.

Then, out of the blue, he learned to his astonishment, that a childless uncle had passed over his two older brothers and made him heir to an estate which included what was left of the Danvers portraits and silver. Overnight, C. S. Crossman had become a man of property. His new affluence enabled him not merely to survive the first briefless years in Lincoln's Inn, but also to enter society as a highly eligible bachelor. An accomplished dancer, which his son emphatically was not, he was also an asset after dinner in the drawing room upstairs, thanks to his agreeable tenor voice, in those pre-radio and TV days when people had to make their own entertainments. Slowly the briefs came: but it was the Danvers inheritance which enabled him to indulge his two great passions in life by regular visits to Bayreuth for the Wagner Festival and to the Swiss Alps for mountaineering. It was his father who introduced Dick Crossman to Wagner, for whom he too had a revealing passion. Years later, on the first day of October 1968, when the rest of us were at Blackpool for a crucial Labour Party Annual Conference, Crossman had to stop work early in London in order to be in the Royal Box at Covent Garden with Sir Claus Moser, one of the then directors of the Royal Opera House, and Lady Moser, to hear *Die Walküre*. Three nights previously, he had had four and three-quarter hours of *Götterdämmerung*, thrilled by the tigerish conducting of Sir Georg Solti. The Secretary of State for the Social Services, as Crossman had become, had taken time off to be the guest of Stanley Sadie, the music critic of *The Times*.

Indeed Crossman's addiction to grand opera was to cause me, as his Parliamentary Private Secretary, untold alarms with our government whips. For instance, on 5 March 1969 there were crucial divisions involving Labour rebellions on Healey's Defence White Paper. I knew – no other MP did – that he and Anne Crossman had given in to the temptation to attend what was likely to be Otto Klemperer's last *Fidelio* in London. He desperately wanted 'to watch this terrific classical figure, barely alive, play with the score, letting it run along under his control'. I also knew that the incomparable second act was expected to start just before the House of Commons was due to vote at 10 p.m. By 10.05 p.m. no Crossman! As the Commons attendants were about to shut the doors, this bulky, dinner-jacketed Cabinet minister elbowed his way past them to record his vote. I tried to tell him that there was a second, even more crucial vote. He says in his *Diaries* that he thought this must have been a formal division on a Tory amendment. Rubbish! I told him. The truth was that Crossman was hellbent on getting back to Covent Garden to hear Klemperer's rendering of the *Leonora No 3* overture and to savour the last scene of *Fidelio*. All hell was let loose that night. It had been remarked that Crossman was not in the lists for the second Commons division. Could this be, the BBC asked me, because he sided with the left-wing rebels in the Labour Party who had caused the vote on defence? The press were agog. I gave the impression that he was absent because he was preparing a major health-service speech. Fortunately, we were not discovered! Only grudgingly at the end of his life, did Crossman admit that his father had lit the spark of a love of opera in him.

Crossman's perception was that his mother worshipped his father. He recollected that throughout their married life, she kept him snugly wrapped in the warm blanket of her love, ministering to his needs, carrying out his instructions, and teaching her children to behave according to the standards of perfection that he set. But because, Crossman thought, she was an able, strong-willed and passionate woman, her life-long submission was punctuated by violent bouts of rebellion and contrition. These she shared with her children. After a family rumpus, she would say to Crossman and his sisters, 'You see how wrong I was to doubt his wisdom!' So it came about, Crossman told me (after he had stayed with my wife, Kathleen, and me in Scotland in 1965, and met my own Edwardian mother), that although her children loved her and hardly knew their father, they came to assume that she was in every way his inferior — intellectually, morally, and also socially. In fact, in Crossman's later, considered judgement, she was not only a finer, more generous character, but possessed just as good a brain as his father, and a great deal more courage and imagination.

Crossman was a respecter of women, wholly unpatronizing, and deeply nice to them. He was certainly much nicer to my wife than he was to me over the years. Frank Longford — Leader of the House of Lords, 1964–8 — endorses this view, with the judgement that his wife, Elizabeth, got on better with Dick Crossman than he did himself. And certainly, although they recognized his enormities and fought with him from time to time, among his most stalwart defenders were some of the remarkable ladies with whom he was to work — Barbara Castle and Evelyn Sharp, Pamela Berry, Mildred Riddelsdell, and Alma Birk. Though no women's rights campaigner, Crossman treated women properly. I suspect that this can be traced to his relationship with his mother.

She was a Howard of Ilford, Essex, the clan that produced Michael Howard, sometime Fellow of All Souls, and Chichele Professor of the History of War at Oxford. As for her ostensible social inferiority, even before the French Revolution the Howards of Ilford had established themselves as pharmaceutical chemists, noted not only for their business integrity and Quaker good works, but for an unusual strain of musical talent and scientific ability. Crossman claimed that his great-great uncle, Robert Howard, and his son, Luke, had been great apothecaries in their day, forerunners of Smith, Kline and French, Glaxo, Beecham and other great benefactor-firms for mankind. All that is certain is that Crossman, aged eight, shot an arrow through the eye of Robert Howard's portrait at Aunt Florence's Christmas party, much to the upset of both his parents.

The plain-living style of the family had prevented her from receiving any formal education. The effect of her marriage was to make her contrast her husband – in her eyes the perfect scholar and gentleman – with her own family of (to her mind) mere businessmen. Crossman did not talk much about his mother, but I was conscious that her life and experience impinged often deeply on his later life. Allow me two stories, five years apart.

In the summer of 1963, I was invited to lunch at the Athenaeum by those heavyweight Oxford professors, Sir Howard Florey and Sir Lindor Brown. Florey told me how ill at ease he thought Dick Crossman had been with them, and I responded that I thought that the only type of person to whom he felt inferior in discussion were the distinguished men of pure science. Trade union leaders, politicians, aristocrats, business tycoons, professors of the humanities were all in his circle of intimate acquaintance, but not the famous and renowned scientists. Florey replied that he was fascinated. Crossman had gone on at length about how in the northeast London suburbs, around Chigwell, Loughton and Ongar, where Buckhurst Hill is situated, they lived among the Howard clan, but were not of them. He told Florey that he and his siblings were constantly reminded by his mother of the wonderful tact and good breeding that his father displayed by treating her family as though the profession of law and the manufacture of quinine were on the same social and ethical level. It was clear to Florey that Crossman's way of telling the co-Nobel Prize winner for the discovery of penicillin that under a Labour government science would be given its proper place, was to show he thought quite as highly of his mother's antecedents, the

13

purveyors of quinine, as of lawyers.

Five years later, in July 1968, I was watching with Crossman a major programme on BBC2 about the National Health Service. It was very much in favour of the hospitals, and took a more sympathetic view of their problems than previous twentieth anniversary programmes on the NHS. However, I realized that the section on long-stay geriatric hospitals had a macabre effect on Crossman.

Viewers were shown an evening in the Cowley Road Hospital at Oxford with the young nurses giving the old people their tea, putting them on their commodes, and then into bed. It was all meant to look hopeful. But Crossman explained to me, as soon as the TV was switched off, that it reminded him of his mother, at the end of her life, sitting there in that dark room in that private nursing home. It was disgusting! In his Secretary of State's room, he said he could almost smell that same stale smell again, and feel how odious it is to grow old and die in a hospital. I have no doubt that the long-lasting controversies over Ely, South Ockendon and other mental hospitals, and Crossman's fanatically effective espousal of the cause of the mentally ill and resources for long-stay hospitals originated in his experience with his mother and a sense of guilt about her. Guilt was a powerful spur in Dick Crossman's actions.

Though his mother also had a considerable private income, both parents were determined that their children should not have more money than was good for them. And from the time that Crossman was despatched at the tender age of seven to the prep school at Buckhurst Hill, he was taught that only unhappiness could ensue from the acquisition of wealth or worldly success. Maybe it was in reaction against this early teaching that he found in his personal life such intense pleasure in earning well and spending freely, while in public life, his Socialism became based on the principle that it was power, not money, that corrupts. Poverty, Crossman believed, since it limits freedom of choice, is the prime cause of human unhappiness.

In 1966, when his own son Patrick was nine, Crossman asked my opinion about the boy's education. Though I myself was happy at Eton, I said that, apart from political embarrassment for a senior Labour Minister, it was silly to abrogate responsibility for the boy's education for thirty-seven weeks in the year, especially when Anne Crossman was such an obviously excellent mother.

Crossman, looking back, now thought that if he had failed to get into

College at Winchester, he might well have remained a contented member of his family, and even followed his father, happily and prosperously at the Chancery Bar. It was Winchester that drove Crossman and his father apart, as public-school education has so often driven a wedge between father and son.

Until 1919, when Crossman was old enough to sit for the Winchester scholarship, everything he did was, in his retrospective view, in preparation for that appointment with destiny. At the beginning of World War One, his father took on the task of teaching him Latin, and the little chair he used for morning prayers was set aside on Saturday mornings in his father's study beside the green baize table. While father worked on his briefs, Crossman learned his Latin declensions. Since he was a docile pupil, and C. S. Crossman a doting father, Crossman recalls that these were happy days. Yet herein lay the seeds of lifelong trouble for Crossman, and loads of trouble for four Labour administrations. Dick Crossman perversely came to enjoy unpopularity and the start of it was during school in World War One. Never one to hide his academic light under any bushel, Dick Crossman, without inhibition, showed off his superior knowledge of Latin. He admitted that he was 'prig enough' – his own words – to enjoy the unpopularity he earned with the rest of his family. He quite welcomed his martyrdom when this priggishness earned some mild bullying at prep school. But then he had a tough constitution and was a natural bruiser – with a mild interest in boxing, almost alone among sports. His superiority in classics, interlaced with a certain insufferable bumptiousness, created the conditions for relative isolation from the small boys. He was a bit of a loner as, years later, even the Bevanites were to find out. He overcame any problems of isolation by persuading his mother, who had developed into an aggressive Anglo-Catholic, to let him be confirmed at the age of eleven, and confess his sins to the school chaplain. Crossman recalled with a malicious glee that he had the feeling that his father, who eschewed any kind of emotional display, was as embarrassed as the school chaplain. But since his piety seemed to please his mother, he gave his sanction. Full approval was forthcoming when C. S. Crossman learned that he had earned thirteenth place in the scholarship exam for College at Winchester – mainly on account of an outstanding divinity paper.

Crossman arrived at Winchester in 1919. A generation of aesthetes and intellectuals was in revolt against the conformity and cruelty of college life, and horrified by what had happened to many of their elder

15

brothers and friends in the war at the Somme and Passchendaele. For any boy arriving at a public school (until recently when the practice of younger boys acting as servants to their seniors, known as fagging, has mostly been abolished), the nature of one's fag-master was a matter of considerable importance. Crossman's first fag-master, the future film director Anthony ('Puffin') Asquith, was not only the senior prefect at Winchester but also the son of the long-serving prime minister and his second wife, Margot Asquith. I heard Crossman describe Puffin Asquith to Asquith's own biographer, R. J. Minney, as a boy with curly, golden hair, bright blue eyes, and the shrill, rather feminine voice of the Tennant family. (Margot Asquith's father was Sir Charles Tennant, MP.) Puffin Asquith became Crossman's protector. Though Puffin was in some ways very feminine and solicitous, Crossman did not think he made love to any of the boys — although Crossman also candidly admitted that he was very insensitive, and did not know what was going on.

One day in the spring of 1920, Crossman fell downstairs with a can of water, and imagined that he was going to get the cane. Puffin Asquith, however, rushed out of his room, and was very anxious about whether he had been hurt. Crossman also recollected how his fag-master's mother had come to tea. Margot Asquith and her daughter Elizabeth found a splendid spread: the fags cooked the muffins and made the cakes; and, after the guests had finished, they were allowed to stuff themselves on the left-overs. If, as a twelve-year-old, you find that the mistress of No. 10 Downing Street for a decade takes trouble over you, it does create a certainly worldly confidence. Fagging to the son of Herbert Henry Asquith, First Earl of Oxford and Asquith, Prime Minister of the British Empire, gave Crossman a sense of his own position in the élite of the nation which never deserted him. For all that he would talk of his bump of irreverence which he derived from his mother, Crossman, deep down, seldom if ever had any doubts about his place at the very epicentre of the British Establishment. Asquith's fag was born into it.

As Puffin Asquith's fag, Crossman was required to read the women's roles in plays by Maurice Maeterlinck, Chekhov, and James Elroy Flecker. Small boys played the parts of girls. The Winchester Shakespeare Society was called Shroggus, and the senior prefects went to read with the headmaster. The Chamber — twelve- to fourteen-year-olds — Shroggus was on Saturday evenings, when the boys went upstairs, sat on their beds, and read highbrow modern plays. Soon Crossman's taste for intellectual iconoclasm began to assert itself. At fourteen, Swinburne and Thomas Hardy were, he claimed, his mentors. At fifteen, Dostoevsky, as he was to tell visiting Russian dignitaries such as prime minister Alexei Kosygin. At sixteen, it was D. H. Lawrence. Inspired by Lawrence's *Kangaroo* and *The Rainbow*, he denounced Christianity as a humbug, and became a theoretical exponent of complete sexual freedom, while suffering all the adolescent agonies of sexual repression. C. S. Crossman could not fault his perfectly conventional and extremely successful school career. But his son believed that he was both shocked and scared by his strident indiscretions. It was at this period in his life, not when he was a don at Oxford, that Crossman developed a pleasure, sometimes plain sadistic, in shocking people — often not to very good purpose in terms of his self-interest.

I went to see James Callaghan in his office in the Commons, during February 1967, about the Vietnam Peace Initiative. I put the case gently. 'Well, all I'll say at the moment,' said the wily Chancellor, 'is that I'll listen to you more carefully than I'll listen to your boss. Dick has an irresistible temptation to say what people do not like to hear. That can be a great virtue. But the trouble is that Dick says it in a way that they least like to hear it. He has indulged his habit of enjoying being contrary, and I can tell you that it has not done your cause on Vietnam any good.' I don't doubt Callaghan was right. Others found this streak of voluble candour, picked up at Winchester College, quite counter-productive.

Crossman tended to presume that all those he came across, at work or socially, liked nothing better than to have their intellectual sacred cows challenged, their arguments questioned, and their assumptions subjected to loud interrogation. His provocative talk could raise the hackles of intellectual equals, and when combined with tactless teasing, could leave a residue of burning resentment.

Shortly after I began to work for Crossman in 1963, I asked for the night off to go to Eton to address the Political Society. This prompted him to ask if I had learned, like most public-school boys, to live a double life when I was at Eton — concealing from my parents what I did and felt away from home? I replied doucely that I was pretty reticent, especially about the times when I was caned at school, even for such misdemeanours as playing football with a squash ball in the corridor. Crossman exploded in a way which prompted me to make a long note of his complaint as soon as I went up to my room at the top of Number 9 Vincent Square, the Crossmans' London home. His own mother had brought up her children according to the ultra-liberal educational theories of the early twentieth century. Determined that they should not be repressed as she had been in the Howard home, she encouraged them to keep no secrets from her, to read anything and everything, and to argue with her on equal terms. Though this made mealtimes bedlam, C.S. Crossman had concurred with his wife's wishes. In the holidays from Winchester, he had to listen night after night as Crossman 'baited' (his word) his mother at dinner, and laid those obvious schoolboy intellectual traps into which, as the father knew only too well, his wretched wife would always blunder. Crossman reckoned that it was during those meals that he forfeited his father's affection. He could not forgive his son for cruelly and deliberately taking advantage of his mother's lack of education. Crossman said to me that night that in his turn he could not forgive his father for suffering in withdrawn silence instead of coming to his wife's assistance when his own values and principles were under attack. Father was appalled by this enjoyment of verbal bullying in his son. Son was appalled by the trait of intellectual timidity in his father that failed to rescue his mother. Father was pained beyond endurance that a Wykehamist son of his could mock the school's motto, 'Manners Makyth Man', and develop a cult of unmannerly bohemianism. Crossman told me that at that stage he was ashamed to have as his father the archetype of the conventional Wykehamist.

Lady (Tess) Swann, daughter of a distinguished Winchester art teacher, R.M.Y. Gleadowe, remembers Crossman at Winchester as being great fun. Yet he seemed awesome, too, and a superb conversationalist. He was not only an aesthete, but good at games, and one of the real grandees of the school, a boy of great consequence. There was at the same time a boy of little significance. His name was Hugh Todd Naylor Gaitskell.

At the end of October 1958, Crossman wrote in his diary: 'I am sorry to admit to myself that I have never felt such a strong sense of personal superiority as I have had this week, looking at Mr Gaitskell or even at poor, soft Nye.' To the rest of the world, Gaitskell seemed an increasingly forceful leader of the Labour Party. For Dick Crossman, he tended to remain the amiable and ineffective schoolboy who, in glaring contrast to himself, had made not the slightest impact while he was at Winchester. When Gaitskell died in 1963, Crossman was neither callous nor vengeful, at least in my presence. He simply observed, 'While there is death, there is hope.' He explained to me that Gaitskell would not have offered him a worthwhile post in the 1964 government for a man of fifty-seven, let alone a Cabinet post; most likely no post at all. I asked him why the relationship had been at best ambiguous, and often sour, though at one moment it was close enough for Crossman's son Patrick to become Gaitskell's godson. Crossman thought if you were at school with somebody who seemed innocuous and insignificant throughout your school life and who since then has been an ascending backroom boy, it is difficult to believe in his greatness. 'I thought for a time that Hugh might be made great by his office, but he became less and less self-assured and, if elected, would have made an unsatisfactory Prime Minister.' Crossman was never to eradicate Gaitskell the schoolboy from his mind. Ironically, in my opinion, Crossman shared with Gaitskell the Wykehamist inability to leave well alone. Both of them were forever redrafting and re-redrafting. The memory of Gaitskell at Winchester was to haunt Crossman in the late 1950s and early 1960s.

Before passing on to Oxford, and Crossman's adult life, it is necessary to consider the family relationship with a friend and suburban neighbour of C. S. Crossman – Major Clement Attlee.

Charles Stafford Crossman was nonpolitical in a strictly judicial way. Like so many distinguished lawyers, he distrusted the speculative mind and resented the questioning of ultimate beliefs. His conservatism was as deep and uncritical as his Christianity. But he played no part whatsoever in politics; and though he got on well enough personally with all the Attorney-Generals under whom he worked, with the arguable exception of Lord Jowitt, he distrusted politicians. Crossman wryly recounted how, as each election approached from 1924 onwards, Mr Justice Crossman had anxious talks with his mother: could he conscientiously vote for such an impossible man? Until his death in 1941, he was never known to have revised his opinion. (But then his last year was coloured by the grief of losing his youngest son on active service.) The 'impossible man' in Mr Justice Crossman's terminology was the local Conservative candidate in the Wanstead and Woodford constituency, Winston Spencer Churchill, a former Home Secretary.

There was, however, one politician whom Crossman came to know intimately. When he was still at Winchester, the Attlees came to live in the same suburban area of southwest Essex as the Crossmans. Since the Crossmans had a tennis court, and the Attlees did not, the two families saw a lot of each other on Saturday afternoons.

It was one of Dick Crossman's nicer attributes that he had the knack of mitigating anger and extending forgiveness with a personal anecdote. In the spring of 1963, I used every Monday morning, as a member of Queen's Club, in Barons Court, West Kensington, to go to play tennis. One Monday, I was asked to practise with Art Larsen, the left-hander and former winner at Forest Hills of the American championship. I was so thrilled at the opportunity of playing tennis in such company, that I cut a meeting on science policy. Crossman was understandably furious, and with colourful bombast threatened to get rid of me. He went over the top. 'So you played with Larsen: well, I played with Attlee!'

Later, he told me that in his late teens and early twenties there were many such afternoon matches. 'Now, young men,' Mr Justice Crossman would say to his elder brother Geoffrey and himself, 'see if you can beat that powerful combination, the Chancellor of the Duchy of Lancaster (which Attlee became in 1929) and the Junior Counsel for the Treasury.' Crossman told me that Attlee had a waspish inaccuracy at the net, but provided he missed the ball completely his father could usually be reckoned to rescue the honour of the second Labour government with his crafty lobs from behind the back line. Later that year, I asked Attlee about Dick Crossman's tennis. 'Erratic – like his politics,' came the laconic reply.

Crossman confirmed that the two families had got along splendidly – with one exception. He was, according to himself, the black sheep in the otherwise blameless flock of Crossmans. His mother and Violet Attlee would chat closely and cosily, sharing the same values. Attlee and C. S. Crossman would talk about the law and the Indian Empire. Off the tennis court, Crossman himself would flaunt his revolutionary views on life and politics. He was, he admitted, insufferably brash. The Attlees never forgave him for causing his parents so much pain – and he reciprocated their disapproval. Crossman was shocked by their stuffiness. The Attlees – Vi even more than Clem – were shocked by what both of them always regarded as the irresponsibility of his public and, even worse, of his private life.

When the Attlees went to Downing Street in 1945, Mr Justice Crossman had already been dead for four years. But the Attlees' link with the rest of the Crossman family continued, particularly closely with his mother. Crossman used to hear with a tinge of resentment of the Christmas cards which they regularly received from the Leader of the Labour Party, when he, as a Labour MP, received no such card or token of esteem. But then he had not only offended the Attlees themselves; worse still, he had done hurt to Ernie Bevin – and that for Clement Attlee was an even more heinous offence.

TWO

Oxford

The Wykehamist
(To Randolph Churchill, but not about him.)

Broad of church and broad of mind,
Broad before and broad behind,
A keen ecclesiologist,
A rather dirty Wykehamist.
'Tis not for us to wonder why
He wears that curious knitted tie:
We should not cast reflections on
The very slightest kind of don.
We should not giggle as we like
At his appearance on his bike;
It's something to become a bore,
And more than that, at twenty four.
It's something too to know your wants
And go full pelt for Norman fonts.
Just now the chestnut trees are dark
And full with shadow in the park,
And 'six o'clock!' St Mary calls
Above the mellow college walls.
The evening stretches arms to twist
And captivate her Wykehamist.
But not for him these autumn days,
He shuts them out with heavy baize;

He gives his Ovaltine a stir
And nibbles at a 'petit beurre',
And, satisfying fleshy wants,
He settles down to Norman fonts.

John Betjeman's poem is not an exact description of Crossman – but the future Poet Laureate had Crossman in mind when he wrote it.

The Oxford where Crossman arrived in the 1920s had recovered from World War One. Most of the boys from the famous public schools, though not as idle as is sometimes supposed, lived a social life. Crossman was an exception. As an undergraduate, he worked ferociously. He did, as Betjeman put it, shut them out with heavy baize.

Lord Zuckerman tells a story of how the brilliant young don, Maurice Bowra, later Warden of Wadham and University Vice-Chancellor, tutor in Greats, invited the brilliant Wykehamist freshman to a party and he went. So he invited him again. But at a third invitation, the hospitable Bowra received a terribly rude letter from Crossman, still in his first year, saying that he had not expected there to be so much gossip and small talk in Bowra's rooms, and he certainly would not be coming again. Crossman did not try to be popular among those doing Greats at Oxford in the twenties. Nor, by all accounts, was he. What no tutor or contemporary could gainsay was the electric brilliance of his mind. This brilliance had its first flowering in May 1937, with the publication of *Plato Today*. It was the first major indication of something Dick Crossman was able to do, as few others this century could – bridge the gap between the scholar and the lay reader, satisfying both.

Today Socialism is relatively bookless – and the poorer for it. In an age of instant television, we can be forgiven for forgetting how important books were to the interwar generation. Jack Brooks, Lord Brooks of Cumnor, agent in Cardiff for James Callaghan for many years and Welsh local government mogul, tells how much *Plato Today* meant to him and other young Welsh working-class socialists. When Crossman came to a rally in the West Lothian constituency, the lilting voice of Councillor Crawford Morgan introduced him, not as a Cabinet minister, not as a man who for a decade had been on the National Executive Committee of the Labour Party, but as a Socialist teacher and author of *Plato Today*. It was one of those books that a generation of the Labour Movement was brought up on. The message was clear. Plato challenged established forms of government and the Platonic ideal could be matched with current political conditions. Personages in fifth-century Athens could be translated into workaday politicians of 1937. The simplicity was powerful. 'Plato looks at British democracy; Plato looks at British education; Plato looks at the family; Plato looks at Fascism': these were powerful polemics, meaningful to the intelligent who had left school at fourteen years of age.

Yet writing which appealed to Labour activists also appealed to two of the heavyweight philosophers of the century, Sir Karl Popper and Sir Isaiah Berlin. Popper, author of *The Open Society and its Enemies* called *Plato Today* an 'interesting book, the first, apart from George Grote's *Plato* [1865], which I have found to contain a political interpretation of Plato that is partly similar to my own.' Isaiah Berlin in 1959 described the book as 'bold, original, and historically important'. He went on:

> Mr Crossman achieved a rare thing: he is a Hellenist who looked at the text of Plato with his own eyes, and not through the spectacles of Platonic tradition, particularly in Victorian England, and was astonished by the arresting relevance of Plato's views to the struggle between Fascism, Communism and Democracy in our time. His thesis, published over twenty years ago, gave rise to a great controversy, which led to a radical revaluation of Plato as a political thinker. During the twenty years that followed, some scholars and philosophers, notably Professor Popper, gave strong support to its central argument, others considered the charges against Plato to be a libellous anachronism. Meanwhile, Europe has been transformed: yet the quality of direct vision, the marvellous readability, eloquence, and validity of Mr Crossman's work seem to me unimpaired, and the issues raised by it have become, if anything, more central today than in the world of Hitler, Stalin, and the Spanish Civil War from which it sprang.

From Plato, Crossman learned the technique of 'elucidating' the minds of his colleagues. He would not be satisfied until the question 'What do you *really* mean?' had been fully answered and until he had probed to the bedrock of a person's beliefs. Even people as clever as Gaitskell did not like it, as Crossman employed this interrogation on the most delicate subjects, and to any draft that he and his colleagues were working on. It was the Oxford tutorial method taken to its extreme.

From Plato, Crossman came to appreciate the value of a good word. For example, in the Labour Party troubles of 1960, Crossman latched on to the word used casually by the Party Chairman, from the Wood-workers' union, George Brinham, that the National Executive were 'custodians' of the 1960 Scarborough Conference decision. How we love a good word, he used to say. The word 'custodian' was as intoxicating for him as 'the commanding heights of the economy' had been in the Clause Four debate. How he used the word 'custodians' for the purposes of functional strife within the Labour Party. There were endless speeches on the importance of being 'custodians of the Party Spirit'.

On the other hand, there was a danger. Such was Crossman's fas-cination with key words that the art of the wordsmith tended to become an art for its own sake. The love of spinning words tended to take him down political paths on which he had never really intended to travel.

Whether a man can be a successful weekly columnist for a tabloid newspaper only if he has done Greats at Oxford is, to put it mildly, open to doubt. What is not open to doubt is Dick Crossman's view on the matter. In 1968, the late Douglas Machray, one of Michael Foot's favourite editors, offered me a weekly political column in the *Daily Record*, the Scottish equivalent of the *Daily Mirror*. I told Crossman that I found it far more difficult than writing a column for *New Scientist*. 'I understand completely' said Crossman, 'I found the *Pictorial* and the *Mirror* infinitely more difficult than the *New Statesman*. But what makes you think you could do a decent popular column? You did not go to Oxford. You did not read Greats!' It was one of those remarks that are half joking but wholly in earnest.

This view I have encountered only once elsewhere. When I was struggling with the learned Commons Clerks about parliamentary questions in the last phase of the Belgrano controversy, a parliamentary opponent and friend came in with his questions. 'Enoch,' I said, 'you need an ability in Greek iambics to do this.' Said Mr Powell gravely, 'You need Greek iambics throughout life.' Crossman and Powell, these glittering Greek scholars, had more in common than either cared to admit.

Crossman, however, was contemptuous of Hegel. For anyone iner-ested in the political philosophy of the state, it was important to read Plato, and then the way was open to go straight on to Marx, disregarding Hegel. Crossman did not accept the conventional wisdom that Hegel was the basis of Marx. He credited Marx with having a meaning which could only mean one thing. Hegel could be taken to mean anything that his reader wished – humanitarian or fascist, conservative or revolutionary, peace-striver or warmonger, according to which particular qualification of which particular proposition the reader wished to see as his ultimate thought. It ought to be recorded that one of Crossman's favourite expressions – he barked it out in a way that I have never heard anyone else equal – was 'Balls!', Crossmanese for nonsense. I had myself been taught in Cambridge by historians of political thought no less distinguished than those at Oxford, but he would repeatedly say, 'Why don't you listen – Hegel is balls!'

Crossman got to know a number of contemporary thinkers, and one among them – surprisingly perhaps, on account of Crossman's agnosticism – was Reinhold Niebuhr, the influential professor of Applied Christianity at the Union Theological Seminary in New York. When he read of Niebuhr's death in June 1971, Crossman told me how nearly forty years earlier he had been heavily influenced by *Moral Man and Immoral Society*. Crossman was attracted to Niebuhr's conviction that democracy has a more compelling justification and requires a more realistic vindication than is given to it by the liberal culture with which is has been associated in modern history. The excessively optimistic estimates of human nature and of human history with which the democratic credo has been historically associated were, for Crossman, as for Niebuhr, a source of peril to democratic society. (All his life I found Crossman unfair, sometimes to the point of being gratuitously vicious, about those whom he saw as 'do-gooders'.) His experience refuted such optimism, and, like Niebuhr, he thought there was a danger that it would discredit the democratic ideal as well.

For example, there was an embarrassing occasion in the DHSS at Alexander Fleming House, Elephant and Castle, in July 1969 when Chuter Ede's former Parliamentary Private Secretary, Frank Douglas, by then Lord Douglas of Barloch, came to see Crossman about anti-fluoridation. The old boy, then seventy-nine years of age, did go on a bit about how he was a passionate believer in composting, and how as Governor of Malta, he had transformed the garden by using compost, after putting his case, I thought rather well. Crossman gave him a rough passage. When he had left, Crossman exploded to me that Douglas was one of 'those birdy creatures with a high laugh, a typical 1920s progressive, fit as a fiddle, hearty and enthusiastic'. So thoughtlessly committed, could such a man really care about fluoridation, children's teeth, or anything else worth worrying about? Crossman's diatribe against the smugness of 1920s progressives was almost demonic, implying that their happy attitudes and self-righteousness were somehow responsible for World War Two.

For Crossman and Niebuhr, a free society required some confidence in the ability of men to reach tentative and tolerable compromises between their competing interests, and to reach some common notions of justice which transcended all partial interests. Some of his intellectual colleagues, including C. A. R. Crosland, would get annoyed with Crossman for often seeming to disparage working-class interests. Yet Crossman followed Niebuhr in believing that a consistent pessimism in regard to man's rational capacity for justice invariably led to absolutist political theories. This was because absolutist theories prompted the conviction that only preponderant power can coerce the various vitalities of a community into a working harmony. Crossman told me that he believed Niebuhr was right in supposing that a too consistent optimism as to man's ability and inclination to grant justice to his fellows obscures the perils of chaos which perennially confront every society, including a free society. Crossman saw a democratic society as particularly exposed to the dangers of confusion. If those dangers were not fully appreciated, they could overtake a free society and invite the alternative evil of tyranny.

Crossman had come to see that a modern democracy required a more realistic philosophical and religious basis, not only to anticipate and understand the perils to which it is exposed, but also to give it a more persuasive justification. For Crossman, man's capacity for justice made democracy possible; man's inclination to injustice made democracy necessary. In most nondemocratic political theories, the state or the ruler is invested with uncontrolled power for the sake of achieving order and unity in the community. But Crossman had seen from history, that too often the pessimism which prompted and was the justification of the policy was not consistent. Seldom was the pessimism applied, as it should have been, to the ruler. If men are inclined to deal unjustly with their fellows, the possession of power simply made this inclination worse. That was why Crossman felt that irresponsible and uncontrolled power was the greatest source of injustice.

In June 1971, I asked Crossman whether it was his contact with Niebuhr, about whom he had broadcast for the BBC, that was the genesis of his obsession about prime-ministerial government. He even saw elements of absolutism in Harold Wilson's premiership. His reply was to the effect that it was wellnigh impossible to apportion intellectual

27

debts, but that Niebuhr had sharpened his questioning of leadership. One point was that the democratic techniques of a free society placed checks upon the power of the ruler and administrator and thus prevented him from becoming vexatious. The dangers of uncontrolled power were repeated reminders of the virtues of a democratic society; in particular, Crossman thought that if a society should become inclined to impatience with the weaknesses of freedom, there was danger. The temptation to choose the advantages of coerced unity at the price of freedom were considerable. For Crossman, over-optimism about our liberal culture has prevented modern democratic societies both from assessing the perils of freedom accurately and from appreciating democracy fully as the only alternative to injustice and oppression. When this optimism was not seriously qualified to accord with the real and complex facts of human nature and history, there was always the danger that sentimentality would give way to despair, and that a too-consistent optimism would come and go with a too-consistent pessimism. These beliefs derived largely from Niebuhr in the first instance, Crossman told me, translated into his political life. Crossman entertained doubts about panacea solutions to political problems. As we shall see, in many a Cabinet conflict, ranging from Rhodesia to prices and incomes policy, he was the pessimist.

Crossman kept up with Niebuhr's evolving thought. Almost uniquely among Cabinet Ministers, he, like Macmillan, simply made time to read. For example, in 1969, when *The Democratic Experience – Past and Prospects* by Reinhold Niebuhr and Paul Sigmund was first published, Crossman had devoured it within a couple of months, and was able to discuss it with another Niebuhr admirer, Sir Edward Boyle, MP, who had been Minister of Education, and who was to become Vice-Chancellor of Leeds University. Profoundly influenced though Crossman was, he did not accept Niebuhr's belief in Christianity.

In his twenties, Crossman had formulated a philosophy of life which explained to him why questions of religion, immortality, and metaphysics were literally meaningless. I doubt if *Plato Today* – and it was certainly Crossman's own view – could have been penned by someone other than an author who had already become involved in public life. From 1934 to 1940, Crossman was a City Councillor for Cowley and Leader of the Labour Group on the Oxford City Council. The author of *Plato Today* and philosophy tutor of New College had won his council seat originally on the promise that, if elected, he would ensure that the housewives of North Oxford would get their rubbish bins emptied not twice a week but three times a week, to cut down the stench of rotting garbage in May to September! Sensitive to the notion that he could be tagged as an airy-fairy classicist, Crossman on the council devoted much of his energy to the practical concerns of his electors. Three decades later, I was fascinated to see the transformation in Crossman when some relatively inarticulate constituent came to see him about a personal problem. He could suddenly switch from a rather fierce and awesome intellectual bully to a kind, considerate and gentle councillor, who would convey the impression to his constituent that all that mattered to him was a solution to the constituent's problem of the moment.

What went awry at Oxford was his personal life. Had it not done so, Crossman might well have ended up as a famous Warden of New College, or more likely Vice-Chancellor of the University of Keele – he was offered the principalship of the then University College of North Staffordshire on the death in 1952 of Sandy Lindsay, ex-Master of Balliol, who had held the post from 1949. (But Max Beloff told me that he knew Crossman as a 'tremendously impressive' young don, who made a powerful impression on the young, and thought he might not have stayed the course in the Oxford life, and was probably more suited to politics.)

Of Erika Landau, Crossman's first wife, I know only what Crossman, Isaiah Berlin and Solly Zuckerman have told me. She was a beautiful, promiscuous German Jew whom Crossman had met in Berlin. As with so much else in his life, their marriage took place on impulse. Within days, Crossman told me, they were quarrelling. The causes of the disputes were not revealed to me, and it would have been impertinent to have asked. Interestingly, however, I was told that Erika, ostensibly a Communist, was enraged by Crossman's approval of certain aspects of the *Hitler Jugend* (Hitler Youth). This is not as shocking, let alone sensational, as one might imagine at first sight. The *Hitler Jugend* in its earliest days appeared to some like a beefed-up Boy Scouts, and if it meant taking jobless youngsters off the streets, so much the better.

But he then became appalled, if ever he had indeed been impressed. Attending political meetings in the Weimar Republic, speakers often had to be shepherded by the police; if they were social democrats, those inside the hall would be apprehensive and frightened by threatening groups of Nazis outside the hall. Besides, Erika was Jewish.

So was Heinz Koeppler, one of Crossman's lifelong friends, who shared rooms with him in the early 1930s. Koeppler became a history don at Oxford in 1937, and in 1940 joined the Political Intelligence Department of the Foreign Office. I knew him from my frequent visits to Wilton Park, Sussex, where he was Warden for thirty years of a discussion centre for members of the Atlantic Community. Of Crossman's first marriage, Koeppler said that the vivacious Erika see-sawed between ebullience and depression, probably as a result of drugs. 'Let us say,' Heinz Koeppler told me once, 'that there were faults on both Dick's side and Erika's side.' But he doubted whether they could ever have made a life together.

Koeppler also complained to me that Crossman, like the rest of the Cabinet, was averting his eyes from the Czech crisis, the Prague Spring of 1968 and its repression by the USSR. After his experiences with Erika, thirty years earlier, Crossman of all people should have known better. The experience of Weimar haunted Crossman. During the student problems of 1969–70, the then Home Secretary, James Callaghan, took the traditional view that he must always permit people to demonstrate, even though he disagreed with them. Crossman did not take a simplistic line. He remembered how the Weimar Republic went down in 1933, and thought that society was entitled to elected leaders who said that we cannot possibly give people the right to destroy democracy. As long as the enemies of democracy were weak, we could afford to let them demonstrate. The moment that they became strong, democratic governments had to be resolute and attack them.

Crossman maintained that it was traipsing around the Continent, looking for Erika, who simply went missing on several occasions, that taught him about Europe. All that remained of her later in the Crossman house was some of her lovely Nymphenburg china.

Of Crossman's second wife, Zita, I have heard far more. Born Inezita Davis, she married, in 1923, John Baker, an Oxford biologist and, like Crossman, a fellow of New College. The received wisdom is that Crossman was responsible for breaking up the marriage, and therefore had to leave New College. I believe it was not quite that simple. Zita, as a young wife, was adventurous. She insisted on going on one of the early expeditions to Borneo. The explorer Tom Harrison, by that time resident in Borneo studying anthropology, thought all possessions were common property – including women! The seeds of the break-up of the Baker marriage were present long before Crossman developed his friendship in earnest.

Long after Zita had died, and indeed until his own death, Crossman had a thoroughly decent relationship with his stepson Gilbert Baker, of whom he used to see rather a lot. Baker, in turn, told me of his respect for Crossman. Whatever the rights and wrongs, his relations with his colleagues were a contributory cause of Crossman getting the itch to leave Oxford. Indeed, at the memorial service for Kingsley Martin, former editor of the *New Statesman*, Crossman described himself as 'the renegade Oxford don who wanted to be defrocked, and found a place in Kingsley's *New Statesman*'.

A part of his life that was enormously important to Crossman was his teaching of classes on behalf of the Workers' Educational Association. In April 1967, he went to the annual dinner of the Chiltern Society in High Wycombe, run by his former secretary, Jennie Hall, to whom he was ever grateful, and her husband Chris. It pleased him immensely to meet again, thirty-odd years later, some of his former students, who had attended the WEA classes which he had given for three years at Slough and Princes Risborough.

Equally, his experiences in 1936, during the course of his lectures at the Hanley Town Hall on local government left an indelible mark. The reason why he went to the Potteries in the first place may have been partly that his pupils might have a say in the selection of Labour candidates in Staffordshire. The end result was that Crossman developed a lifelong concern for the victims of silicosis, pneumoconiosis, emphysema and chronic bronchitis, the afflictions of pottery workers and mine workers.

Crossman was a radical leftist who, ever since he was a young New College don, believed in the value of the Workers' Educational Association in training so many people for the responsibility of self-government. For that purpose, Crossman thought it was realistic, not optimistic, to use education in order to substitute genuine social democracy for oligarchy.

Crossman's application in the mundane work of the Oxford City Council on bread-and-butter issues impressed activists in the Labour Party whose background was very different from his own. The late George Hodgkinson, a great political figure in the West Midlands, who was one of the groups of councillors who superintended the reconstruction of postwar Coventry told me 'We selected Dick Crossman because he had been an excellent candidate in Birmingham, and because of his capacity to do a job on the Oxford Council, as much as

31

on account of his academic achievement.'

Denis Howell, MP, Minister for Sport in the Wilson and Callaghan governments, remembers as a young teenager working for Crossman, delivering leaflets, and accompanying his father to meetings. Howell is an authentic Brum politician with impeccable working-class credentials. 'All those years ago, the Birmingham working-class voters did not understand what Crossman was talking about; but they thought he was great.' Throughout his life, it was precisely the absence of condescension or an air of noblesse oblige that endeared Crossman to the most unlikely audiences.

Sir Austen Chamberlain died at the beginning of March 1937 and the new National Government candidate was Councillor Walter Higgs. The West Birmingham Labour Party were without a candidate, and readily accepted the offer of a twenty-nine-year-old Oxford don. In 1929, Sir Austen's majority had fallen to 43, in a seat which he had represented since 1914. All twelve Birmingham seats were held by the National Government in 1935, and few thought that the 7,371 majority would be threatened, not least because the Birmingham Unionist machine, created by Joe Chamberlain, was still very efficient.

One of Crossman's main planks in his platform was that increased industrial activity was being accompanied by a rise in the cost of living to the detriment of the workers. Attlee, Dalton, Shinwell, Greenwood, Ellen Wilkinson and other Labour Party notables went to speak for him. His election address referred to the 'appalling dangers in which we now live', making it doubly necessary for the electors to think carefully before casting their votes. The address stated that under the National Government we were surely but slowly drifting into war, and that the Government's 'colossal rearmament programme, which will saddle the country with an expenditure of £1,500,000,000 during the next five years' was proof of this. Crossman added that he could support rearmament only on three conditions: that it was combined with a real League of Nations policy; that the armament industry was brought under national control and the profit motive taken out of war; and that the rearmament programme was financed wholly out of taxation. The address, which was light years more adult and serious than the obvious sloganizing of most current election addresses, concluded:

I will try to sum up the gist of my message in two questions.

Do you believe that war can be prevented by democracy answering the blusterings of the Fascists with the cool and resolute determination to maintain international law and to uphold the League of Nations?

If you do, I would ask you to vote for me...

Are you content to accept the meagre and short-lived 'prosperity' of the armaments 'boom' which must finally lead to war or slump? Or do you believe with me that we must plan for the future of this country with courage and foresight so as to enable all – whatever their class or stations – to enjoy their due share of security and comfort?

I am confident that you will find the right answer to these questions, and will give a lead both to Birmingham and to this country in upholding the cause of peace and progress.

Pericles could not have put it more succinctly.

Biographical details set out beside a portrait of the vigorous-looking candidate on the front page of the address included the following: 'Popular BBC lecturer on democracy – accomplished linguist; has travelled all over Europe – exposed German Nazis in sensational broadcast – athlete and distinguished sportsman.' I suppose being a lusty second-row forward in the New College First XV does qualify one for the description as 'distinguished sportsman'!

However, Crossman never indulged in yah-booh politics. Maybe this was because he recognized in his first parliamentary opponent, Councillor Walter Higgs, a man of quality. Of Walter Higgs, the current representative of Tory Birmingham and its commercial classes, Anthony Beaumont Dark MP says: 'He was a man who thought what he said, and said what he thought.' He was the anointed heir of the Chamberlain tradition. It was to be the first time in sixty-one years that West Birmingham had not been represented by a Chamberlain. One can hardly imagine today's Labour Party putting out a pamphlet that eulogizes their own candidate but by implication heaps praise on the deceased Conservative member. Richard Crossman proclaimed: 'The name and repute of the West Birmingham division will not fade into the limbo of forgotten constituencies, but will ring through the nation once more, synonymous with the cause of virile progress.' Besides, Crossman believed that young candidates, in particular, gained nothing by calling their opponents names. No epithet should be used, except with the object of making, with wit, a clear political point. It was very much a bell and loudspeaker campaign: Crossman, accompanied by groups of canvassers, went round the streets, using the bell to call the electors to their doors, and the loudspeakers to tell them why.

By loudspeaker and on doorstep, and at amazingly well-attended meetings, Crossman denounced the National Government for doing nothing to prevent Japanese aggression in the Far East, and allowing Mussolini to massacre the Abyssinians. Edgar Heelas, a distinguished Birmingham inspector of schools, told me that as a young man he had attended many of Crossman's meetings. It was one of the few occasions when the candidate outshone in knowledge and delivery the visiting speakers: 'Compared to Crossman, Attlee looked and was simply pedestrian!' As in later life, Crossman's oratorical triumphs did not endear him to those who had to share his platform, and bear comparison accordingly. 'He was too good for his own good' was a frequent comment from Labour party cognoscenti.

Supporting Crossman, Norman Thomas, the American Socialist leader and former candidate for the presidency of the United States, made a moving speech to the constituency workers, and volunteered to help in putting circulars into envelopes.

Crossman always retained a soft spot for Birmingham, which had given him his chance. Twenty-seven years later, within weeks of the 1964 general election, Harry Watton, Leader of the Labour Group on the Birmingham City Council, took him round housing in the very area where he had campaigned. He told us in one of the streets how it was in exactly the same state as he had seen it in 1937 — which meant nearly thirty years worse. It made him even more determined to try to improve the housing stock of the inner city.

As things turned out the by-election result was:

W. F. Higgs 12,552
R. H. S. Crossman 9,632
Conservative majority 2,920

as compared to the 1935 general election:

Sir Austen Chamberlain 16,530
O. G. Willey 9,159

However, the industrial recovery was apparent in Birmingham perhaps earlier than anywhere else in the country, and long before re-armament began. The improvements had been gradual and substantive. Since 1932, the unemployment figures had fallen by 58,000 and by the time of the by-election were standing at 16,000 out of a population of about 1,000,000. West Birmingham, home of Lucas, which employed 12,000 people, had more than shared in the recovery.

For Crossman himself, the West Birmingham by-election was a watershed. He had caught the bug of desire to go to the House of Commons and confirmed that he was more interested in political life than academic life. (I believe that no person should become a Member of Parliament unless they have contested a seat that they could not expect to win. Until one had actually been a candidate, no person, in my opinion, can be sure about becoming an MP.) He had made a memorable reputation and more important, political friends in the West Midlands. It was therefore no surprise that in the wake of the by-election he was approached by the Coventry East Labour Party. In 1929, Philip Noel-Baker had taken the seat from the incumbent, A.B. Boyd-Carpenter, but had lost it in 1931. Since then, it had been held in the Conservative interest by Captain William Strickland, sometime of the Camel Corps, by a slender 2,400 votes in an electorate of 90,000. Given the prospect of boundary changes, Crossman was being offered a safe Labour seat, (where in 1945, he was to get 60.5 per cent of the vote), and entry to Parliament in 1939 or the spring of 1940 at the general election then due to take place. But that was not to be.

THREE
Plato Today

Crossman treated Plato not as the father of all academics, the venerated first Academic, but as a 'politician *manqué*'; he once told me that in certain respects he had Herbert Fisher in mind. He related Plato's political ideas to his life. And why, asked the irreverent Crossman, if Plato's political and educational theories were so good, did they have such disastrous results when anyone tried to put them into practice? It offended the conventional wisdom of the University of Oxford's philosophy faculty that Crossman should portray Plato's Academy as 'a school for counter-revolutionaries', and Plato's *Republic* as 'a handbook for aspiring dictators', as he put it in his Introduction to the (lightly) Revised Edition of 1959. His view had the subsequent powerful if qualified support of Sir Karl Popper, author of *The Open Society and its Enemies: From Plato to Marx* (1945/1966). However, if Plato was a failed politician, Crossman conceded to his senior academic colleagues that he was the founder of theology, the theory of knowledge, ethics and semantics. Crossman also told me to reread Plato when he was irritated with me for being, as he saw it, self-important – which, alas, was not too infrequent. *The Republic*, he believed, was an antidote to self-importance!

I suggested to Crossman that he ought to properly update *Plato Today*. He thought about it in 1970, after leaving office, and rejected the idea on much the same grounds as in 1954. When he wrote it, he could read Greek easily, and had begun Greek philosophy seriously when he went up to New College in 1925. Forty-five years later, he doubted if he could read Greek texts easily, if at all. 'In the 1930s, I could not be faulted for lack of scholarship: now the classical scholars would have every justification in challenging my scholarship.' He would obviously have been hurt by the deteriorating opinion of the tiny but, to his self-esteem, important classical scholarship community. Incidentally, Crossman's claims to Greek scholarship were corroborated to me by unchallengeable sources. In the 1960s, I used to return often to King's College, Cambridge, where the former Vice-Provost, Sir Frank (F. E.) Adcock, and the former senior tutor, Patrick (L. P.) Wilkinson, remained friends. Both, separately, vouchsafed that Crossman's scholarship was superb. Since Adcock, vastly erudite, pernickety, pedantic, the best code-breaker of all at Bletchley during the war, edited the *Cambridge Ancient History*, and since Wilkinson was a formidable academic politician, their opinion was significant. And neither thought that I was safe in Crossman's hands: Adcock because he was an old Tory, Wilkinson because he thought Crossman himself had some of the shortcomings which he rightly ascribed to Plato!

The nub of Crossman's first book (1937) lies in the contrast between Plato and Socrates. The latter's execution was not in vain: 'By his death, like another conscientious objector, four hundred years later, [Socrates] immortalized the idea which he served.' For Crossman, 'the legend of Socrates became the inspiration for all who believed in reason. But the man who first formulated the Socratic faith into a systematic philosophy was fundamentally different from [Socrates himself]. Just as Paul of Tarsus created an orthodox Christian theology strangely remote in spirit from that of Christ, so Plato [like St Paul] modified the Socratic ideal of philosophy into a new Platonic system.'

For a man who when I first knew him was a humanist, Crossman was extraordinarily interested in religions (and had himself a Christian send-off in 1974). Plato and Paul were both converts to a faith, but each of them, Plato and Paul, changed the faith of his master almost as much as he was changed by it. With attribution to Crossman, whose *Plato Today* he recommended, this was a point made by the gentle, quiet voice of Dom David Knowles, Regius Professor of History at Cambridge, and Fellow of Peterhouse, who used to pack Mill Lane's largest lecture room three mornings a week at 9 a.m.

In the history of both Platonism and of Christianity there was a strange tension between the ideals of the master and of the disciple; and at recurring intervals there was a movement to get behind the disciple's dogma to the real personality of the master.

[**A digression fast-forward**: Thirty years after writing *Plato Today*, Crossman entered the Ministry of Housing. He was forever wanting to know what younger, junior, clever people in the ministry thought. One fine November morning, Crossman asked Freddie Ward, then an Assistant Secretary, what he really thought about what he, Crossman, had outlined on rents policy. (A recollection of Bob Mellish, later Chief Whip, the Minister of State at Housing, tallies precisely with my own. We were both in the room.)

'Come on, tell me,' said Crossman, at his most insistent.

'Well,' said Ward, 'Minister, if you really want to know, I think you are talking complete bollocks!'

So did Mellish, vastly experienced as a fixer and dockers' MP and chairman of the London Labour Party. So did I!

'Oh,' said Crossman, 'if you think I'm talking bollocks, then I want you to go away and write me a White Paper on what *you* think the Government's policy on rents ought to be!'

Ward demurred.

'No, go away; you've told me I'm talking bollocks; so let's see what you can do!'

Exit Ward and sundry bemused officials.

'Dick!' chimed Mellish and Dalyell, 'you can't do that! Tell a junior official to produce a Government White Paper!'

'Oh, why not?' said Crossman.

Mellish resorted to the picturesque blunt language associated with the Millwall docks. A knock on the door. Enter Dame Evelyn Sharp, black as thunder.

'Permanent Secretary, I'm told by Mr Mellish here and Mr Dalyell that I should not have told Ward to prepare a White Paper. Have I offended you?'

'I should think you have!' growled the Permanent Secretary.

'All right, very well . . . !' and the inferno gradually subsided. Mellish, who had loathed Crossman in the 1950s, came to like him very much, and in my opinion was exceedingly good for him, injecting common sense and street wisdom in colourful language.

Mellish told Crossman that the Ministry of Housing and Local Government was most certainly not an extension of a university. Until Government experience disabused him, I do not think Crossman imagined that a minister could treat civil servants as an enlightened Wayneflete Professor of Metaphysical Philosophy might treat his colleagues. But the Socrates in Crossman conceded more and more to the Plato in Crossman as time went on!

Mellish was another politician who had his power base in the Party and, being unsackable, could speak his mind to Crossman and Wilson. Unfortunately, Mrs Thatcher's Ministers have their portfolios at prime-ministerial whim.]

We must return thirty years, to Crossman's perception of these two men, Plato and Socrates. 'No two personalities could have been more sharply opposed: Socrates, the humorous citizen of Periclean Athens, who knew and loved all sorts and conditions of men; Plato, the aristocrat, who shook the dust of democratic Athens off his feet: Socrates, the man who knew that he knew nothing; Plato, the systematic exponent of an authoritarian creed: Socrates, the conversationalist, and Plato the master of the prose style: Socrates, the personification of life itself, and Plato, the remote observer of all things living.' Drily, Crossman thought it would be 'no surprise to find that the Socratic ideal under Plato's hand has suffered some startling transformations'.

For Crossman, who often, very often, would talk of himself as a Socratic man, Platonist was a term of deep criticism. When he was angry with Michael Stewart, he would tell me what an awful Platonist he was. On the occasion of Michael Stewart's going to the Oxford Union televised debate and putting the case for the Americans in Vietnam more eloquently than any American had ever put it, Crossman referred to him as an arch-Platonist.

I have always liked Michael Stewart, and particularly since I was his deputy for a period, when he led the British Labour delegation to the European Parliament. But Crossman did not warm to him, though he admired the clarity of his mind. Michael Stewart, most honest of men, even now tells me that quite simply he did not like Crossman. This was a pity for the Labour Government, especially as it made certain that Crossman's influence could not be brought to bear on foreign affairs. Both were Oxford Firsts in Greats. The trouble was partly that Michael Stewart had aroused Crossman's resentment for being on the front bench for the 18 years Crossman was on the back benches. But at another deeper level, Crossman was of the school of Socrates, and Stewart of the school of Plato – in Crossman's mind at least.

Though he admired scholarship, I (in the superbly well-qualified company of Isaiah Berlin) rather doubt whether Crossman continued to be interested in academic philosophy. It was the pedantry of the philosophers which he came to detest. On several occasions when I commended friends and parliamentary contemporaries of mine, he would say shirtily, 'I found him a pedantic young man.' That meant a gamma rating.

This was often unjust. Then Crossman's taste in some people and distaste for others seemed not good to me. It was arbitrary – and in my view he was too often dismissive of people for frivolous reasons.

On one matter, everyone without exception to whom I have talked about it, friend or foe, agreed: that Crossman was a riveting lecturer at Oxford in the 1930s. How much his lectures actually taught the undergraduates is open to doubt. His capacity to inspire is not in doubt.

FOUR

Coventry

I believe that Labour candidates should not be selected for safe or winnable Labour seats unless they have fought in a hopeless or marginal constituency. This is for a very practical reason. No one can be certain about how they react to the test of elections until they have actually been involved. And not only does one find out about oneself, but the party finds out about the candidate. Crossman had acquitted himself well in the eyes of the party in the Midlands by his performance in West Birmingham. He was clearly a good candidate, with the all-important quality of a temperament for politics. So it was under-standable that a West Midlands marginal/winnable seat like Coventry East should select him later in the year as a prospective parliamentary candidate for the anticipated 1939 or 1940 general election, which was postponed to 1945 because of the war.

But, as usual in politics, chance played a critical role. One of the organizers of the Coventry Labour Party was the then 43-year-old son of a chimney sweep, who as a child had helped his father clean the flues of factory boilers. The Coventry Labour Party loaned this organizer, the future alderman George Hodgkinson, hero of the 1940–1 Blitz and future lord mayor of Coventry, to the West Birmingham Labour Party for the election. (I came to know George Hodgkinson, by then in his mid-seventies, very well.) Thirty years later, I seldom saw Crossman so upset with Harold Wilson as when he discovered that the knighthood due to Coventry in the honours system distribution had been bagged for a senior local government official, in the face of his recommendation that it ought to go to George Hodgkinson.

Working together in the by-election was the origin of an important lifelong friendship. Hodgkinson liked Crossman from the start, as he knew enough about Oxford to know that Crossman had burned his boats with New College over the West Birmingham candidature, and was going wholeheartedly at the by-election. Crossman's mettle as a candidate had been proved. so a firm invitation went to him from the Coventry Labour Party, on the understanding that there was one other possibility, G. T. Garratt, author of *Mussolini's Roman Empire*.

Crossman was selected by a substantial majority. His brutal candour had its appeal. At the selection conference, held at the Railwaymen's Club in Coventry, one of the accredited delegates confronted him with the oft-put question, 'How much money can you put into the Coventry Constituency Party's funds?' Quick as a flash, without hesitation, Crossman said, 'None!' Whereupon Pearl Hyde, later herself to become an alderman (1952) and distinguished lord mayor of Coventry (1957–8), loudly observed, 'And a jolly good job too. You are not buying us.' When Pearl Hyde was tragically killed in a road accident in 1963, Crossman reflected that, had he answered differently or prevaricated on her question, his whole life would have been different. He would not have been selected.

The Coventry Labour Party regarded it as a matter of honour not to ask for donations from the candidate. Dirty, greasy, thumbmarked collection sheets were circulated in the factories and offices of Coventry. These sheets had the caption 'The workers' pennies can beat the bosses' millions.' These soiled papers were the symbol of Labour enthusiasm and independence.

Shortly before he died, George Hodgkinson told me about Crossman as his candidate. He was a dynamic personality who became a 'miserable creature' when he had no work to do. At all times, he was open, frank, get-at-able, a good mixer and transparently honest.

Crossman was soon to realize that Coventry politically was not Birmingham politically. Thirty years later, when I addressed a large meeting on the Lady Godiva Festival Day, I was indeed told not to refer to the 'Birmingham Area' on pain of dismissal from being his PPS. It was not simply a matter of local pride. There are some unique characteristics of the urban and industrial development of Coventry, which made Coventry's brand of Socialism strikingly different from the Socialism of Birmingham, 15 miles to the northwest, or the Socialism of Rugby, 12 miles to the southeast. It was a difference that was to have a considerable influence on Crossman as a politician. Had he remained candidate for West Birmingham, he would surely have won that seat in the landslide of 1945, and the constituency pressures on him would have been to be a loyal, more staid, certainly less rebellious member of the Parliamentary Labour Party, and more obviously concerned with bread-and-butter issues. Coventry not merely allowed Crossman to be left-wing and 'disloyal' – he would have had a very uneasy relationship with his Constituency Labour Party had he not been so. It suited Coventry Labour Party to have a nationally known rebel.

Prewar and postwar, Coventry had become, of all British cities, the most American in its outlook. Crossman told me that visitors from the States sensed an affinity in Coventry to the way of life on the other side of the Atlantic. This was not simply due to the presence of the motor-car industry, or to the fact that ownership of a motor car ceased to be an exclusively middle-class characteristic in Coventry at least a decade before this change in customs took place anywhere else in Britain. What the American visitor recognized as familiar in Coventry was the combination of trade-union militancy, demanding ever higher wages and improved conditions on the one hand, and on the other a willingness to welcome new techniques of production, and a hard-headed recognition, unusual in Britain of the middle years of the century, that high wages can only be paid out of high profits, which themselves were a function of ever-increasing productivity.

Not only in his constituency but elsewhere – he was never a man to choose to say one thing to one audience and another elsewhere, for the sake of courting popularity – Crossman objectively, in his view, spoke of Coventry's virtues. One reason why wage levels and earnings were substantially higher in Coventry's engineering factories than they were in Rugby or Birmingham was quite frankly because, if Coventry trade unionists managed to winkle more out of their employers than trade unionists in the rest of the West Midlands, the Coventry people gave employers better value for money.

For twenty years, I represented the British Motor Corporation Truck and Tractor plant at Bathgate, which became British Leyland. With the encouragement of the Macmillan government, and subsequent Labour governments, and with massive financial help, a number of major employers moved to Merseyside and to Scotland, reducing their labour costs at least in terms of wages paid. I have to admit that not one major employer ever claimed to me that in terms of efficiency their move was justified by the lower wages they were able to pay away from Coventry. There was the piquant but true story of a senior communist Coventry shop steward visiting the Rootes factory at Linwood in Renfrewshire, and innocently enquiring what was the cause of the go-slow. It was the normal pace of work he was seeing!

Crossman had little doubt about why the trade unionist in Coventry behaved in a more go-ahead way. What made him tick was the aftermath of the mass immigration to which Coventry had been subjected since the motor-car and aeroplace engines replaced the bicycle as its main product. In most of the British Isles, industry had been rooted in particular regions. The textile worker of Lancashire or the Durham miner normally worked where he was born, and often inherited his father's trade. What made Coventry different to almost any other city in Britain during the time Crossman was a Coventry MP was the unique proportion of its families and single people who were born into a rooted industry somewhere else, experienced unemployment there, and flitted to Coventry because someone told them that the streets were paved with gold.

Crossman doubted very much whether the ethos of Coventry when George Eliot stayed with her friends at Foleshill, now within the Coventry city boundary, and composed *Middlemarch* (1871–2) was much different from that of a number of other ancient boroughs which had recently pulled down their city walls. It was a borough of watch-makers, ribbon-makers and weavers. The skills of the watchmakers gave birth to one of the first genuine machine-tool industries in Europe. Then came the bicycle. Then the motor car, following the skills of watchmaker, machine-tool maker, and bicycle maker. Then the aero-engine manufacturer. It was the expanded demand for labour in the First World War, the surge of incomers from the Welsh valleys, Tyne-side and Lancashire in the 1920s, which was responsible for the emerg-ence of an extreme-left shop-steward movement.

As prewar candidate, Crossman made public speeches repeatedly contrasting his experience as a Workers' Educational Association tutor, going each week to Staffordshire mining villages where he took classes, and the booming full employment of Coventry. This was one of the best arguments for Socialism and planning. 'The rooted miner rotted in the Kidsgrove Community Centre, where I taught him the elements of Plato's *Republic*. Less than fifty miles away there was a job waiting for him, as there was for the unemployed of South Wales, of Durham, of Lancashire or of Glasgow, provided they were prepared to share a bed in a Coventry lodging-house and do an unskilled job before graduating into a motor-car factory.'

Crossman believed that those who came to Coventry showed, by definition, that extra bit of initiative. After the immigrants from other parts of the United Kingdom had uprooted themselves, they looked back with horror to their home areas and the distress which they had left. In Crossman's view, the parents of most of his constituents had accepted both the management's demand for ever-increased intensity of labour in return for a swelling wage-packet, and the collective solidarity and discipline which the shop stewards had insisted upon, *ab initio*, as the passport of admission to the excellent wages of the mass-production line.

Crossman was fond of quoting the story of Captain Sir John Black. (Crossman had a sneaking admiration and penchant for tycoons, and like me, was an early fan of Captain Robert Maxwell, MC, for all his enormities.) John Black was a ruthless business tycoon. He was deputy chairman and managing director of the Standard Motor Company; he was chairman and managing director of the Triumph Motor Company, and he was chairman of the crucially important wartime Joint Aero-Engine Committee. John Black was a favourite of Stafford Cripps at the Ministry of Aircraft Production, of Lord Beaverbrook and of Winston Churchill, and at the same time, he was the open confidant of a left-wing shop-steward movement, dominated by an alliance of Communists and Irish Catholics, giving them the power to hire and fire so long as they produced satisfactory production figures in return. Later he was expelled from the Employers' Federation, and had a row with the Communists. However, for Crossman, John Black's history encapsulated the special qualities characteristic of Coventry trade unions – a blend of a hard bargaining spirit with a black-and-white sense of right and wrong, as well as an ability to combine genuine shop-floor democracy with collective impatience of minority opinion.

Unlike Maurice Edelman and Elaine Burton, his fellow Coventry Labour MPs, Crossman steered clear in public, at any rate, of local trade-union affairs – and, above all, did not dream of getting involved, unless he was asked to become involved by the official trade-union officers. He thought the behaviour of Labour MPs who took up shop-steward and unofficial causes, to the embarrassment of the full-time officials, simply wicked.

To many Labour MPs, honourably immersed in their own constituencies, Crossman's appeared to be a high-and-mighty attitude, far too remote for a tribune of the people. However, there was a personal factor. It so happened that for much of his earlier period in Coventry, the relevant full-time official of the important Transport and General Workers' Union was one of the most commanding and effective trade-union leaders of the century, James Larkin Jones. No politician in his right mind would think it wise to meddle uninvited in Jack Jones's business in his own patch. As I was to find when we were both members of the Mikardo Committee on the Docks in the 1960s, Jack Jones is an exceedingly able, self-assured and, in my view, charming man. But he never did suffer pretentious fools gladly. And I was intrigued to notice how careful Crossman always was in Jack Jones's presence. It was not, latterly at any rate, that he had anything to fear from Jones's possible criticism and antagonism — it was rather that he respected him as an equal if different mind, and wanted to be well regarded by Jones. He was. Jack Jones told me that the idea that Crossman was casual about the industrial situation in Coventry was rubbish. 'When we wanted his help, we asked him and he gave us his full and prompt attention. Though you will understand that we could call him "The Professor", he was held in good repute by the trade unions in Coventry all the time I was there.'

But it was not only in domestic affairs that Coventry politicians were active. It was important to Crossman and to his parliamentary image as a foreign-affairs expert that Coventry City Council had been particularly active in international affairs and had sent delegations to many countries. Groups of councillors and officials went to Stalingrad and many other places in Eastern Europe, to the extent that the headquarters of Coventry Labour Party was christened the 'Kremlin of London Road'.

The trade-union movement which Crossman found in Coventry was, unlike trade unions of the time in many industrial areas, never exclusively concerned with wages, conditions and authority inside the factory. From 1917 there were contacts between Coventry and Russian workers and soviets. Crossman said that, try as he might to interest his local party members in Swedish or West German social democracy, their natural place of pilgrimage remained to the communist countries of the Eastern bloc. It was typical that, though Coventry was twinned with both Kiel and Dresden, it was the latter, the East German relation-ship, which commanded fonder care and patience. It was clear to Crossman that so long as the shop stewards remained the praetorian guard of the Labour movement in Coventry, this instinctive link with Communist ideology and proletarian class consciousness was likely to remain the ideological basis of the Coventry Labour movement's atti-tude to international affairs.

As Coventry's first Labour MP who had an overall majority, Philip Noel-Baker, 1929–31, was Arthur Henderson's Parliamentary Private Secretary, and able to dedicate himself to foreign affairs to an extent that would be inconceivable for a 1980s MP. Forty years later, when Noel-Baker was Chairman of the PLP Foreign Affairs Group, and I was on the committee, he confirmed to me that his crusade for disarmament chimed perfectly with Coventry Labour movement's belief in inter-national working-class solidarity and opposition to capitalist war. After 1931, the ignominious collapse of the Ramsay MacDonald Government only confirmed the basic suspicion of council heavyweights such as Sidney Stringer and George Hodgkinson that a Labour Cabinet would always be an unreliable instrument of social revolution. If there were to be left-wing change, it would have to be achieved on a local basis.

Crossman was a considerable admirer of the way in which the Coventry Socialists rejected Herbert Morrison's pattern of Cabinet government in local authorities through committee chairmen, and believed in rotating jobs. He compared the Coventry Socialists to the Athenians of the period of Pericles, who took it for granted that, in a genuine democracy, expertise must be subjected to the rule of the inexpert average man or woman. It this meant transferring an out-standing chairman of the Housing Committee to a less important job, and replacing him with a Labour party 'hack', so be it. The justification was that the loss of expert leadership would be more than compensated by the knowledge that in this way the will of the majority had been secured. Like the shop stewards' movement, in which many of them had been brought up, the Coventry councillors rejected elitism. They were determined to stymie any *de facto* move to Cabinet government. Considerable men like George Hodgkinson and Sidney Stringer had, like Pericles, to rely not on the power that ministerial office would have given in national politics, but simply and solely on their personal authority and persuasive abilities. The will of the majority of Labour councillors was binding on them, and sometimes they had to accept defeat in the secret Labour caucus which preceded open council. But, as Crossman acutely observed, neither Hodgkinson nor Stringer ever doubted that their occasional defeat was infinitely preferable to the weakening of democracy inside the party which continuity of leadership in office inevitably brings.

I have no doubt that it was Crossman's experience and perception of Coventry politics during the postwar rebuilding which prompted both his scepticism and his profound curiosity about Cabinet government, and his championship of the rights of backbenchers even when exceedingly inconvenient to the Wilson Government in 1967–8.

The years in which Crossman combined being parliamentary candidate for the whole of Coventry, which was a one-seat constituency before 1945, and then for Coventry East, with local government as leader of the Labour minority on the Oxford council were for him a period of exhilarating creative activity. He claimed it was more satisfying in terms of collective effort and personal achievement than any period of his life, with the exception of the years in which he was crusading against Ernest Bevin's policy on Palestine. Certainly, what he learned in Coventry was put at the disposal of the less developed trade unions in the motor-car industry at Cowley, who were becoming increasingly aware. However, the very fact that Crossman derived such stimulus from opposition in Oxford Council and opposition in Coventry, in my view, damaged him. His experience was against authority. He had never actually run anything.

As his years in Parliament went by, Crossman became more and more of a national figure. This is what Coventry wanted from its MP. Crossman eschewed the notion that an MP should be a glorified welfare officer. He did not think (not do I) that it is any part of an MP's job to second-guess an elected council in what the council itself was elected to do. But he never missed the Coventry Labour bazaar. He held regular advice clinics, and I know that for constituents who really needed their MP to fight for them in a just individual cause, Crossman could not be bettered. He did not seek personal publicity in such cases, as many modern MPs do. If he got in adequate answers from government departments, he went to great lengths to get satisfaction.

As time went by Crossman thought that Labour support in Coventry was growing squashier and squashier. The reasons were national, and are considered elsewhere. However, in the 1959 general election, Crossman's majority in Coventry East rose by 1 per cent to 7,762 votes.

48

This has to be compared with Maurice Edelman's majority in Coventry North falling by 4.2 per cent to 1,241 votes, while in Coventry South, Elaine Burton lost the seat to the Conservative, Philip Hocking, by 1,830 votes, the Labour proportion of the poll faling by 3.2 per cent, and the Conservatives making a 3.3 per cent gain. Crossman attributed his comparative success to his activity on pensions.

It is a strange experience being a long-serving MP. As a young man or woman, one is selected by the party elders, and for the first few years the people in key constituency party posts are generally of a senior generation. Then an MP spends fifteen years working with his own contemporaries. Then, and often suddenly the MP finds himself or herself working with a new generation, who had no part in the original selection conference. By the time of the second election of the Wilson government, thirty years had passed since Crossman was first selected, and the dramatis personae of Coventry politics had changed. Something else had happened, as Crossman himself was characteristically candid enough to confess : Prescote.

FIVE

Psychological Warrior

The war altered Dick Crossman's life, and it made him a different person. Crossman never had been an identikit intellectual of the Left, saying and believing in all the right things. His questioning mind and his former experience saw to that. But the war made him a strategist and added a new dimension.

Crossman was one of the Socialists who from the mid-1930s had not the slightest doubt that he might be called on to fight in a war. I was quite appalled at his dismissive attitude towards people like Philip Noel-Baker, an arch-priest of the League of Nations, and later of the UN, MP for Derby from 1936. The award to Noel-Baker of a Nobel Peace Prize in 1959 simply exacerbated Crossman's contempt. Noel-Baker remained 'washy', an adjective expressing extreme opprobrium in Crossman's vocabulary.

Chance is a major factor in all our lives. I asked Crossman how he became involved with the Political Warfare Executive in the first place. It happened like this. While he was having dinner at a friend's house, a fellow guest was called away during the meal to Broadcasting House, to translate Neville Chamberlain's pre-Munich explanation of why he was going to negotiate with Hitler, Mussolini and Daladier, and to read it over the airwaves. That simple action in the autumn of 1938 was the beginning of the European Service of the BBC. Until that moment, the British, still less the Americans, had not felt the slightest need to try to counter Nazi (or Communist) material by a British Government-controlled campaign. Crossman said that the contemporary notion was that 'Truth would prevail'. Nothing of the kind would happen. It dawned on those present with experience in newspapers, business and politics that truth seldom prevails when it cannot be heard. The requirement for a propaganda service became obvious over the following weeks, though there was a sense of being struck by light on the road to Damascus that night.

When war broke out in 1939, Richard and Zita Crossman occupied a flat, later to be blitzed, above the *New Statesman* offices, where he was Kingsley Martin's assistant editor. Wryly, Crossman recalled that he and Zita went away for a weekend after they had just completed furnishing the entire top floor. They hastened back during the bombing, just as the building was beginning to catch fire. Crossman vividly described how he came across an exhausted fireman. He asked the fireman if he could not do something, and pleaded with him to extinguish the fire before it got hold of the building and destroyed his flat. 'I'm from Reading, not London, Sir, and my nozzle does not fit.' Crossman approached another fireman. 'Sorry, Guv, the water's run out – and that geyser won't let us into his house because he says we may flood it.' Crossman's flat burned.

But how was Crossman recruited to Political Warfare? By the old-boy network. One of the recommendations for Crossman to be taken into this embryo area of activity came from the hard-bitten Sefton Delmer, chief foreign affairs reporter of the *Daily Express* and high in the esteem of Beaverbrook and of his great editor for a quarter of a century, the remarkable Arthur Christiansen.

Crossman was a controversial choice when he became head of the German Section of the PWE – the Political Warfare Executive, which he often called Psychological Warfare Executive. In early 1941 he was the object of ferocious criticism by elements in the Executive led by the German adviser, F. A. Voigt. The Chairman of the Executive Committee, the legendary Sir Robert Bruce Lockhart, was appalled by the vehemence of Crossman's response, but decided that he should stay and Voigt should go. They had accused each other of being trivial, disingenuous, cheap, misguided, and amateurish. Voigt might have been thought to know more about Germany, but in Bruce Lockhart's view, Crossman had soon become a supreme propagandist. Open propaganda was handled by the BBC, but Crossman was able to form a first-class working relationship with Ivone Kirkpatrick, the BBC's Foreign Adviser, who had been appointed as link between the BBC and the PWE. Kirkpatrick was given the authority to resolve disputes between the regional directors and the BBC editors, who had a right of appeal to the Executive Committee.

Because he came to understand the needs, requirements and conditions of the broadcasters in the exigencies of the war, Crossman was different to, and I thought better than, any other of his Cabinet colleagues, twenty years later, at handling the heavyweights of the Corporation, such as Sir William Haley and Hugh Carleton Greene. He was a respecter of the rights of broadcasters, and thought Harold Wilson was often petty and childish in his petulancies against the BBC from the time of the D-notice row of 1967, (involving Colonel Sammy Lohan, Secretary of the Services Press and Broadcasting Committee, and Chapman Pincher of the *Daily Express*) right through to the end of his premiership.

At thirty-three, Crossman was extremely sophisticated in his approach to Germany, partly because he knew so many Germans, among them Adam von Trott, Rhodes Scholar at Oxford, who was to be executed for his role in the 1944 bomb plot against Hitler.

Crossman believed that the Germans must be told not only that they faced a long war, but that the very system of Nazism implied a situation of war without any foreseeable end. If Germany won the struggle of 1940–1, another armed conflict would follow. In the absence of war and conflict, Crossman perceived that the whole apparatus of Nazism had no meaning. Certainly, Crossman told me, he conceded that Germany might make great conquests. Yet the conquered peoples, subjugated and humiliated, would be her resentful enemies, and would in due course rise against Germany. Crossman's theme was that it was only on account of Hitler and the Nazis that the war continued.

British propaganda experts in general believed that the war at sea and in the air were by 1941 likely to be of overwhelming importance for the purposes of political warfare. The government view was that the British blockade and the weakness of the German counter-blockade should be emphasized. It was Crossman who entered a crucial caveat. As a Socialist, he understood that the Royal Navy must not be portrayed as the tool of the British upper classes who planned to starve Europe with their blockade. Crossman argued strongly against the sense of trying to poke fun at Italian or even German sailors, preferring to spotlight the brutality of U-Boat attacks on merchant shipping. Psychological warriors, Crossman believed, should forever ask themselves the question on what was the probable effect of their words on potential

listeners. Throughout his ministerial life, Crossman would berate colleagues for failing to reflect on how their actions looked to others. There
was, however, an extraordinary lacuna – he was often extremely naive
about how he himself would appear to others.

It was his ability to put himself in his listeners' shoes, superimposed
on his German experience and his basic desire to appeal to moderate
Germans, that led him to clash with colleagues over the role of the RAF.
(I also think that the death of his younger brother, Flight Lieutenant
T. E. S. Crossman, in 1940 gave him a prejudice against unnecessary
flying, or aerial combat that was only of marginal advantage.)

The issue that emerged was no less than the role of the RAF and the
United States Air Force in the bombing of Germany. The conventional
wisdom was that PWE must make the most of the Battle of Britain, in
which Germany suffered her first military setback since 1918. Crossman
went along with this, and claimed he thought up the phrase 'The Aerial
Marne' to describe the Battle of Britain. Where Crossman parted
company with the wisdom of his colleagues was in highlighting the
bombing raids, from an early attack on Emden in 1941 on German
cities and towns. He told me that he had asked the military what they
hoped to achieve, pointing out that whenever he had gone back to
Coventry, as a parliamentary candidate, he had found that the Blitz
had made the people more determined, not less, and that production
had consequently gone up. Why did anyone imagine that German
cities would react differently to Coventry? Being subject to bombing
simply herded people together in common cause, flushed out the
less-than-essential jobs, quelled internal criticism and enhanced production and the war effort. 'At first,' said Crossman to me, 'bombing
simply winkled the waiters out of the Hamburg restaurants into the
Wehrmacht.'

Though no uncritical admirer of Crossman, the late Lord Ritchie-
Calder, who was in charge of the Political Warfare Intelligence Directorate planning department at the time, told me, 'More than any of us,
Crossman pointed out the folly of carrying out a propaganda assault,
like bombing raids, directed at the German population as a whole.'
Ritchie Calder and Crossman were the proponents of trying to get the
listeners to *do* something, rather than trying to get them to *feel*
something. Crossman saw their objective as trying to create a climate
of opinion in Germany through which, at the appropriate moment, the
Allies could promote internal opposition to Hitler. Propaganda ought

to be geared so as to persuade Germans to believe that they shared a common enemy with the Allies, and should concentrate their hatred on that enemy, Nazism, and not upon the British people. Unlike some of his Foreign Office colleagues, Crossman saw clearly that propaganda could not achieve ambitious objectives; all it could do was to play upon and widen such differences as already existed. He foresaw that these differences would only become important in terms of undermining the German effort, when it became clear that the Germans could not actually win the war through military action. Crossman's ambition was to help to create a substantial element inside Germany which, if only surreptitiously, looked forward to an Allied victory, thus avoiding a long-drawn-out period of war.

Crossman did not swallow the notion being peddled as early as 1941 that the German people could be frightened into Armistice. At best, they might be made to feel uneasy. To harp on about the guilt of the Germans as a nation would be the same as bringing into British propaganda the selfsame hate theme which was at the core of German propaganda. Crossman believed it would shatter any hope of an alternative regime acceptable to the moderate Germans whom he had come to know in the decade before the War. Besides, harping on about the guilt of the German people might well have the effect of helping to drive resistance groups into the arms of the Communists.

In 1970, when the controversy of the rights and wrongs of the bombing of Dresden was reopened, Crossman angrily recalled that the PWE was shackled by the inability of the Allies to agree on a statement of war aims which he and his colleagues could use to highlight and give credibility to the 'divide and conquer' motif. Crossman thought that the war could be shortened if blame for the war was placed fairly and squarely on the shoulders of the Nazis, not the entire German people. The truth, as Crossman saw it thirty years after the event, was that there was no satisfactory way of allocating degrees of guilt between the Nazis and the citizens of Dresden or any other part of Germany. His job had been to put over the view that the Nazi Party had dragged a reluctant German people into a war for which they had had little appetite. However questionable this premise, Crossman's concern had been the exploitation of words and ideas, not teaching the Germans truth. He hoped that many would oppose the Nazis, looking to their due reward when peace came. Morality and loss of life apart, Crossman judged the bombing of Hamburg and other cities — and much later

Dresden – as clumsy, ill-conceived, and counterproductive in terms of his objectives at the time.

Nor was Crossman enchanted by black propaganda, which he would generically sum up as 'enjoyable pranks', but which, he complained, diverted an enormous amount of talent and energy. However, he did admire the black leaflets – that is, printing whose British origin had to be hidden – of Ellic Howe. In the summer of 1941, Mr Howe had become a sergeant-major in the Anti-Aircraft HQ, which was unable to make the best use of his unusual talents. He was a printer who had worked on the continent in order to travel and see Europe, and had thus come to have an expert knowledge of continental typographical styles and conventions. Crossman discovered that Howe, in an experience comparable with his own in chasing Erika Landau round Europe, had become fluent in German, Italian, and French. He had also made a study of forgery techniques when he became hard up. Crossman used his influence to get Howe installed in Bush House, the Aldwych HQ of overseas broadcasting, with a staff of three, among whom was an equally unusual German lady who was brilliant as a type designer and graphic artist. Howe, besides forging passes and postage stamps for postal operations contrived by the Special Operations Executive (SOE) inside Germany, printed highly subversive booklets written in collaboration with Crossman. With a pride which he never surpassed, and as a senior Cabinet minister, he showed me a booklet, somewhat dog-eared, which claimed that it had been printed in Germany, and purported to bear the imprint of a Frankfurt printing firm. 'It was printed at Dunstable and written by me and Howe,' he purred. In general, however, Crossman believed that black propaganda achieved little more than amusing the Gestapo.

It was his background in PWE, and his scepticism about black propaganda and the unwisdom of using language which implied that we would take action that we could not and never would take, that prompted Crossman's first-ever intervention in Cabinet. The most pressing business at the Thursday Cabinet on 22 October 1964 concerned Ian Smith and his proposal to declare Rhodesia independent. Arthur Bottomley, the Commonwealth Secretary, had produced a draft paper, which amounted to a gesture bullying the Smith Government. Crossman asked the pertinent question of why the Bottomley draft was formulated in terms of revolt and rebellion, whereas the Defence Committee minutes made it clear that it was a 'unilateral declaration of independence'.

Crossman told me that he had quietly and politely demanded to know whether it was prudent for the Labour Government to use language that suggested that Britain could undertake a military strategy of which we were simply not capable and which we would never undertake. Ought we to treat the White Rhodesians as rebels? It was an obvious question, Crossman chuckled — for an old psychological warrior.

All his life he had a militant aversion to phoney posturing. He would divide his Cabinet and parliamentary colleagues between the categories of realists and gesture-makers. It was his experience of black propaganda that made Crossman so antagonistic to gimmicks and stunts. In June 1965, Harold Wilson, as Prime Minister, announced he would lead a Commonwealth Mission to Vietnam; this was to include Sir Robert Menzies, the Australian Prime Minister, who had himself led a Commonwealth delegation to Egypt at the time of the Suez crisis in 1956. Crossman was worried that the Prime Minister would be *hors de combat* on the domestic political front for some weeks. Within hours, the whole scheme had, not surprisingly, foundered on the refusal of Pham Van Dong, the Prime Minister of North Vietnam, to receive the Commonwealth delegation in Hanoi.

Crossman told me some days later of a conversation that concerned him greatly. Wilson had told him that he would only have been away on the Vietnam mission for a couple of weeks. Crossman then said that Wilson had added, 'Anyway, I think we have got most of the value we can out of it already.' It was the first occasion since he had become Prime Minister that I had heard Crossman contemptuous of Wilson. For Crossman, Vietnam could have become an issue as awkward for the 1964 Labour Government as the Korean War had become for the 1945–51 Labour Government – and even more divisive inside the party. Intuitively, he suspected Harold Wilson knew perfectly well that the chances of success of a Commonwealth initiative were so slim that they did not justify the role that the Prime Minister had allotted himself. Crossman did not think Wilson saw Vietnam as an issue, and was simply content to move from emergency to emergency, picking up bright ideas as he went along. This did not please Crossman. Nor the following month was Crossman enchanted by the Prime Minister's disclosure that he had sent Harold Davies to Hanoi. I stuck up for Wilson, and vouchsafed the opinion that Harold Davies had close relations with Asians long before his current job as an Under-Secretary at the Ministry of Pensions, and actually knew key Vietnamese personally. Crossman was rather wounding to me, telling me not to be a naive boy, and to recognize stunts, even if they were 'dignified by being Prime Ministerial stunts'. All of us are products of our past lives to some extent, and the aversion to black propaganda displayed by Crossman the psychological warrior, left an indelible mark on Crossman the Minister.

White propaganda – millions of leaflets, miniature periodicals and newspapers, for which the British government could openly accept responsibility – was something Crossman believed in with fervour. Later, when he was Secretary of State for Social Services, he often urged the Department of Health and Social Security to produce leaflets to cope with controversial issues. Crossman's view on white propaganda is of crucial importance to understanding how he operated as an issue politician.

The key to success in psychological warfare, he believed, against a state such as Hitler's Germany, or Mussolini's Italy was to reach objectivity in two senses. First, the material must appear to be objective, not to some scholar in Washington or London, but to the proverbial man or woman in the street in Berlin or Rome under Fascism. In turn, this required a second objectivity, a sensitivity to and knowledge of the varying emotions, constantly going up and down according to events, of the men and women to whom the message was being sent. This level of sensitivity and knowledge could not be achieved in the absence of a substantial and well-organized research staff, trained to think and feel itself into the mind of Germans or Italians, or those in countries occupied by the Axis. Crossman wanted a combination of integrity (which he defined as stating accurately the Allied case) and empathy (which he defined as stating the case in terms that the audience in Europe would readily understand). This combination was the ideal which had to be constantly aimed at.

Throughout his Cabinet and policy-making life, Crossman was to organize a research staff, and his favourite researchers were those who he thought saw into the minds of the relevant audience. For example, when he was doing Labour pensions policy in 1957, he relied hugely on Professor Peter Townsend, author of the penetrating study of Bethnal Green, *The Family Life of Old People*, who had become immersed in an elderly community in east London. For Crossman, white propaganda was an aggressive weapon, circumscribed by the fact that it could only achieve positive results when combined with a diplomatic or military offensive. It was utterly misconceived to try to use psychological warfare, white or black, as a substitute for military or diplomatic success. It was a fatal error to use psychological warfare to try to cloak military or diplomatic embarrassment. Crossman thought that use for defensive purposes of psychological warfare simply drained goodwill, and showed up division and weakness. From this belief, he deduced that in a defensive period, or in a period of stalemate, white propaganda had to be strictly confined to the objective of accumulating goodwill, by the open and accurate reporting of defeats or other embarrassing events. Crossman held the view that if setbacks were reported objectively, before they were reported by Germans, Italians or Japanese, considerable advantages in terms of credibility could be gained later on. If catastrophes were hidden in a time of adversity, then the aggressive use of white propaganda in a later period of military success would be devalued.

As we shall see in Chapter 16 on Crossman's period as Secretary of State for the Social Services, this philosophy was most emphatically translated into action on mental health, at the time of the revelation of alleged scandals at the Ely, Friern Barnet and South Ockendon Hospitals. White propaganda should never be directed in a way geared to satisfying the home public. If it was to be effective inside Germany, the manner of presentation and tone would necessarily seem intolerably appeasing and inadequate to the public of Britain or the USA, which had an image of Germany that was far from reality. Crossman had some qualms about the decision of the British Government and Brendan Bracken, Minister of Information, to classify as secret the leaflets distributed in enemy territory. But he grasped the need to avoid a situation in which an ill-informed and therefore ill-tempered public opinion created problems for those involved in conducting a psychological war. This justified establishing secret departments in the Government ministry which supervised psychological warfare, so that their work was not subject to detailed scrutiny by elected representatives. I was myself responsible for placing Crossman on the horns of a most awkward dilemma over Porton Down (Chapter 14 – Leader of the House of Commons). Though he was in favour of open government, it was more difficult to champion it when it might embarrass political colleagues. Crossman, if left to himself, would probably have had no such inhibitions.

In World War Two, British white (and black) propaganda was organized as an auxiliary secret division of the Foreign Office. He thought it should be placed under the Chiefs of Staff. The reason he gave was revealing. Psychological warriors tended to be prima donnas. Prima donnas could be more easily disciplined if they wore uniform and were subject to a clearly understood military hierarchy. Again, Crossman thought there was a difference of temperament between trained diplomats, who often had an inbuilt antipathy to psychological warfare, and service officers, who were more comfortable about using it as a weapon of war. Finally, as a result of his experience at the Allied Forces Headquarters in Algiers, he came to believe that the most crucial psychological warfare activities have to be directed from supreme headquarters in the various areas of operations.

Combined with the fact that provincial cities like Coventry or Birmingham did not want to be run from London, his enthusiasm for regional decision-making, on the other hand, also stemmed from his time in Algiers. He was an enthusiast for satrapies, provincial governments. Harold Macmillan had been a 'marvellous satrap in Algiers'. (Curiously, these two men, who had known each other well, liked each other and admired each other in Algiers, only had one significant conversation during the years 1945–63, when they were both members of the Commons – such is the adversarial nature of British politics at the top. During the course of it, Macmillan gave Crossman the advice, 'When you have got a really good speech, go on repeating it, time after time, until all of it gets printed.' (Crossman did exactly this!) However, in March 1960, Crossman trekked down to Oxford to register his vote for Macmillan against Sir Oliver Franks in the election for the chancellorship of Oxford University – to the chagrin of Franks's supporters.

Fascinated by the French television series *Les Rois Maudits*, Crossman once launched into a diatribe in which he asserted that the counts of Flanders and the dukes of Burgundy were more cost-effective rulers than the kings of France, and that the Electors of Brandenburg and the Margraves of Baden were to be infinitely preferred to any Hapsburg Emperor, as a form of government. Significantly, when I raised all sorts of objections to national assemblies or parliaments in Edinburgh or Cardiff – Crossman was a parliamentary John the Baptist of devolution, to my dismay – he would justify his position often in terms of the Algiers experience of 'getting things done'.

White propaganda could only be used to maximum advantage when it had become obvious to the enemy that they could not win outright victory. At that point, Crossman claimed, psychological warfare became more and more important as a means of imposing the will of the USA and Britain on the minds of the Germans and on the people of occupied Europe. During a campaign, the chief task would be to create the deepest co-ordination between psychological warfare strategy, and the strategy of the commanders in the field. Making sure that there were no 'stunts' and that there was correct timing would be a priority task of the military command. In such a situation, Crossman believed that the 'market research' into the minds of the Germans, painstakingly built up before the military and diplomatic attack, would repay its value.

The firm subordination of psychological warfare to the policy of the Chiefs of Staff was straightforward. But to make sure that such conformity did not degenerate into a lifeless uniformity of output was, in his view, an altogether more daunting proposition. Overcentralization had to be eschewed. An organization which might seem to be untidy – with its executive units operating at Army, Army Group, and Supreme Headquarters level, as well as back at home base – was infinitely to be preferred to an organization so tidy that it defeated the very object for which it was set up in the first place. That object was to give the enemy the feeling that he was not listening to propaganda, but to honest men, simply telling him the truth. Crossman remained in charge of the German and Austrian regional directorate of PWE until he was transferred to Allied Forces Headquarters in Algiers in 1943.

Though the initiative came from Paul Vellacott, Director of Political Warfare in the Middle East, who thought he could harness Crossman's talents, Crossman himself, conscious that he was a future parliamentary candidate for Coventry East, and that many electors in Coventry had suffered bombing or been posted abroad, was anxious not to be accused of fighting his war at home. Crossman was lucky in that he worked well with his *de facto* boss, Robert A. McClure, a tough Scottish-American brigadier from Illinois, whom he had first known as the military attaché at the American Embassy in London in 1941–2, and who was eventually in 1944 to become chief of the Psychological Warfare Division of SHAEF (Supreme Headquarters, Allied Expeditionary Force).

Twenty years later, Crossman instructed shell-shocked officials of the Ministry of Housing that all minister's papers should have in front of them a two-page staff study, the structure of which he had borrowed very largely from the SHAEF soldiers like Robert McClure. It was not quite what the young men of Whitehall anticipated from an incoming

Labour minister. But it made sense. Crossman wanted to ascertain precisely what the vital issue was, and how the ministry suggested that it should be dealt with; when that had been given to him, he could dig into the documents at will. The traditional Civil Service view on home departments was that a minister must not complain if he does not know about a matter until it is ready for him to digest. Crossman was simply not prepared to have *faits accomplis* presented to him, like pre-cooked food, and to discover that he was merely a final court of appeal on matters which had in fact been decided before he had been granted access to them.

Crossman was a man with few heroes. Chaim Weizmann, first president of Israel, was one. Another was, of all people, an American General, Eisenhower's chief of staff, Walter Bedell Smith: 'He was quite simply the best organizer of work I ever saw in action.' Bedell Smith was an exceedingly tough soldier from Indianapolis, who had worked his way up the American military ladder from being a private in the Indiana National guard at the age of fifteen. Crossman told me that it was from Bedell Smith that he got the habit, rare among politicians – George Brown also had it – of asking basic, pertinent questions of complete or almost complete strangers, within thirty seconds of meeting them. It was extremely productive, if disconcerting. Crossman said of Bedell Smith, 'If he found the initial answers of some interest to him, you came away thinking he was wonderful. If your answers were of little or no interest, you came away thinking he was an unmannerly and boorish thug.' Crossman could easily have been describing himself – and knew it! Bedell Smith, like most senior officers, demanded an 'appreciation' of any situation. Crossman often had to respond, and quite an ordeal it could be. Fifteen years later, in preparation for the 1959 General Election, Crossman was frequently asking for 'appreciations' of the political situation. I have the impression that Hugh Gaitskell and Harold Wilson, neither of whom had been in the army, were mildly irritated by Crossman's habits of military terminology.

For his part, Crossman came to suspect at AFH and then SHAEF that the task of a general was relatively easy, compared to those further down the hierarchy. He compared the job of a Minister with that of a general. It suited his temperament. Like a general, he would sit at his desk and pull out a mass of papers from a red box, and find that he had to decide on whether a city should have, for example, new housing land. Such decisions were pleasant and interesting. The staff work done by others was more arduous, and could cause the morning panic, from which he suffered as a journalist, and before that as a member of Eisenhower's staff. Given a difficult ministerial decision, he would consciously ask himself *sotto voce*, but in my hearing, 'How would Bedell Smith have handled this?.'

There was something else that contact with this formidable, no-nonsense Midwesterner taught Crossman, which was not really comprehended by his Cabinet colleagues of the 1960s, and least of all by Harold Wilson. It was that in any crisis, the interests of the United States would come first; and the British, like others, could pick up any crumbs that were going. It was Walter Bedell Smith who disabused Crossman of any illusions about a 'special relationship' between Washington and a Labour Government. It was Bedell Smith who sowed the seeds of Crossman's antagonism to the development of the Anglo-American alliance along Bevinite right-wing lines and to much that was to emerge in the 1960s: the Vietnam War; the cutting back of the British aircraft industry to the advantage of American industry; and much else.

As early in the 1964–70 Labour government as January 1965, Crossman came back at night, aghast that he could not get the cash needed for housing. And why? It was really the overseas commitments and Denis Healey's Defence demands: Hong Kong; Sarawak; Malaya; Singapore; the Maldive Islands; the Persian Gulf; Aden; Cyprus; and many more! Crossman thought Healey and Fred Mulley, the defence ministers, with approval of the troika of Wilson, Brown and Callaghan, had simply capitulated to their advisers, who said, 'Oh, minister, you can't cut that!' Crossman reckoned that no serious cut was being made in defence. On the contrary, he realized with a sinking feeling that the Wilson government was being sucked into an overcommitment in overseas expenditure more burdensome than that to which Ernie Bevin had committed Britain in 1945 – and deep down for the self-same reason: on account of their attachment to the Anglo-American special relationship and their belief that it was only through the existence of this relationship that Britain could survive as an international power outside Europe. This prompted me to go to the Borneo War in 1965, and see for myself what 'confrontation' was about. It was this event that baptized me into the Awkward Squad and shaped my political destiny as a frequent critic of my own government.

The following month, in February 1965, Crossman was angry about cutbacks in the aircraft industry, not least because they affected his own

Coventry East constituency. And why? Because we had to concentrate on maintaining our imperial position East of Suez. Again, why? Not because we needed Singapore and other bases ourselves, but because US President Lyndon Johnson could not defend the Far East on his own. Had it not been for Crossman in Cabinet – and the late Sir Maurice Oldfield as head of MI6 in the Far East at the time – I suspect that Wilson might even have been tempted to accede to Johnson's request 'to send a British contingent to Vietnam, even if it is only a battalion of bagpipers'.

Twenty-one years after he left SHAEF, on 15 June 1966, Crossman sat on the Cabinet platform in Committee Room 14 of the House of Commons and listened to Harold Wilson attempting to justify remaining East of Suez. I was one of the ringleaders of the minority in the Parliamentary Labour Party who wanted to withdraw from Singapore. After the meeting, Crossman said to me, 'When the Prime Minister sat down, had I not been a Minister, I would certainly have put my hand up in the vote with you and your friends.' Crossman lambasted the east-of-Suez stance as a grotesque illusion. How could anyone regard Britain as a great power East of Suez, when we could not even maintain the Sterling Area, and George Brown was gallivanting round the capitals of Europe, trying to get us into the EEC? I gave Crossman the unwelcome advice that if he felt like that, he should resign from the Cabinet and make his reasons for doing so very explicit. It was the only occasion that I talked to him along these lines, and he took it like a lamb. He observed that if I had waited nineteen years for office I would not be quite so quick in my recommendation and referred me to the patient, wear-'em-down virtues of the Roman general Fabius Cunctator (Fabius the Delayer).

Though he admired his SHAEF colleagues, Crossman was not dazzled into becoming one of the Socialists who flocked to NATO from 1948 and tended to jaunt on the circuit at NATO expense. It was Crossman's first-hand working relationship with the Americans – often his friends – which aroused his scepticism towards the Labour government's excessive devotion after July 1945 to the Anglo-American special relationship. This caused him to move an amendment to the King's Speech in November 1946, and to compound the fury of Attlee and Bevin by his co-ordination in April 1947 of the *Keep Left* pamphlet.

Crossman was critical of NATO from its inception. He challenged the assumption which underlay the concept of interdependence. He sensed that many supporters of NATO wished to transform it into an Atlantic confederation, supposing it to be a latterday Roman Empire, whose frontiers were coterminous with the limits of civilization. Outside were the barbarians. He summarized this attitude towards Western defence by a true story which I heard him tell on several occasions. In 1929, at the age of 22, he went to Germany for his postgraduate year. His father had arranged for him to live for six months at the house of a well-respected Jewish judge, who later committed suicide when Hitler came to power because he was the kind of German Jew who could not face up to leaving his own country. Every Sunday, the judge and Crossman used to go for a walk on the Taunus mountains. Along the great desolate saddle at the top, there ran the long line of a Roman *limes* (barrow-and-ditch fortification), with a magnificent view towards the valley of the Rhine. Crossman vividly recalled standing there on a Sunday morning, as the judge said to him. 'Things have not changed much since the Romans left. This side, my dear Dick, civilization. The other side, barbarism. It was true then. It is still true today.'

Crossman told me that his host's attitude encapsulated a clear and precise notion of Western defence. The job was to defend the lines of civilization, the place where the West ends and slavery begins. For him, it was the simplicity of their strategic concept which maintained Roman morale for so many hundreds of years. The legionaries of Rome knew what they had to do, and why they were doing it. As for Rome, so for John Foster Dulles, US delegate at the UN and later Secretary of State for Eisenhower. At the centre of Dulles's thinking was a world dominated by a simple conflict between good and evil, along a line that divided the 'free world' from its enemies. The philosophy don, the psychological warrior, the traveller in prewar Germany did not believe this simplistic gulf. Besides, the MP for Coventry – a city twinned with Stalingrad and the recipient of a Sword of Honour from the Russians – would not in 1945 have tolerated an MP whose world view displayed such anti-Soviet tendencies.

SIX
Palestine and Israel

When in 1963 I was being given what can only be described as a 'viva voce' by Crossman to ascertain whether I was a possible Parliamentary Private Secretary, one of the questions he asked me was: 'You are a gentile: are you an anti-Semite?' 'No,' I said a little primly, slightly offended. 'How do I know?' he said. 'Almost all gentiles are anti-Semitic – I am.' I was disconcerted and had I not known from my own stay in Israel in 1956 that Crossman was something of a hero there, I would probably have decided there and then that it was impossible for me to work for the man. I explained that I had stayed on two kibbutzim, and who my Israeli friends were, such as the family of my student contemporary, Michael Bruno, now Governor of the Bank of Israel. After this inauspicious start, it quickly became clear that Israel was one of the very few matters in life that really did touch Crossman deeply.

Some weeks later, when I had got to know Crossman rather better, I said I was curious to know why he had asked such an unwarranted and aggressive question – feeling that his approach could be the end of relationships for him with less relaxed Members of the Parliamentary Labour Party. He replied, as he often did, rather disarmingly with a reminiscence. At his first meeting with the president of the World Zionist Organization and future president of Israel, Chaim Weizmann, which went on throughout most of the night, he had said to Crossman, 'Are you anti-semitic?' Crossman, like J. S. Mill when asked if it were true that he had said his working-class electors were extremely lazy, replied 'Of course.' Crossman thought that his friendship with Weizmann had begun at that moment. 'Because,' recalled Crossman, 'Weiz-mann believed that if a gentile denied his latent anti-Semitism, he must either be lying or deceiving himself. Weizmann thought that the only honest attitude for a gentile to adopt was to confess to an unconscious prejudice against Jews, and to make certain that this in no way influenced his behaviour by consciously making allowances.'

Frankly, one of the problems I have in writing about Crossman's life before I myself knew him is that one cannot be sure about the absolute accuracy of what he said – or wrote in books. The story of gentile and anti-Semite is true in substance. I do not doubt that Crossman came to believe it was true as he told it. What may have been embroidered was the dating of the story, pinpointing it to his first meeting with Weizmann.

I once put the question to Herbert Morrison, 'Why on earth did the 1945 Government soon after it was elected appoint Crossman to the Anglo-American Commission of Inquiry into Palestine?' In that avuncular Cockney voice, Lord Morrison chuckled, 'You will learn at your age [I was 30] that in politics men do not always turn out as you think they will. Bevin said the Americans had asked for him; Attlee said he knew the fellow and he was a nuisance; and therefore I was glad to get him out of the way, causing me trouble in the House here, by giving him something to do. It was as simple as that, my friend!'

It rings true. Their immediate convenience is a powerful motive for major politicians making appointments. Some thirty years later, Harold Wilson and James Callaghan, then Foreign Secretary, decided that as Vice-Chairman of the Parliamentary Labour Party I should go to the European Parliament, as Deputy Leader to Michael Stewart of the indirectly elected British Labour Group – because by doing so they reckoned that they would get me out of their way and stop me being a nuisance on the Scotland and Wales Bills. I also understand the opprobrium that such activity on matters of deep political principle, such as support for the Jewish nation or the future constitutional relationship of England, Wales and Scotland, can generate.

Crossman was tagged the man 'who stabbed Ernie Bevin in the back'; and I was told by Roy Hattersley that one of the side-effects of my forty-seven days on the floor of the House of Commons, opposing Devolution, had been to bring down the Labour Government. The charges are equally preposterous and unfair.

Sir Isaiah Berlin told me that some time after Crossman had returned from the Anglo-American Commission and was creating trouble, Bevin was asked why he had given Crossman the appointment in the first place. At that time, Bevin replied with the benefit of hindsight that he was testing him to see whether Crossman was capable of working in a team. I do not doubt Berlin's information. I do suspect that it may have been an excuse or justification from Bevin, given to those who thought he had brought his troubles from Crossman on to his own shoulders. Sir Isaiah also told me of a revealing episode from 1946 before relations between Crossman and Bevin had irretrievably broken down. Bevin and Crossman had agreed that each of them would do something to oblige the other. Crossman carried out his side of the bargain, Bevin reneged on his. When they next saw each other, Bevin put his hand on Crossman's shoulder and said, 'Sorry, but that's the way these things go in politics.' On which Crossman commented disingenuously, 'That's the type of politician I admire!' But relations were to deteriorate and become very sour indeed.

Any explanation of how Crossman became involved in Israel would be incomplete without reference to another leitmotif of Crossman's early and middle life – though progressively less marked later on. Quite simply, Crossman was one of those people who adored fishing in troubled waters. He found a thrill in struggle and strife. He was exhilarated to become involved in areas where there were issues. He was one of Mother Nature's stirrer-uppers. Turbulence for its own sake provided the kind of environment where Crossman felt comfortable and in his element. Disputatious and fractious peoples interested him. Never mind danger and the foreboding of death: this added spice to life. Above all, constant, serious argument. On these criteria, Israel and the Jews suited Crossman perfectly.

It is part of the pattern of Crossman's life that when he was pitched into a situation, he became wholehearted. This was true at Housing, at Health, at SHAEF and on other occasions; above all it was true when, with a hitherto empty mind, he was pitched into Palestine. It was to become what he still called at the end of his life certainly the most thrilling and probably the most useful episode in his existence. He was an observer and then a participant in the birth of a new nation.

On the mantelpiece of his study there was for all the years that I lodged with Dick and Anne Crossman, a sepia photograph of an Edwardian gentleman. At first I naturally assumed that it was Crossman's father – before I discovered the father/son relationship!

One day I referred to Mr Justice Crossman's photo. 'That's not my blood father, it's my spiritual father. It's Chaim Weizmann.'

Born in 1874 in the Pale, the only part of Russia where Jews were then permitted to live, and spending his childhood in the time of black reaction which came to a head with the pogrom in Kishinev, Weizmann escaped to Germany, and became a student of biochemistry at Berlin (and Berne). Amazingly, this young Russian chemist arrived in Manchester with his German degree, with no contacts even with British Jewry, no money and no knowledge of English. But within six months he was teaching Lancashire students chemistry and his wife, having taken her medical degree for the third time in a foreign language, was in charge of Manchester's clinics. The New Zealander Rutherford, then doing his seminal work on the atom at Manchester, and C. P. Scott, the legendary editor of the *Manchester Guardian*, were among his friends. In the middle of the 1906 election campaign, he had one conversation with Arthur Balfour. Crossman was fascinated that out of their personal friendship in Manchester, and his position as Director of Admiralty Laboratories (1916–19), grew the fabric of Zionist policy which was to set the pattern of British Middle Eastern diplomacy for the two decades after the First World War. Weizmann was president of the World Zionist Organization and later also of the Jewish Agency for Palestine in 1921–31 and 1935–46. He became the first President of Israel in 1948.

Crossman told me that in 1952 when Weizmann died, it was one of the few occasions in his adult life when he dissolved in tears: 'He is the only great man I ever knew well, and I am not likely to know another.' He had spent 'many, many hours' with him, and grieved that it was over: 'Life's worth living when there is a cause like that [of Israel] to fight for, where you have no inhibitions of any kind and you feel that you are absolutely right.' More than any other single individual, it was Chaim Weizmann who inspired Richard Crossman to be an issue-politician rather than a position-politician.

Years later, in the Drury Lane Theatre, on the occasion of the Zionist Federation Fiftieth Anniversary Celebration of the Balfour Declaration in November 1967, Crossman paid tribute to his hero. It was an unforgettable evening. Daniel Barenboim conducted the English Chamber Orchestra, himself playing the solo part in Beethoven's C major Piano Concerto. Then Sir Barnett Janner led Crossman, Julian Amery, Bob Boothby and Abba Eban on to the stage. The Theatre

Royal was packed to capacity. Crossman said that as Leader of the House of Commons, he was the holder of a great ministerial office; but that was no greater honour than the love and respect of the Jewish community. 'By luck or Bevin's choice' – at which there was a knowing roar of laughter – he had participated in an act of atonement by the Christian communities of the West. He supported not the claims of the hawks, but the vision of the doves, and as a disciple of Weizmann pleaded with the Jews present to use their influence to get the Israelis to enter into direct negotiations with the Arabs. He implied that it would be a mistake to rely on the United Nations. The next day, Crossman told Abba Eban that he had had his speech cleared as official Government policy. Eban retorted that he had already seen the Foreign Secretary, and asked whether the speech was a personal statement or whether it represented official Government policy. George Brown solemnly assured Eban. 'I worked over it with him word by word. Indeed, there was nothing left for Dick to do but to deliver it. Did he deliver it well?' To the Jews, Brown took full credit for the speech. To the Arabs, the Foreign Office revealed that they had sent a telegram asserting the speech – 'Crossman's Declaration' as the *Jewish Observer* dubbed it – represented no change of policy; and Hugh Foot, Lord Caradon, the UK Permanent Representative at the United Nations, duly disowned it. Crossman had expected little else. He had been telling the Israelis for twenty years that they would be foolish to rely on Perfidious Albion.

As a member of the Anglo-American Commission, Crossman had first met Weizmann in Rehovoth in the winter of 1945–6. At first, he could not comprehend how Weizmann combined an admiration for the civilization of England and Germany with a distaste for assimilation. Weizmann struck Crossman as a man of the fanaticism and power attributed to Lenin, with the sophisticated charm attributed to Disraeli. He found a man who seemed to have more time for British gentiles than for assimilated Jews. As the relationship with Weizmann deepened, Crossman told me that he thought we were regarded as Goyim, for whom allowances had to be made. English and above all German Jews, whose Jewish patriotism was supercharged by national loyalty, were in a different category. Not only in private but in the public hearings of the Commission, Weizmann made an indelible impression on Crossman.

In his diary of 8 March 1946, Crossman wrote: 'Today we had Weizmann, who looks like a weary and more humane version of Lenin, very tired, very ill. He spoke for two hours with a magnificent mixture of passion and scientific detachment. He is the first witness who has frankly and openly admitted that the issue is not between right and wrong but between the greater and lesser injustice.'

The more Crossman saw during the 120-day sojourn in Palestine, the less neutral and more committed to the Jewish cause he became. It is put around political circles that he behaved badly to the British forces, who were doing a difficult job. It so happens that I arranged for Crossman as Minister of Housing to combine a political rally in Bathgate, in my West Lothian constituency, with a visit to the prize-winning New Town of Cumbernauld on Saturday 13 February 1965 – about which the dour Secretary of State for Scotland was to complain in Cabinet about Crossman's PPS arranging a 'Royal Progress through Scotland for the Minister of Housing.' (Harold Wilson told me this with a twinkle, and said I'd better be tactful to Willie Ross, the Scottish Secretary.) Knowing that the then chairman of the Cumbernauld Development Corporation was Lieutenant-General Sir Gordon Mac-Millan of MacMillan, a family friend of ours, and that he had been in Palestine in 1946 (and was GOC there in 1947–8), I rang him up to make sure that he would not object to Crossman's coming. 'On the contrary, I shall be glad to see him. He behaved impeccably, as far as I was concerned, when he came with the Anglo-American Mission.'

To acquire a full picture of how Crossman's opinions were formed and transformed on Palestine in 1945–6, it is essential to read his own book, *Palestine Mission* (1947).

Returning to Britain, he demanded to see the Prime Minister, with results described elsewhere (pages 71–2). Crossman was concerned about the issue. The Prime Minister was concerned about totally different matters, in particular that Crossman had offended Ernie Bevin. And anyone who offended Ernie, who was the bedrock of his own position in Downing Street, could not be taken to be submitting a serious case.

Crossman, on his return, naturally went to Bevin, who after all had appointed him, and who he at first imagined was actually interested in his opinions. 'But, Ernie, I've seen it for myself. The Palestine Jews have grown into a nation, and if you refuse them partition, they will fight for their lives.' The massive and dogmatic leader of the Transport Workers' union, who was not used to be contradicted by anyone in the Labour movement, let alone MPs of one year's standing, gruffly replied, 'No. There's only a Jewish religion and not a Jewish nation. And if

those Jews in Palestine are not religious, they ought not to call themselves Jews!'

After years of struggle and the burden of the Ministry of Labour
during the war, Bevin was getting tired, heavy and short-tempered, and
Crossman had crossed him. When a serious and persistent critic crosses
a senior Minister, it is difficult to stop personal relations breaking down,
or at least the deaf talking to the deaf. Twenty years later, I was myself
to go through a similar agony with the Bevin-like Denis Healey (though
a Balliol first, he would not be displeased at the comparison), when we
were in disagreement over the Anglo-French variable geometry aircraft,
the Borneo war, the Argyll and Sutherland Highlanders, Aldabra atoll,
and chemical and biological weapons.

Bevin and Healey thought they had better things to do than answer
the merits of a case put up by parliamentary colleagues on their own
side of the House of Commons, who were issue-politicians. It would
have been better for Britain and unquestionably better for the Labour
Governments and Labour Party if Bevin and Healey had listened with
care to what Crossman and Dalyell were actually saying. Equally, in
retrospect, I am conscious that I certainly (and probably Crossman)
was irritatingly self-righteous in those days, and did not help my causes
by being overmuch of the knight in shining armour. Ex-public school
boys in their thirties are often not very reflective about how others may
perceive them when they know that they are right and that great
men with huge responsibilities are wrong. More than most, the issue
politician, embarked on a crusade, had better be careful about his
good manners and personal tact. Harry Nicholas, later to be General
Secretary of the Labour Party and for years one of Ernie Bevin's friends
in the TGWU, told me that Crossman had never appreciated the simple
human fact that Bevin was personally hurt that the Jews showed so
little gratitude for all that Britain had done for them. This, as much as
the pro-Arab prejudices of the Foreign Office, accounted for his putting
the shutters down to Crossman. I suspect Harry Nicholas was near the
mark.

I know for a fact that Attlee felt this lack of gratitude acutely, because
Arthur Royle, his PPS and close friend, told me so. Crossman ruefully
recounted the very first Commons lobby encounter with Attlee after
he had rejected the Anglo-American Commission report. The Prime
Minister's opening remark was, 'I'm disappointed in you, Dick. The
report you have produced is grossly unfair!' Crossman told me – and I

believe it because he was genuinely concerned with issues per se – that he was honestly puzzled and said, 'Unfair, Prime Minister, to the Jews or to the Arabs?' With venom, Attlee had snapped, 'No, unfair to Britain, of course. You have let us down by giving way to the Jews and to the Americans!'

Crossman was genuinely shocked at the cynical lack of interest of the prime minister in the rights and wrongs, pros and cons of the issue. He never got over it. Typically, he did not sit back and sulk. Nor did he indulge in self-pity, a common and most destructive disease among politicians. Instead he moved an amendment to the King's Speech in 1946, which some remembered against him all his life. Herbert Morrison, who disliked Ernie Bevin and was basically sympathetic to the aspirations of the Jewish people, wanted Crossman to be an Under-Secretary in the Foreign Office at several different points, and most decisively when he himself became Foreign Secretary, according to Eddie Shackleton. Attlee would not hear of anything of the kind and preferred safe old Haileybury boys like Christopher Mayhew.

By the autumn of 1946, Attlee's irritation against Crossman had developed into sustained hostility, and Bevin's into violent rage at the very mention of Crossman's name. Percy Wells, a Labour MP from Kent and Bevin's PPS, later told me about his boss's spluttering fury with my new boss, Crossman, and mimicked Ernie Bevin's incoherence at the mention of the Coventry MP. What the bloody hell were the industrial workers of Coventry sending a bastard like that to the House of Commons for? He would get hold of them! The immediate straw-that-broke-the-camel's-back was the repeated refusal of the Jewish settlers in Palestine to be grateful for British protection and to conform to the plans that Bevin had made for them. By 1947, Bevin had become anti-Semitic. Some would say he was under strong provocation – others would be less charitable. The Jews had rejected his pet solution to their problem. The provocation grew when Bevin discovered that the Russians were exploiting the issue against him and, even worse, that the Americans were ganging up with the Russians. Goaded by a perilous mixture of fury and extreme self-pity, Bevin got it into his head that the Jews were organizing a world conspiracy against poor old Britain and in particular against poor old Ernie! Crossman was an instrument of this diabolical plot.

Crossman was partly inhibited by the fact that two British sergeants who were murdered in July 1947 in dreadful circumstances came from

Coventry. What happened to Clifford Martin and Mervyn Paice was to haunt Crossman throughout the 1940s. For the sake of the Jews, Crossman had burned his political boats. They knew it and rewarded him with friendship. However, the qualifications are encapsulated in a story which I heard both from Crossman, and from Yigael Yadin, the archaeologist-general who excavated Masada, one of Crossman's (and my) favourite places.

In 1948, almost at the end of the Jewish War of Independence, Crossman was staying with Weizmann at Rehovoth. A party was given for him. A well-known Jewish matron advanced on Crossman and said for all to hear, 'I would like to introduce Yigael Yadin, our commander-in-chief to our pro-Jewish guest, Mr Richard Crossman!' It was the first time Crossman had met Yadin, the beginning of a lifelong friendship. Crossman says that he looked into the large, quizzical eyes of the remarkable archeologist-turned-soldier, and was agog to know what he would say. Yadin's version to me was that he thought Crossman would want to hear the brutal truth. So, his first words were: 'Mr Crossman is not pro-Jewish: he is pro-British. After all, he was the prime author of the Anglo-American Commission's Report, and I remember that when we were discussing our attitude to it, Dr Weizmann remarked on the ruthlessness of some English politicians. "This report," Dr Weizmann told us angrily, "was nicely calculated to concede the minimum to the Jews in order to obtain their acquiescence."'

The truth was that the report had gone about as far as the House of Commons would stomach. Twenty years later when Sydney Silverman died in the middle of February 1968, I was taken aback at the way Crossman snapped back his refusals to write an obituary when asked to do so by several daily and weekly newspapers. Crossman said he liked Silverman only with his head and not with his heart. He then, to my chagrin, because I thought the particular criticisms were not fair, launched into a diatribe that in order to be effective backbenchers, men like Silverman and Dalyell had to have unpleasant characteristics – being personally difficult, inordinate vanity and unco-operative bloodymindedness.

You and Sydney are the type of people who have tremendous individual egotism, driving you along and concentrating your energies on a few objectives. If you can work in a team, a man would want to be in government, not to succeed on the back benches. The only people who can really live the back bench life must have the unattractive characteristics of a George Wigg, a Sydney Silverman or yourself.'

I must be allowed one further personal reference to myself, as a springboard for what I am going to say. In 1986, I was invited to speak at the quarterly constituency Labour Party meeting of the Cardiff South and Penarth Labour Party on, of all things, 'Official Secrets'. I was introduced to the meeting by the local MP, who said, 'You've never asked me to talk to you on official secrets, but I do realize that it is more interesting to have the Sydney Silverman of our time. It is a pleasure to introduce my friend...' Since that particular local MP had only held the offices of Foreign Secretary, Home Secretary and Prime Minister – not to mention Chancellor of the Exchequer – and was James Callaghan, I would gladly have disappeared under the floorboards with embarrassment. However, there is an element of truth in what Crossman and Callaghan say. In order to stand up to the House of Commons when it is baying its hatred of Jewish terrorists or Argentine juntas you have got to have a kind of mental tenacity and guts, intertwined with a kind of vanity and egotism, which leads one to believe that one is right when all others are out of step. When Ernest Bevin decided to send the *Exodus* back to Hamburg with its shipload of Jewish immigrants, the Commons boomed its approval, as it did on 3 April 1982, when Margaret Thatcher responded to a hostile interruption from me on the Falklands and the sending of the battle fleet.

Sydney Silverman, latterly on capital punishment, was an inspiration in standing up to unpopularity. Crossman was never a good enough Commons attender to go through this experience. Indeed, leadership of the pro-Israel cause in the Commons was left to Sydney Silverman, Maurice Orbach and others. I felt that Crossman's admiration for Israel was enhanced by a remarkable phenomenon. He had seen a land where thousands of young men and women had been trained to practise illegal violence, and had learned to lie and to spy, to bribe the police and corrupt the established authorities. Crossman found it astonishing that as soon as the need for resistance and illegal activity was over, these young men and women went back to their normal occupations and reverted to the accepted standards of civic right and wrong. A way of life was emerging which was military without becoming militaristic. As Weizmann had predicted to Crossman, the standing, the self-confidence and the morale of Western Jewry had been vastly strengthened by the existence of Israel. The popular stereotype of the Jew as a clever cosmopolitan and slick moneyspinner had been undermined in the gentile mind by the earthiness and toughness of Israeli democracy. The victories of the Israeli army had done more to combat anti-Semitism in Christian countries than the combined effort of all organizations for reconciling Christians and Jews. Later, Crossman was to note the many thousands of people in Britain who regarded Suez 1956 as a reckless crime but who could not suppress a glow of admiration for the Sinai campaign.

Crossman was not a rubber-stamp of all the Israelis did and said. For example, during the 1967 War, Harold Wilson told Abba Ebban that he might be surprised if he knew who in Cabinet had been among those who advocated a passive British stance. Eban guessed at once – Crossman!

A year later, Crossman again infuriated some of his Israeli friends during the marathon negotiations on the selling of Chieftain tanks to the Israelis. Bluntly as ever, he told his colleagues that if they sold tanks to Israelis they should not be surprised if the darn things were properly used. They had been buying Centurion tanks for a long time, and they would buy the best available. Their requirement was 200 Chieftains to replace the Centurions in 1970 and 1971.

On account of my experience as national-service tank crew with the Royal Scots Greys, I told Crossman that he could not deny the Israelis new tanks, and that there was nothing worse than trying to make do with clapped-out tanks, with tracks, turrets, and everything else jamming. Besides, the Israelis said that they were out-tanked four or five to one now that the Russians had rearmed the Egyptians after their resounding losses in the Six Day War. Crossman saw it as a major issue. He asked for and got all the papers, which would not normally go to the Social Services Secretary, because Wilson thought he would be a potential friend in Cabinet to the sale. However, what Crossman saw as the merits dominated his advice. Quite simply, to let the Israelis buy Chieftains would give an extra turn to the screw of the armaments spiral in the Middle East. To give military ascendancy to the Israelis was hazardous.

By the summer of 1969, Crossman thought that the military threat to Israel had increased to the point where either the British or Americans should sell them tanks. But characteristically he was for telling the Israelis that the British would always let them down. Crossman accepted the Foreign Office line that we could not afford to supply them with tanks, because of our own desperate situation with the Arabs. The British should tell them that, although we were their friends, we could not help them and they had better get arms elsewhere. Ironically, this put him in the company of the pro-Arabs in Cabinet. Superficially, and to many serious colleagues, Crossman's attitude was inconsistent. However, what he was consistent about was preaching to the Cabinet that rather than postpone decisions, they should tell the Israelis the honest truth, that we British feared for our oil supplies and having our installations burned down. Crossman was scornful of those who attempted to get the best of both worlds; in this case, appeasing the Arabs by postponing the decision and leading the Israelis along on a string. He thought Michael Stewart, George Brown, and the Foreign Office were implying all kinds of promises and then letting the Israelis down.

On the other hand, the Israeli representatives were very shrewd people, who would be able to judge the British as we actually are. The Israelis were unlikely to be led down the garden path. But the British duty was to warn them in advance that we were a bad ally. I know Crossman was cut to the quick by Golda Meir's remark as she sat in the plane at Heathrow: 'I don't want to set foot in a country where there is a Labour Government whose name is synonymous with treachery.'

The Israeli arms saga prompted Crossman to reflect how ministers do get used to assuming that they can stay in senior ministerial positions by accepting a whole important area of Government policy, even if they know in their heart of hearts that it is thoroughly misconceived.

Crossman was a deep friend of Israel, yet not one of the Israeli lobby. He was outraged at the efforts being made to unload millions of pounds' worth of the most sophisticated armaments on Arabs who really were not capable of handling them. This was what he saw as the ignominious tradition of old-fashioned Foreign Office strategy, in conjunction with a cynical merchant-of-death arms sales policy. I asked him what he would have done if he had been Foreign Secretary. He admitted that he would not have flagrantly taken the Israeli side, threatened our contacts with the Arabs, and risked seeing our embassies throughout the Arab world in flames. He would have attempted to have extracted Britain from the Persian Gulf and would have placated and appeased during this period. As though it concluded the matter, and almost met the situation, Crossman defiantly enunciated the difference between himself and his colleagues: he would have carried out the same policy without trying to pretend that we could really do anything for the Israelis meanwhile. Semantics were too often something of a bolt-hole from difficult decisions.

Crossman thought that the House of Commons lived in a world in the 1960s of wish-fulfilment and illusion, discussing ways in which Britain could shape the future of the Middle East. Parliament was forever demanding emergency statements from ministers, in reality for no better reason than that parliament had to feel important. He found it embarrassing.

SEVEN
The Bevanites

Number 9 Vincent Square is one of those nineteenth-century, somewhat jerry-built London houses, which has a dining room-kitchen in the basement, a drawing-room one floor up, a toilet and, a few steps above that, a bedroom, bathroom, and a top flat – occupied successively by the Jacobsons, the Hetheringtons and the Dalyells, during Crossman ownership. It is within twelve minutes' walking distance of the House of Commons, past the Horseferry Road Magistrates' Court and up Millbank.

The drawing-room was elongated and comfortable and held for Crossman treasured memories. Sometimes – and even more frequently in the last year of his life – he would point to a particular place or chair, and would recall, not really nostalgically, that a comrade sat there. I had the impression that the Keep Left group held fonder memories for him than the later Bevanites. It may have been partly that Keep Left was more concerned with fundamental aims and long-term goals rather than the day-to-day tactics which appear to have dominated the later Bevanite Group. Nye would sit there, and Jennie Lee there. That's where Stephen Swingler and Dick Acland would sit. Tommy Balogh, Dudley Seers, and David Worswick would be over there. Harold Wilson would sit in that chair; Ian Mikardo, a key member, influential and an organizer, there. This was a gathering of the central core of the intellectual Left.

Yet, at the risk of Crossman's shade rising and bellowing at me in disagreement, I don't think he was in the first instance or by nature one of the Left of the Labour Party. He was, though, in the first instance, a serious foreign-policy critic of the Attlee–Bevin regime.

It was on a grey 18 November afternoon in 1946 that Crossman made a speech in which he crossed the political Rubicon into opposition to the Labour Party hierarchy, and thus shaped the future pattern of his life. On the fifth day of the King's Speech debate, dealing with foreign policy, he moved at the end the following amendment: 'and express the urgent hope that His Majesty's Government will so review and recast its conduct of International Affairs as to afford the utmost encouragement to, and collaboration with, all Nations and Groups striving to secure full Socialist planning and control of the world's resources and thus provide a democratic and constructive Socialist alternative to an otherwise inevitable conflict between American Capitalism and Soviet Communism in which all hope of World Government would be destroyed.'

There is another reason why I am coy about offering any clear-cut treatment of the Keep Left–Bevanite period. Like Crossman, I have been a Member of Parliament for more than a quarter of a century. Like Crossman, I have been elected to the National Executive Committee of the Labour Party (alas, for a much shorter period!). Like Crossman, I have been a weekly columnist on a tabloid daily (the *Daily Record*), and a weekly (*New Scientist* for 22 years). Unlike Crossman, I was not a member of the Tribune Group. Therefore a certain reticence may be seemly.

To understand Crossman's Cabinet life, and indeed his unanticipated promotion following the death of Gaitskell, it is necessary to delve back to those lunchtime Tuesdays at Vincent Square where each person chipped in six shillings and sixpence.

A crucial event occurred in April 1954, exquisitely described by Ian Mikardo, in *Back-Bencher* (1988), in terms not different in fact from what Crossman recalled to me:

Under the standing orders of the Parliamentary Labour Party the vacancy in the Shadow Cabinet created by [Nye Bevan's] resignation would be offered to the highest unsuccessful candidate in the last Shadow Cabinet election, and in this case that was Harold Wilson. In my innocence I took it for granted that Harold couldn't possibly distance himself openly from Nye by taking that place, particularly as he had strongly supported Nye on the issue of policy in South-east Asia which had led to the resignation. I went along to that week's lunch meeting in Vincent Square assuming that that matter wouldn't occupy more than a minute of our time and then we'd get on with the other things we had to discuss.

Not so. It soon became apparent that Harold had quickly decided to take the vacancy: he had had a talk about it with Dick, though with no-one else, not by way of consulting him but merely to enlist him as an intermediary to break the news to Nye and to arrange for the three of them to meet... [At a subsequent lunch meeting] Dick alone supported Harold's decision: the rest of us, however critical we were of Nye's resignation and of the manner of it, believed – and we were proved to be right – that Harold's action would inflict serious damage not only on Nye but on the Left as a whole. But the decision was Harold's, and he made it by himself and for himself..

...Except that Nye never fully recovered his trust in Crossman ('too clever by half'), each of the two sides in the Wilson-acceptance argument showed an understanding tolerance of the other: we accepted that each of us had acted in what he believed, rightly or mistakenly, was in the best interest of all of us and of the Party as a whole.

Mikardo refers to the eternal struggle on the Left between the principled and the pragmatists, and saw that it would eventually boil over:

I always had the feeling, though I was never courageous enough to face it and bring it into the open, that sooner or later the strains in our group between the principled and the pragmatists were bound to drive a wedge between them.

An amendment to the Royal Address from a supporter of an administration was without precedent. The Prime Minister was livid; unforgivingly livid. Ernest Bevin blew his top. And anything that upset Ernie not only upset Attlee, the linchpin of whose leadership Ernie was, but it upset all those who were upset when Ernie was upset.

In moving the amendment at 4.19 p.m. when he had sat down after 37 minutes, even though he later offered to withdraw it after the Prime Minister's lengthy reply, Crossman had ensured that he would never, never be the meanest parliamentary secretary in a government headed by Clem Attlee. When Herbert Morrison asked for him in 1950, as a junior minister in the Foreign office, Attlee refused point blank with a monosyllabic 'No.'

Actually, Crossman had made a formidable case, which Attlee did not attempt to answer. The Prime Minister's attitude and ill-treatment drove Crossman into the arms of the serious Left, where he found, as I have done for twenty-five years, a number of simply the nicest, most congenial, honourable, gentlemanly men and similarly generous women in the House of Commons – and certainly the wittiest and most amusing. But I understand the Left were not altogether pleased with Crossman. Michael Foot told me that Crossman had in effect made an apology for moving the amendment. The slightly sour taste was left in their mouth that even at that stage, having well and truly burned his boats, he was still hankering after office.

I have the impression that, unlike the principled Left, Crossman did not quite ever make up his mind about whether or not to crawl for office. Bombastically he used to say, 'The way to become a Minister is either to lick the arses of the leadership or kick them in the political goolies – you can't do both.' Correct, in my view. But he may have fallen between his two rules.

This book is not the place to dwell on the important influence of Keep Left and the Bevanites on British politics. Michael Foot's great biography, *Aneurin Bevan* (1962–73) provides first-hand information. So does Ian Mikardo's deliciously written and fascinating autobiography, *Back-Bencher*. Both Foot and Mikardo were themselves major participants. Both are supremely honest and candid men. Though they knew his faults and shortcomings, both were well disposed towards and liked Crossman.

Truth to tell, Crossman, when a senior minister, did not always like to have his Keep Left incarnation thrown in his face. And yet he was generous enough to admit that there was an uncanny similarity with the situation when he was himself a backbencher in the Keep Left Group of 1946–7. In me and my friends such as Joel Barnett, Bob Sheldon, Edwin Brooks, he thought he saw the same kind of Left growing up in the Parliamentary Labour Party. He saw the young MPs as protesting that Britain was under the heel of the Americans, and that Harold Wilson and Michael Stewart, as Foreign Secretary, were carrying out a Bevinite policy, but from a far weaker position than Britain had in 1945. He sympathized with the new backbenchers of the 1964 and 1966 intakes who were saying 'No' to an East-of-Suez policy costing us £250 million a year, and he felt strongly that when the confrontation between Malaya and Sukarno's Indonesia had ceased, there was no excuse for keeping troops east of Suez at such cost.

Harold Wilson was probably Crossman's least favourite guest. He was certainly regarded then nothing like as warmly as Nye Bevan, Ian Mikardo, Barbara Castle, Dick Acland and some others. Crossman found his constant references to his time at the Board of Trade, which he dragged in regardless, quite insufferable — not least because those MPs who have not had the opportunity to be a minister find it hard to take endless reminiscences from younger men who were given office.

Crossman was even ruder about Wilson and his indecision. He likened the future prime minister to a spherical little thing which kept twirling in dismay. It was no good bullying him. Someone who does not want to stand, could not stand. But stand he did.

Unedifying though it may have been for the Tuesday lunchers, Crossman had not only given support, but critical support, for a step which was a crucial milestone on the road to 10 Downing Street. Had Wilson rejected the place in the Shadow Cabinet, I was told by several colleagues when I was a young MP, he would not have become Shadow Chancellor, which was to pave the way to the Leadership of the Opposition. In politics, adversity and unpopularity created a bond. Such a bond was created thirty-five years ago.

Crossman thought that Wilson, though vain, was not conceited; though enormously intelligent, he was certainly not an intellectual. He would also say cheerfully that one of Wilson's great merits was that he was not afraid of his (Crossman's) brutal brain power. He thought (mistakenly, in the light of later years) that Wilson would stick to the agreed party line; and that he genuinely felt that when policies were worked out and compromises were agreed, the line had to be observed by everybody, including the leader. There was also a negative bond between Wilson and Crossman: neither was an Aldermaston marcher; Crossman, because marching was not his scene, and anyway he never thought there was much difference between the latest fire-bombs and atomic/hydrogen bombs. Dresden in 1944 was, he believed, worse than Hiroshima or Nagasaki in 1945.

Crossman also, for all his hatred of Attlee, knew the truth about the legend that the Labour Government of 1945–50 had deceived Parliament over British manufacture of the atomic bomb. Crossman found out that in 1948, when the decision to make the atomic bomb was taken, there was a meeting of the Cabinet's Defence subcommittee in the late spring. The full Cabinet was made aware of its decision at its next meeting by the normal circulation of the subcommittee's minutes. Attlee, who presided at this subcommittee, raised the question as to the best way of informing Parliament. It was agreed without dissent that this need not be done in a formal ministerial statement, but that it should be conveyed to the House at the first available parliamentary opportunity. On 12 May 1948, the following exchange was reported in Hansard:

ARMED FORCES (MODERN WEAPONS)

44. *Mr. George Jeger* asked the Minister of Defence whether he is satisfied that adequate progress is being made in the development of the most modern types of weapon.

The Minister of Defence (Mr. A. V. Alexander): Yes, Sir. As was made clear in the Statement Relating to Defence, 1948 (Command 7327), research and development continue to receive the highest priority in the defence field, and all types of modern weapons, including atomic weapons, are being developed.

Mr. Jeger: Can the Minister give any further information on the development of atomic weapons?

Mr. Alexander: No. I do not think it would be in the public interest to do that.

Not one MP – Labour or Conservative – challenged the statement or sought further information. The Government had no reason to make any further announcement during the subsequent three years of its existence during which the painfully slow development of the British atomic bomb took place. It is true that the cost involved was not stated in the Defence Estimates, because for obvious security reasons the cost of the development or production of specific weapons was never isolated. Crossman, in my view, does not emerge from this controversy in a favourable light. Almost alone among MPs, he latched on to the truth. He had the potential for massive press coverage. Yet he kept quiet. I am afraid it was because he did not want to get entangled with the Left on such an emotional issue.

Crossman never thought the Russians wanted war. He was exceedingly angry that Attlee should not have made more effort when in August 1954 the Labour party delegation entertained Chairman Malenkov, First Secretary Khruschev and future Vice-Chairman Mikoyan to dinner in Moscow. Elitist, perhaps, but Crossman was right in supposing that most of his colleagues were floundering out of their depth. (He always excepted Ian Mikardo, who was appalled by Crossman's elitism.) Wilson also knew the truth about the Labour Government and the Bomb. And he had an excellent working relationship with Mikoyan, with whom he had negotiated wheat agreements. So Crossman and Wilson had a lot in common.

There is another basic simple fact. These two men, though they could get mutually exasperated, liked each other. At the top, it is difficult in British politics to have friendships which go deep. And it may be that their friendship was the better for the fact that both men understood the parameters. Crossman, I vouch, liked Wilson. Wilson liked Crossman – until, at any rate, the posthumous publication of Volume Two of *The Diaries of a Cabinet Minister* (1976) some of which was hurtful.

Both Crossman and Wilson understood that if friendships in politics are to last, those friendships are best kept cool and detached. Crossman said it was a terrible mistake of his to get Hugh Gaitskell as his son Patrick's godfather. When I, without knowing this, said that Kathleen and I would like him to be our son Gordon's godfather in 1965, he declined.

Politicians in Parliament can be like ships that join a convoy and later become detached: they can converge for a particular cause or relationship, and then drift apart. But Wilson never saw Crossman as a rival for his crown. Nor was he a contender for the deputy leadership. The Labour Party could not swallow two Oxford dons as leader and deputy leader. When he became leader of the party, Wilson needed Crossman. With the exception of Fred Lee, all the elected members had voted for Brown or Callaghan and against him. It was like trying to run a Bolshevik revolution with a tsarist Shadow Cabinet.

The single most influential commentator for the Labour party during 1964–70 was a man Crossman first described to me as the rare phenomenon of a *Daily Express* Beaver-worker joining the *Guardian* – Ian Aitken. (Aitken used to phone Crossman every Sunday about midday, and when Aitken went to hospital for an operation, he was visited by the Prime Minister without publicity.) In a review of Volume Two of the *Diaries*, Aitken writes, under the heading 'Richard the Unbuttoned': 'For Dick Crossman liked Harold Wilson. Harold liked him and both men were aware of the other's personal affection. No other explanation is possible for the fact that Wilson persistently put up with needling from Crossman, in Cabinet as well as in private, which would have destroyed the ministerial career of almost anyone else.'

It also helped that Harold Wilson's immediate entourage, particularly Marcia Williams, liked Crossman. (The exception was Trevor Lloyd-Hughes, the press chief at Number 10, whom I thought Crossman maligned.) So did Burke Trend, whom Crossman referred to as the Grand Vizier, head of the Cabinet secretariat which was the Prime Minister's Praetorian Guard.

Crossman never, to my knowledge, considered resigning. George Brown had exemplified the fatality and futility of resignation. But there were weeks – not longer to my knowledge – when he got very angry with Wilson. Before Christmas 1965, he thought Wilson was going the way of Lloyd-George and casting off his radical past – if he ever had one. Crossman thought he wanted to become a national fixer with all the power in his hands. None the less, the old Bevanite bond and relationship, unforgotten at times of difficulty by either Crossman or his Prime Minister, remained.

EIGHT

NEC and Party

Crossman's life was at Transport House, then the Labour party head-quarters, rather than in the House of Commons. He was elected to the National Executive Committee (NEC) of the Labour Party at the Morecambe conference in September–October 1952, and then proceeded to make a well-remembered gaffe.

From personal experience, I know exactly the difficulty. The results of elections to the National Executive Committee were announced on the Tuesday morning of conference week – now with computers on the Monday afternoon. But a newly elected member of the NEC has to wait until the following year to take his place on the platform. It is a difficult position, since one is not quite speaking for oneself, and one is certainly not speaking on behalf of the National Executive of the Party. I resolved the dilemma by not signalling to go to the rostrum at all. Crossman succumbed to the temptation to participate in the foreign affairs debate on the Wednesday. He told me that he had prepared the substance of what he was going to say carefully, and limited the content well within the allowed five minutes. He had touched upon rearmament, the need to resist American pressure, to expand East–West trade, and was seconding a resolution which was to be accepted by the Executive. However, on the way to the rostrum, after he had been called by the chairman, he was applauded by delegates as a successful NEC candidate. He thought on the spur of the moment that he ought to respond to the applause. So he thought he would begin with a sentence or two meant as a gentle joke. The joke took the shape of suggesting that now that he was suspended between the platform and the floor, he would have to be 'less controversial'. The chemistry of the Labour Party Conference is such that the cheers, like some substance changing colour with an additive, were transformed into boos. The joke seemed to contain the arsenic of insincerity.

Crossman's left-wing supporters in the constituencies, who had given him his seat on the NEC, were dismayed; his opponents were jubilant. Hugh Dalton, whose place on the NEC Crossman had taken, was convulsed with mirth. Attlee gave his only smile of the Morecambe conference. The delegates were serious. They had put Crossman there for a purpose, and that purpose was change – not to provide humour. It was a nightmare of a start to his time on the NEC. But the NEC was to be the centre of his life, because in the House of Commons itself the Bevanites were a small and resented group.

Crossman thought that Attlee had behaved worse than he did. When the obituaries were read out at the beginning, they included the names of Sir Stafford Cripps and of George Tomlinson, who had been Minister of Works 1945–7, and Education 1947–51. To let these names pass and continue to doodle when the conference chairman asked the leader to say a few words was awful, and a missed chance to pull the conference together.

Back in the House of Commons, the Bevanites had a grievance. They were repeatedly lectured and accused of disloyalty to the Party. But why in that case did so many of their colleagues ask them to speak in their constituencies? The answer was quite simple: the members of the Party back home wanted to invite them.

Crossman never let elections to the National Executive dominate his life, to the extent that it was a chronic disease with some of his colleagues. On the other hand, Crossman told me it would be self-deception to imagine that he did not care.

Crossman was horrified by Gaitskell's pledge that a Labour government would not increase taxation. At every subsequent election, he was repeatedly warning his colleagues against giving the impression of last-minute bribes and concessions. At all costs the Labour Party had to avoid giving the impression of carefully calculated pre-election hedging on difficult issues. He did not make a moral-issue meal of it. He was rather scornful of knights in shining armour. It was simply that the Labour Party lost votes by either trying to avoid or seeming to try to avoid awkward questions. For reasons of hard electoral calculation, it was better to stand by a Party policy, unpopular but right.

On 11 June 1964, Crossman told me that if Gaitskell had lived, he would probably have dropped the same brick in another form. Then he observed, with no tinge of callousness, 'While there is death, there is hope.' (A favourite saying, which Isaiah Berlin tells me originated with Maurice Bowra, and maybe before that with some sage of Ancient Greece.)

After Zita's (much-regretted) death in 1952, he travelled widely. It irritated his MP colleagues that when he went abroad virtually anyone was prepared to see him at the drop of a hat. Not because he was an MP, but because they knew of the *New Statesman* and his *Sunday Pictorial* column. In Italy, for example, in June 1953, in three days he saw Fanfani, Gronchi, Nenni and Togliatti. He left his glasses in the Socialist Nenni's office, and they were there for him when he got to the Communist Togliatti's villa. That told him a good deal about the cosy nature of the Italian Left. (He had not been one of the 'Nenni-Goats', Labour MPs who in April 1948 had sent a telegram of congratulations on the left-wing Socialists' electoral pact with the Communists.)

At that period, Crossman used to refer to Gaitskell as 'Our St Sebastian' – which was definitely not a term of approval. It was partly that during this period Crossman did not feel he himself was leading a particularly useful life, and that he was neither fully engaged nor committed.

In a curious way, Crossman mellowed towards Gaitskell after a period as a Minister. He used to get mad with him as Leader for saying so often, when a difficult subject arose, 'That's an issue that no responsible person can decide until he sees the Cabinet papers.' After twelve months of himself reading the Cabinet papers, he told me that he thought Gaitskell, who had been a senior Minister, had been right; and that, he who had come to ministerial office late in life, had been wrong.

NINE

Journalist

Quite a number of Labour MPs have been journalists before entering the House of Commons. Some have contributed columns to *The Times*, the *Guardian*, or even occasionally the *Daily Telegraph*. Others have contributed occasional articles to the tabloid press. Fewer have had a temporary column. One or two have had a regular column. Crossman's journalistic career started with the *Sunday Pictorial*, now defunct. But in 1947 the *Pic* was read by millions and by virtually every Labour MP.

Hugh Cudlipp, one of the great editors of the twentieth century, was his patron. Sydney Jacobson, the politically astute and aware Political Editor of the *Daily Mirror* (1952–62), taught him his craft. Ellis Birk, the experienced *Mirror* lawyer, generally succeeded in keeping him out of the courts. From 1955–59, their good opinion counted greatly with Crossman, the period when he wrote for the *Mirror*. It was Cudlipp who taught Crossman a lesson, fine for journalists but fraught with peril for a politician – that personalization is the secret of readability. Crossman realized only too well the dangers of personalization; and after he was transformed from a journalist into a Minister, eschewed personalization in or out of the House of Commons when dealing with colleagues, preferring to leave personalization to his then-secret diaries. Yet, for all this marvellous back-up, the flair was Crossman's. He was a peerless wordsmith. I never saw anyone anywhere go to such trouble to find *le mot juste*. Pacing up and down, dictating he would drive his secretary to the end of her tether, altering and altering and altering again in those pre-word-processor years. Either writing his articles or drafting party documents required a lot of skill and a spark of inspiration. But *Mirror* or *Pictorial* articles or party manifestos or policy documents were in his experience sheer hard work; trying, retrying and trying yet again was the only recipe for success. Yet no Member of Parliament ever has had such a long-running, frequently front-paged, and above all widely read regular column as Crossman. First in the *Sunday Pictorial*. Then in the *Daily Mirror*. No MP, on account of his journalism, earned for himself the pitch of animosity that Crossman accrued. He could write what he liked in the *New Statesman* or the *Manchester Guardian*, or *The Times*. But the *Mirror* sold over five million copies – and was devoured in what was still only the early Television Age by most members of Constituency Labour Parties. His capacity to cause trouble at t'mill knew no limits. It reached its apogee in an article on trade-union MPs (5 July 1957) which was still the cause of consternation when I became a Member of Parliament in 1962, and which Crossman never really lived down until the end of his days.

Crossman did not care for dealing with people who said things or adopted attitudes because they were unprovocative. In his view, the soft word and the soft approach did not sharpen thought. He was therefore given to wilder exaggeration and greater acerbity than was justified. His comment was blunt, his sense of irony direct, his sentences crisp and easily understood; and that is the most difficult, time-consuming kind of writing to do well. But he could not be altogether surprised that he concentrated fury on himself, as if he were a lightning conductor.

By the spring of 1953, Attlee was making snide little comments in the NEC about politician journalists.

[A **digression**. With the honourable exception of Michael Foot, every Labour leader seems to become ridiculously uptight about the press. When Crossman was taken ill with a recurrence of ulcer trouble in 1968, I was summoned at midnight to Downing Street, since the caring Harold Wilson – a most decent man in such situations – wanted to know what was wrong. I was invited in to his little study, upstairs in Downing Street, to find the PM listening to the BBC midnight news, and scouring the first editions, fuming at this, that and the other – it could not have been good for him. Equally, like Attlee, Neil Kinnock was forever during my year on the NEC (1986–7) making unflattering remarks about the press, though unlike Attlee he owed a lot in his early days to the press. It seems to be an occupational hazard.]

Crossman tackled Attlee in early March 1953, saying he was puzzled by his references to journalists on the NEC. What did the former prime minister mean? Attlee muttered that he thought that for a member of the NEC to write every week in the sensational press put them in a very difficult position. Crossman, in recounting the episode, told me somewhat haughtily, that he told 'the bastard' that he supposed he had a higher opinion of the press than Attlee had. Attlee, according to Crossman, said he had no opinion of the press. Crossman persisted. Why was it more difficult to write a Sunday column than to make a weekend speech compatible with one's responsibility? 'Because,' said Attlee, 'the speech is made on Labour platforms, and most of you write in the non-Labour press.' Crossman, by this point, not bothering to conceal his anger, told Attlee that the *Pic* was not a Tory paper, and that Cudlipp gave him no directive. Attlee then, according to Crossman, said like Colonel Blimp that the newspapers preferred reporting bad things to good things about the Party, and wanted to create trouble, and that's why politician journalists always chose to write about the most mischievous topics. Crossman recalled that they had been walking very fast along the corridor, since Attlee wished to escape him. 'And when he reached the door of his room, Attlee disappeared with a bang!'

Personally, I am on Attlee's side of this particular argument. Though vociferous on some subjects when I was on the NEC, I was inhibited on other subjects simply because repetition of what I really thought would have been damaging to the Party. When I was on the NEC, no member, as far as I know, wrote about party affairs for money.

The ferocity felt against Crossman was understandable. He was not only participating in the NEC's internal rows in the public press. He was seen as exploiting the Party's wounds in the capitalist press, and being paid a substantial sum of money into the bargain for his willingness to do so. Colleagues on the Executive, such as Ray Gunter, never really forgave him for this.

In July 1955, Crossman went to the *Mirror*. Kingsley Martin, the editor of the *New Statesman*, was not the only one who told him that he was degrading himself by doing so. Crossman did not see it as degrading himself. On the contrary, when he went to the Conservative Conference at Bournemouth in 1955, with the columnist Bill Connor ('Cassandra'), Sydney Jacobson, and Vicky the cartoonist, he was agreeably astonished how much room the *Mirror* took up in the minds of politicians and how seriously it was regarded in the Conservative Party. Indeed, Crossman's cup of joy was full when R. A. Butler, during his major conference speech as Chancellor of the Exchequer, said that he would carry his economic policy through, despite the *Daily Mirror* editorials; more poignantly, Butler added that he was not afraid of Vicky. It was one of those things that politicians say half-jokingly and wholly in earnest. Moreover it was Butler's only public reference to the press! The Conservative Party regarded the *Daily Mirror* as one of their most formidable opponents. Being on the *Mirror* gave Crossman far more kudos than being on the *New Statesman*, and Crossman enjoyed kudos.

On a relaxed occasion when Tom Driberg, not only chairman of the Labour Party during a famous Scarborough Conference of 1958 but a master of English prose, came to our home in Scotland for a meal, I asked him how he rated Crossman as a columnist. Driberg was a connoisseur. It was patently obvious to him that Crossman took infinitely more trouble about the *Daily Mirror* than about the *New Statesman*. Interestingly, Driberg thought that Kingsley Martin was justified in being annoyed by the rough and slipshod nature of some of the writing that Crossman was latterly submitting to the *New Statesman*, and that he did not deserve later (1970–2) to become editor.

Though he continued to do occasional articles for them, the *Mirror* under Cecil King's influence dropped Crossman's column after Labour's election defeat in 1959. Many MPs smiled and heaved a sigh of relief. Some of the more reflective did not. I recall being told by George Darling, MP for Sheffield Hillsborough, and a constructive and successful Trade minister, 1964–8, that as soon as Crossman's column was dropped, he and a number of others tumbled to its importance. He told me he did not care for Crossman in some respects. But Darling recognized that though he might dislike the content of Crossman's column, it was one of the few places where over a period of years a systematic attempt was made to explain the Labour Party's policies to the public in intelligible terms. The withdrawal of the column left a gap which no one else had subsequently been able to fill. Having done a political column for the *Mirror*'s Scottish sister paper, the *Daily Record*, for eighteen months, I can only marvel at how Crossman sustained his effort. Crossman told me that, oddly enough, Gaitskell was one to appreciate this aspect of his work. Few others did until 1959 and it was too late.

There was, however, a deep and serious reservation held about Crossman's journalism, seldom expressed. It was this. A journalist is a man whose very profession makes him want to be ahead of events. James Callaghan and other contemporaries thought that this persistent urge was incompatible with being a responsible politician.

Crossman saw it differently. Politicians had a duty to inform the public about the choices open to them. That is why, years later, as Leader of the House of Commons, Crossman was to see parliamentary reform and the television experiment as part of a single process. That is why he favoured including topical debates during morning sittings and ministerial statements appropriate for transmission on regional television. There is something else to be said in exculpation of Crossman, which Callaghan did not quite appreciate. The problem was not irresponsibility. The problem was speed. In journalism, decisions have always had to be made very quickly. Crossman, before he became a minister and even after, gave the impression of jumping at things. He bullied. He tugged. He shoved. He pushed. But that was the ethos of Fleet Street, in which environment (the word was popularized later!) he worked.

On several occasions in the late 1960s, Harold Wilson greeted me in the Commons corridor with the barbed question 'How is your compulsive communicator?' I knew exactly what he was referring to. As PPS, I used to sit in on many of Crossman's cosy briefings of James Margach, chief political columnist of the *Sunday Times*, Harold Hutchinson of the (then-Labour) *Sun*, Ian Aitken of the *Guardian*, and other key journalists. Contrary to widespread belief, he was not a leaker on these occasions, and I can think of no occasion when he indulged in venom to the disadvantage of a Cabinet colleague. Basically, Crossman was one of nature's explainers. It was his deep-seated beliefs as a professional journalist that prompted him to want Standing and Select Committees of the House of Commons to be televised. It was as a journalist rather than as a politician that Crossman was so dismayed when on 10 November 1966, his proposals for a television experiment in the House were cold-shouldered by the Cabinet. I never saw Crossman so white with rage as when on Thursday evening, 24 November, his television proposals were turned down by 131 votes to 130 – and, to add insult to injury, not a single other member of the Cabinet stirred himself to vote in favour of the proposals, on a 'free' vote, unwhipped. Not that Crossman thought that television was the most important medium for a politician who wanted to put a message over, as opposed to being seen. On a radio programme, such as the late Bill Hardcastle's

'*World at One*', a politician could say more in five minutes than he could in ten minutes on television. One in the ear was worth two in the eye!

About television in particular and presentation in general, there is an age-old controversy which often assumes unfortunate personality overtones. The media 'experts' held that in the world of television it was personalities that counted rather than policy arguments. This is what leaders from Gaitskell and Bevan onwards have wanted to hear. Crossman took the view that if they really knew anything about advertising or psychological warfare, they would realize that getting an audience was only the first stage. The second and more important stage, argued Crossman, was getting an idea across to the audience. If on television, or during a party political broadcast, one was merely content to see that the leader made a good impression, one was doing no better than his paper, the *Mirror*, did if it won a bigger circulation on account of its non-political news. The real test had to be how much serious politics was injected. The litmus test of Labour MPs appearing on television or on the radio was how much Socialist belief they could convey without upsetting the goodwill of those who saw and listened. Crossman thought it was a terrible error of judgement for Labour leaders to suppose that all they had to do to achieve power was to make amiable appearances on television, and avoid committing themselves to anything that would be deemed controversial.

TEN
Class

Certainly Crossman had terrible relationships with some working-class colleagues, such as Ray Gunter (until almost at the end of Gunter's ministerial career, when, after a long talk, both of them realized they had ridiculously misjudged one another). Yet the decade of bad blood between the two had little to do with class *per se*. On Crossman's part, it was because he saw Ray Gunter as a ruthless thug who chaired the dreadful Org. Sub. (Organization Sub-Committee) of the NEC in a capricious way, spiteful to the Left. Ray Gunter – who was incidentally always nice to me, in spite of knowing me to be Crossman's henchman, and particularly helpful as Minister of Labour in relation to the problems of the motor industry at Bathgate – saw Crossman as an archvillain, encouraging dissident elements in the party.

In 1957, Crossman made a gaffe of thermo-nuclear proportions in the Labour Party, but writing as follows in his *Daily Mirror* column of Friday, 5 July (I quote the entire column, since he also touches on overseas affairs in the final section):

CROSSMAN SAYS...
THE UNIONS MUST SEND BETTER MEN TO PARLIAMENT

'WE must have more trade union M.P.s.' This was the demand which Sir Thomas Williamson, Chairman of the Trades Union Congress, made to the Labour Party on Wednesday.

What Sir Thomas Williamson said in his speech at the Miners' Conference sounded rough. But I am glad he has aired a grievance which trade union leaders have been harbouring for months.

What they resent is the behaviour of the Constituency Labour Parties.

More and more, in selecting candidates for Parliament, these local parties prefer the bright young Socialist with a university or co-operative background to the sponsored trade union applicant.

What adds insult to injury is the fact that these union-sponsored candidates are rejected although each can contribute up to £250 a year to the constituency's expenses as well as paying eighty per cent of the bill for the election campaign.

No wonder the trade union leaders are sore when – even in strongholds of trade unionism – they see the intellectual with the university degree preferred to the trade unionist with £.s.d.

What can be done to put things right?

I agree with Sir Thomas that if the Labour Party is to remain a real labour party and the next Labour Government is to have the confidence of the T.U.C., there must be a fair balance in Parliament between the industrial and political wings.

Yet in order to restore that balance, the trade union leaders will have to face one unpalatable fact which Sir Thomas Williamson failed to mention on Wednesday.

It is not merely the number of trade union candidates adopted by constituencies that has declined but their quality as well.

It is this decline in quality that is gravely affecting the Parliamentary Labour Party.

To see this we have only to compare the situation now with that in 1945.

Of the ninety-seven sponsored trade union M.P.s in Parliament today, only four – Mr James Griffiths (Miners), Mr Aneurin Bevan (Miners), Mr George Brown (Transport Workers) and Mr Alfred Robens (Shopworkers) – suggest themselves for key jobs.

In contrast, Mr Attlee in 1945 was able to allot eight important ministries to sponsored trade unionists. Here is the list: ERNEST BEVIN at the Foreign Office (Transport Workers), JAMES GRIFFITHS at National Insurance (Miners), TOM WILLIAMS at Agriculture (Miners), ANEURIN BEVAN at Health (Miners), JOHN LAWSON at the War Office (Miners), BEN SMITH at Food (Transport Workers), GEORGE ISAACS, Labour Minister (Printers), ELLEN WILKINSON at the Ministry of Education (Shop Workers (sic)).

The truth is that trade unions are no longer sending even their second best men into politics.

If an outstanding trade unionist does become a sponsored M.P., he is only too often recalled from Parliament to a job in the union before he has made his mark.

Has Sir Thomas Williamson forgotten that he himself was pulled out of Parliament to take up a union appointment?

* The lesson is clear. The men who can restore a proper balance in the Labour Party are the trade union leaders.

* If they release a dozen of their ablest lieutenants for work in Parliament I predict there will be no difficulty whatsoever in finding twelve constituencies eager to select them as Labour candidates.

The New Stalin?

Having liquidated Stalinism, Mr Krushchev (sic) has decided to make himself as all-powerful as Stalin.

That is my guess at the realities disguised by the Kremlin communique on the top-level sackings in Russia.

That communique, of course, is palpably untrue. It is ridiculous to suggest that Molotov and Kaganovitch (sic), two Old Guard Bolsheviks, who thought Krushchev had departed too far from Stalinism, had anything in common with Mr Malenkov and Mr Shepilov, who wanted to go even further.

Krushchev has learnt from Stalin (and also from Hitler) that the best way of achieving supreme power is to invent a conspiracy, accuse all your various enemies of being members of it, and hold them responsible for all the failures of the regime.

He is achieving absolute power by Stalinite methods in order to carry out an anti-Stalinite revolution.

However, this *Mirror* article did not injure his relations with the trade union leaders, some of whom (it was whispered to me) were in clandestine agreement with Crossman about their own trade union-sponsored MPs then in Parliament. (The picture is totally different today, with rigorous selection of sponsored MPs.)

Sir Alfred Roberts, chairman of the Trades Union Social Services committee, Sam Watson (who admired Crossman on Israel), Frank Cousins, and Edwin Gooch of the Agricultural Workers came to think of Crossman not as an intellectual who talked down to the working class but as a Socialist who got things done – like pension plans which mattered hugely to them.

The lacuna in Crossman's make-up was rather that he was curiously impervious to the effect that his talk might have on other people. I have checked the following story with, among others, Mrs Gwyneth Dunwoody, MP, daughter of Morgan Phillips, the famous general secretary of the Labour Party in 1945–62.

In February 1957, Crossman made arrangements to attend the conference in Venice of the left-wing Italian Socialist Party led by Pietro Nenni. Representing the Socialist International was Morgan Phillips. Travelling out together, they shared a compartment on the Orient Express. In an unusually personal conversation – Labour politicians in England, as opposed to those in Scotland and Wales, tend to know rather little about one another's personal lives – Morgan Phillips started to tell Crossman about his son. He had won a scholarship to Downing College, Cambridge. Crossman was delighted. What was the boy going to study? Classics! Whereupon, for some inane reason, Crossman, of all people, expostulated thoughtlessly: 'Classics, Morgan? You should be ashamed of yourself! I am a Classic and the one thing it has taught me is how to write articles in the *Daily Mirror*. A Classic can really express himself accurately!'

Was Crossman a snob? My wife, who liked him and to whom he was always charming, thinks he was a snob. I think he was not. His friends, colleagues and posthumous enemies – a large and distinguished company – have been most willing to talk about him, and are divided on whether he was a snob. Few are neutral.

I should say that I myself was uneasily aware that a number of well-disposed Labour MPs did not think it quite appropriate that one of the two Old Etonians in the parliamentary party should work for a Wykehamist Cabinet minister in a ministry such as Housing. It was put into words in an avuncular and friendly way by Herbert Morrison, by then Lord Morrison of Lambeth, but a regular luncher (as ex-MPs in the Lords are entitled to be) in the members' dining room. 'You'll be bad for Crossman. He should get a working-class boy as his PPS, not you, Tam. And you ought to work for a working-class Minister like Ray Gunter or Tom Fraser!' I put this to Crossman, and he would have none of it, with the comment that Herbert Morrison could not talk since he himself had chosen as his own PPS the Radleian and Oxonian Eddie Shackleton – a life peer and now a Knight of the Garter, and still a Labour Party member, to his credit.

My view is that Crossman did not have any feeling of difficulty with working-class constituents or colleagues. For example, he personally liked Frank Cousins, Eric Heffer, Stan Orme and others – though it might be thought that my examples are working-class colleagues of a certain 'aristocratic' tendency which appealed to Crossman. He was genuinely concerned to know what Heffer thought; there was no hint of condescension.

Back on the Orient Express, Morgan Phillips gave exactly the reply that Crossman deserved. 'Do you think I don't know that? Do you think it isn't always a terrible thing that we can't express ourselves like you?' Crossman commented that this told him a lot about Morgan Phillips's character. He suspected that Morgan felt hurt and injured and took offence fifty times a day at things which one had no notion would hurt him. Crossman was always quick on the draw to suggest that other people had acute inferiority complexes – often absurdly, in my view. This was one such occasion. I fear this episode tells us more about Crossman than about Morgan Phillips – he could pile insensitivity upon insensitivity. He was at his most gauche in dealing with the Welsh – native or expatriate – who were and are great powers in the Labour Party. To some, it seemed that Crossman lived in his own imagination in the Italy of the 18th century: there was the oligarchy in control, and the masses were below the level of political articulacy.

I don't think Crossman had the ethics of a gent, and in this he is almost alone among Labour's ex-public schoolboys. He could be terribly rude to those who he knew full well could not answer back. I once cringed with embarrassment when he bawled out a veteran tea-provider in the Privy Council office for having a slightly cracked milk jug. As soon as the ministry attendant was out of the room, I remonstrated with him, and told him his conduct was reprehensible. Without a word to me, he shouted, 'Arthur!' The attendant opened the door. Crossman called out, 'Sorry. Forgive me'; and the man retreated, bewildered. His gross bad manners were usually unconscious. Sometimes he would retrieve the situation; more often, not. And yet when he was feeling well no one could be nicer or more chatty. I noticed he was a great favourite with railway staff on trains, with whom he got on particularly well for some unfathomable reason – maybe because he adored train journeys.

If Crossman was not class-conscious, paradoxically I have known few men so acutely conscious of class. In 1964, the night after he had first set foot in the Ministry of Housing, I asked him on his return to

Vincent Square how he had got on with Dame Evelyn Sharp, whom, as a member of the Public Accounts Committee, I had questioned when she appeared as the accounting officer. The nature of Crossman's reply tickled me. Nothing about her intellect. Or her command over the Ministry of Housing. Or her position in Whitehall, or anything of that kind. 'Well,' said Crossman, as if it were the most natural comment in the world for a minister to make about his Permanent Secretary, 'well, you know, she dresses as middle or upper-class professional women do dress, quite expensively but rather uglily!' When I then compared Lady Sharp to my Cambridge supervisor, the formidable Joan Robinson, he replied, 'Yes, these intellectual upper-class do-gooders, if they are able like that, have all the obstinacy of their class!' That in Crossman's view was one of the factors which made Dame Evelyn Sharp so tough in negotiation. But, irritably, he would add that Dame Evelyn would turn out to be very public school when she was asked by the Treasury or by Sir Laurence Helsby, the head of the Home Civil Service, to make a sacrifice in her departmental interests for the good of the nation or for the interests of the civil service.

Crossman held the view that far too many working-class ministers, if not putty in the hands of the civil service, were at least too pliant towards their officials. In this respect, he was particularly concerned about Fred Lee, a former shop-steward convenor from Trafford Park, the AEU-sponsored MP for Newton-le-Willows, who was Minister of Power. Resignedly, showing genuine anxiety as to whether the government was doing the right thing, Crossman would query why we thought it necessary as a Labour government to carry out even more drastic pit closures than those proposed by the Tories. Was it because Fred Lee was working class that he succumbed to the accelerated pit-closure policies, attributable to the officials of the Ministry of Power? When Crossman was honoured to be the guest speaker at the Northumbrian Miners' Picnic in 1969, he could hardly contain himself the following Monday. Fred Lee, Dick Marsh and Roy Mason, working-class trade unionists all, had presided over a pit closure rate which was 'outrageously fast'. It might cost, reckoned Crossman, a significant sum to keep some pits going – but what about the real costs of young men walking out of the industry, and all the costs of voluntary redundancy?

Crossman discriminated in his view of working-class colleagues, quite shrewdly in my view. He respected Roy Mason, albeit in disagreement. He was scathing about Richard Marsh, and said he was a cheeky brat

100

whom the prime minister should sack for impertinence. He thought George Brown in his day superb – having had fisticuffs with him in the lobby during Bevanite times in the previous decade. However, Crossman believed at the time that Ray Gunter's resignation as Minister of Power in June 1968 (apart from its manner: 'I do not wish to serve in Harold Wilson's Government') was an even greater loss to the Cabinet.

It was partly that Ray Gunter did represent a working-class view. But it was also the realization that after he had left the Ministry of Labour and gone to Power where he was a square peg in a round hole, Barbara Castle had become an antagonist and not a conciliator. George Brown and Ray Gunter may not in Crossman's perception have been a very big fish in the trade union pond, but in the political Labour government pond, they certainly were big fish. They carried a lot of weight.

Had Gunter remained at the Ministry of Labour, I believe the whole history of the Labour Government would have been different. At the time, Crossman wanted Gunter out of the Ministry of Labour, but not out of the Cabinet. At first he showed blind loyalty to Barbara Castle and was terribly abusive to me for expressing grave doubts about the government's policy. (In the early summer of 1967, I nearly packed my bags and left Vincent Square. Crossman accused me of being gutless and chicken-hearted for agreeing with the West Lothian Constituency Labour party that we should legislate exactly down the line on Lord Donovan's 1968 Report on Trade Unions and Employers' Associations. I admitted that it did matter to me what my CLP thought, but added that some of them knew more about what was acceptable and not acceptable on the shop floor than Crossman!) Peace was restored between us in a bizarre fashion. He gave me a long lecture/tirade as to how the Prices and Incomes issue was between the Socialists in the Labour Party, supporting Mrs Barbara Castle, and the do-nothing muddlers-through, led by Callaghan and Gunter, who were the proletarians in the Labour Party. 'As an Old Etonian, Tam, I accept you are a natural proletarian in such matters!'

Actually, Crossman emerged from the prices and incomes argument within the Labour Party without much honour. He gyrated from one side to another, and on this occasion – though not on as many others as his enemies liked to suggest – earned the nickname, Double Dick Crossman.

As I saw it, in truncated form, what happened was this. When the

101

Labour Government had the heaven-sent report of Lord Donovan and his colleagues and were about to legislate sensibly along those lines, there was a hiccough at the crucial moment. A couple of score of men in the greatly important but medium-sized Girling Brake Company went on unofficial strike. This created bottleneck troubles in the car and vehicle industries. The general issues which should have been separated in the Cabinet's collective mind, of prices and incomes and of trade union penalties and trade union legislation were thrown into the melting pot. Mrs Castle produced her White Paper, *In Place of Strife*. To say that the atmosphere between Labour Government and trade unions became sour would be an understatement. It became rancid. And the internal wounds paved the way for defeat in 1970.

Crossman was excluded from the formative discussions of the policy. I am told this was because the prime minister thought that he would leak information prematurely to James Margach of the *Sunday Times* or Ian Aitken of the *Guardian*, who phoned him up every Sunday forenoon at Prescote for background. But, unconsulted, and possibly being uncharacteristically vague about the proposals, he went along with his chums Barbara Castle and the prime minister – basically, because they at that stage, not Ray Gunter and James Callaghan, were his Cabinet friends. When he discovered more about the actual substance of what his friends were up to, Crossman got cold feet, not because of political *force majeure*, but because he ceased to be a believer in the idea of what had developed into 'bashing the Trade Unions'. In spite of the fact – no, I have the sneaking suspicion, maybe because of the fact – that George Woodcock, General Secretary of the TUC, was an ex-pupil of Crossman's at Oxford, Crossman had little relationship with Congress House at this period. 'Gnarled George Woodcock will not talk to me,' Crossman would complain. The situation changed when Crossman's old friend, Vic Feather, moved up from the number two position at Congress House to the General Secretaryship. They talked. Crossman reflected and virtually changed Cabinet sides. This is the kind of behaviour that had some of his usual allies spitting with anger. If he was going to go cool, why did he not convey to them his doubts in the first place?

Part of the difficulty over the controversial economic measures was that Crossman, unlike James Callaghan, would not be coaxed by me or others into going into the Commons tea-room to chat, let alone to use the members' cafeteria. When I used to tell him that he ought to listen more to what people he knew less well in the Parliamentary Labour party were saying – James Callaghan to my certain knowledge gave him the same advice – he would brush me aside impetuously. If he went 'slumming in the tea-room' he would talk shop as he did in his own Minister's Room 21a. He had to dispense whisky and water, or sherry, in his own style. He steadfastly refused to change habit. Had he been more gregarious, his position on the economic controversies which beset the Wilson government would have been more consistent from an earlier stage.

I believe that the experience of the rows with the trade unions made Crossman realize that the working class was underrepresented in the Wilson Cabinet Mark II. It was certainly in the context of the trade union legislation fiasco that Crossman told an incredulous and amused group of junior ministers who came to his room for a get-together – a welcome innovation – that one of the troubles of 'this Government is that there are too many Oxford firsts in the Cabinet'. Who did he have in mind for removal, asked one waggish Parliamentary Secretary. Wilson? Stewart? Crosland? Jenkins? Healey? Or himself?

Paradoxically, perhaps, Crossman did not believe in the proposal, on which the Prime Minister was determined, to get rid of political honours. When the idea was first mooted, after the 1966 election, Crossman consulted Len Williams, who was General Secretary of the Labour Party. (In March 1969, I saw Sir Leonard Williams in Mauritius, where he was Governor-General, and we discussed the subject of governorships and honours.) Williams pointed out that the regional officers of the Labour Party and agents were very cool. Apart from MPs, what the abolition of honours really amounted to was the exclusion of regional organizers and those who had worked hard for the Labour party, and virtually nobody else. Crossman had agreed that an end to political honours would be bad for morale among the vital full-time staff of the party. And so it has proved. Politics is an honourable profession. If we are going to have Sirs and Dames, why should not those who have toiled in the electoral vineyard be recognized? Crossman was an undoctrinaire, pragmatic socialist. Crossman's great friend, Doug Garnett, Eastern Area Organizer for the Labour Party, for whom Crossman did a host of meetings in Norfolk and Suffolk when the Labour Party was still a power in East Anglia, persuaded Crossman to write to the Prime Minister formally, in an official minute. Crossman did. Wilson dithered and prevaricated. He was in a genuine difficulty.

Elements in the Labour Party were and are very much against political honours. Crossman's class prejudices escaped. If a man came from the same sort of 'petit bourgeois milieu as Harold, with the associated cultural values, and was at the same time a Labour prime minister, of course he would make up his mind about honours with difficulty'. Alas, Crossman did not live to see – and doubtless write a comment about – Harold Wilson in the robes of a Knight of the Garter! *Plus ça change*...

Unlike some other of Labour's ex-public schoolboy MPs, Crossman believed in having good personal relations with the Tories. This was partly because he lived in more civilized political times than we do since Mrs Thatcher became prime minister and overtly takes every opportunity to downgrade the Opposition. It was partly because not only had he entered the House of Commons when the 280-odd previous members had worked together in wartime, but the rest had served together to defeat Hitler. It was partly because he himself – who as a back-bencher could fill the chamber of the House of Commons – would get a better hearing if he had decent personal relations with Tory MPs. It was partly that his Commons pair, Sir Alec Spearman, MP for Scarborough and Whitby, was an influential man, leading partner in the stockbrokers Grieveson Grant, later to be part of Kleinwort Benson. Spearman just believed that he could and should, for the good of Britain, introduce certain Labour MPs – John Strachey was another – round the City. Lady Spearman tells me that Crossman was the subject of genuine interest and curiosity round Tory dinner tables, even before he became a minister. Not surprisingly, there was also an element of strong antagonism.

Crossman envied the Tories their great country-house parties. This was not because he was a *bon viveur*. Other than highly political parties given by Pamela Berry and George Weidenfeld, Crossman declined invitations to gatherings. What he envied was the relaxed contact with colleagues, which created better and different relationships. How much we in the Labour Party miss the great country houses which we do not have, he would say wistfully. In particular, he regretted the prime minister's determination to have everything in terms of business.

In some ways, Crossman was one of nature's Whig grandees. He used to refer at intervals to the times spent at the magical Buscot Park, home of Gavin Faringdon, where in idyllic surroundings the Keep Left Group of Labour MPs would hammer out their most convincing policies.

Crossman had an ambivalent relationship with the elders of the Labour Party. They could not make up their minds about one another. Wing-collared Chuter Ede, Parliamentary Secretary to Rab Butler at the time of the 1944 Education Act, and subsequently Attlee's Home Secretary, told me in 1963 that at times he was proud to have a man of Crossman's intellect and talent as a colleague of the Parliamentary Labour Party, and there were equally times when he devoutly wished that Crossman would get back to Oxford.

It was the same old story, put into words by Herbert Morrison, when Eddie Shackleton brought him to 9 Vincent Square, late at night on 31 January 1952. At the end of an argument on the Middle East, Morrison said, 'I can't help liking you even if I disapprove of you!' To which Crossman replied, 'That's exactly the way I feel about you, Herbert!'

ELEVEN

Shadow Education and Science

I doubt whether Harold Wilson ever really intended to make Crossman the Secretary of State for Education and Science in a Labour Government. But Crossman's frenetic hard work between February 1963 and October 1964 is still worth considering. Crossman and his team changed the Labour Party's standing in the scientific and educational world of that time. The prospect of a Labour government generated an excitement in opinion-forming circles, without which Wilson's own speech at Scarborough in 1963 on the white heat of the technological revolution would have fallen on stonier, less receptive ground. And without this groundswell of enthusiasm, Wilson would probably not have got his knife-edge electoral victory in October 1964.

I believe that the serious work – chiefly in education but also, and crucially, in science policy – outlined in this chapter, swung the 1964 general election, and therefore altered the political history of Britain.

Crossman believed that Britain faced a national emergency in education, as a result of the shortage of teachers in the early 1960s. Public opinion had to be alerted. The brutal truth was that unless we could recruit the teachers, any talk of modernizing our schools, and providing that equality of educational opportunity about which C. A. R. Crosland wrote so eloquently in his book, *The Future of Socialism* (1956), was completely meaningless. For Crossman, ex-Oxford don, it was equally meaningless to talk – as Sir Edward Boyle, the Conservative Secretary of State, did – about providing higher education for every boy and girl who could benefit, if, at school level pupils were being taught in classes of forty or over. True to his basic belief (and ceaseless refrain during the conferences on National Superannuation), Crossman reiterated that the small classes which were then the privilege of the few must be made the right of every boy and girl in Britain. That required an enormous increase both in the quantity and quality of the entrants to the teaching profession.

Many senior politicians would have been content simply to mouth sage speeches. Not Crossman. Friend and foe could only marvel at his sheer drive and energy. Immediately Lord Robbins's Royal Commission had announced its plans, ambitious and far-seeing, for Higher Education, Crossman persuaded the National Executive Committee of the Labour Party to set up a working party that would study in depth the problem of the shortage of teachers, and come forward with proposals on how to meet the problem. Crossman assembled not only members of the National Executive and of the Parliamentary Labour Party, but a number of leading experts of the day, using the width of his acquaintanceship. Voting Labour was not a necessary qualification, let alone membership of the party; good will towards a potential Labour government was.

From the universities and colleges came Professor Lionel Elvin, director of the London Institute of Education, and W. B. Inglis, the erudite head of Moray House College in Edinburgh; from the Local Authorities, Mrs Marjorie McIntosh, Barbara Castle's sister, and chairman of the LCC Education Committee; from statistics, Professor Claus Moser; from social science, Professor Richard Titmuss; and from the Advisory Centre for Education, its director, Dr Michael Young.

I was a regular attender and witnessed Crossman, postilion-like, driving a coach-and-four at maximum speed. Crossman was determined to be decisive. Deadlines were sacred. Had it not been so, the work would simply not have been completed before the 1964 general election. Crossman used to boast that he was literate, not numerate – until, in my first row with him in the spring of 1963, I told him that it was nothing to be proud of, and anyway it was not true. Soon he became adept at using figures, about which he was unusually scrupulous, to demonstrate his theme. For example, this is how he deployed his concern about the gravity of the educational emergency, and the fact that it was getting worse, and not better.

In England and Wales, twenty years after R. A. Butler's 1944 Education Act, Crossman trumpeted up and down the land that there was a shortfall of 55,000 in the number of teachers required to reduce classes to the maximum laid down under the Act, forty in primary classes and thirty in secondary classes. In 1963, half the classes in secondary schools, and one in five of the primary school classes exceeded the maximum figure.

Crossman always believed in giving credit where credit was due. He had been taught by Aneurin Bevan to look for an opponent's strongest point, and attack at that point, not necessarily at the weaknesses or absurdities. Yes, he said, it was true that the government of Sir Alec Douglas-Home did have plans for recruiting teachers which would reduce the overall shortage by the year 1970 to 30,000. But the raising of the school leaving age in 1970–1 would increase it once more to 50,000. Further, a decision to carry out the Crowther Committee's recommendation that there should be compulsory day release for two years after school leaving would, at the very least, require a further 20,000 teachers and so raise the total deficiency to 70,000. Crossman was a fervent advocate of day release. He was rather tepid about the raising of the school leaving age, but recognized that it was a party imperative.

[**A digression.**   I have only twice had the rough edge of James Callaghan's tongue – which can be very cutting indeed. Once was when, as chairman of the PLP Education Group in 1965, I suggested that instead of raising the school leaving age, pupils ought to complete the year in which they were fifteen, with the advantage that teachers did not have to take fourth or fifth year rump classes, where morale deteriorated as groups of pupils left in driblets, when their birthdays arrived. 'It's all very well for you and Dick Crossman who have had the best of university advantages – only a man like me who had to leave school at sixteen really understands what we've missed. Over my dead body!' He was Chancellor at the time.]

Crossman's technique was to set out fairly and clearly his opponent's options. Most politicians resort to the cheap laugh when setting out the opposing view. It was not his style. The jocular technique was the after-dinner speech technique. And Crossman never, ever made a formal after-dinner speech, nor an informal speech on any public occasion until November 1964, when he was fifty-six years of age! He absolutely refused. On Tory education plans, he simply said: Consider their four options. First, to postpone the start of primary education from the age of five to the age of six. Second, to postpone the raising of the school leaving age. Third, to postpone any attempt to introduce compulsory day release even by stages until after 1971. Or fourthly, to recruit more teachers by lowering standards – for instance, by an emergency two-year training scheme.

Crossman, in countless speeches, would set out the educational grounds on which he rejected all these proposals. If our average children were to be given the teaching they deserved, primary as well as secondary school classes had to be reduced to a maximum of thirty, and we had to set ourselves a time limit for achieving such a figure.

Crossman inveighed against the discrimination which gave a middle-class child six times as good a chance of reaching higher education as a working-class child. Wagging his fingers and using his hands to emphasize a point, as few politicians have done more effectively, he would stress that if the increased provision of higher education, recommended by the Robbins Committee were implemented, while the size of primary and secondary classes in working-class areas were left unchanged, this discrimination would get worse and not better. With genuine socialist conviction, Crossman rejected every proposal for dealing with the teacher shortage by lowering standards or postponing the improvement of the school system. Having courteously examined the case put forward by the opposition, Crossman would turn to his own case. He believed that in the years 1965–75 it was essential for Britain to advance simultaneously along the whole educational front. Certainly he would carry out the crash programme recommended by the Robbins Committee. (Crossman would have been appalled, had he been alive, to observe how Mrs Thatcher refuses to appoint Royal Commissions to examine difficult and important areas of policy and report on them.) He was in favour of abolishing the eleven-plus by re-organizing secondary education on comprehensive lines. (His own children were to attend the local comprehensive school.) He would raise the school leaving age to sixteen. He would move forward the compulsory day release for sixteen- to eighteen-year-olds. And he would reduce the maximum size of classes to thirty in primary as well as secondary schools.

Crossman was an orator who disarmed serious critics by anticipating criticism. Making eye-to-eye contact with his hearers he spoke from headings of one, two or three words – he would exclaim confidentially in a stage whisper, 'Of course it is easy to announce these aims. But we agree heartily with Ronnie Gould [Sir Ronald Gould, the long-serving and heavyweight General Secretary of the NUT] that to do so without facing the problems of teachers' supply is sheer political hypocrisy.' Crossman was genuinely hostile to those who put forward imaginary soft options which ducked an issue. Anyone who rejected, as he did, all the proposals which involved the lowering of educational standards, or the sharpening of educational inequality, had to be prepared to demonstrate the sincerity of their intention by advancing a realistic and practical plan for recruiting teachers. Crossman was against gimmicks, and was never one to propound a single simple solution. The immense increase of teachers required could only be obtained through a combined operation under which a whole number of measures, which would be ineffective if taken in isolation, were co-ordinated in a single con-centrated effort. This is how I heard Crossman present his case at many of the thirty-four Two-Way Traffic in Ideas Conferences, which I was instrumental in helping to organize up and down Britain in that spring and summer of 1964.

The late Sir Ronald Gould, whom I knew through my work with the Educational Institute of Scotland before I knew Crossman, com-mented to me: 'I've heard many Education Ministers and spokesmen. I've never heard any of them cause teachers to listen with such rapt attention as Crossman. He makes it so *interesting*.' And it was the interestingness – or capacity to interest – of Crossman that was a key ingredient of the success of the 'Bonnington' Science Conferences, so called after the hotel in Southampton Row, Bloomsbury, where the first conference between politicians and scientists generated excitement. That – and the fact that they thought that the chances of a Labour Government were extremely high – was why the heavyweight scientific establishment accepted an invitation, almost without exception, to the stuffy basement of the Bonnington Hotel. The names helping Crossman and Labour that weekend rippled through Whitehall and academia and added to the credibility of the parliamentary Opposition. To mention only a few, they included: Sir Eric Ashby, FRS, Master of Clare College, Cambridge; Dr Thomas Balogh, Fellow of Balliol, Oxford, economist; Dr Vivian Bowden, Principal of Manchester College of Science and Technology; Sir Nevill Mott, FRS, Nobel laureate, Cavendish Professor of Physics and Master of Caius, Cambridge; Captain Robert Maxwell, MC, chairman, Pergamon Press; and Fred Willey.

Had Crossman become the actual Secretary of State for Education and Science, I have little doubt that he would have harnessed the talents of such people, as he was to use the abilities of Asa Briggs, as chairman of the Committee of Inquiry into Nursing Services when he became Secretary of State for the Social Services.

However, as fate and Harold Wilson were to determine, this was not to be. His legacy was different.

Reg Underhill – now Lord Underhill – veteran National Agent of the Labour Party, saw a good deal of Crossman in the West Midlands. Underhill reckons that there could be all sorts of views about Crossman as a politician – but no doubts at all about him as a great teacher and great educator.

TWELVE
Housing and Local Government

That Harold Wilson should have cast Dick Crossman for the role of Minister of Housing and Local Government in 1964 was a cause for astonishment. Education and science had been his Shadow portfolio. Pensions had been his expertise for seven years. Defence and foreign affairs were the areas where his opinions had mattered for two decades and more. But housing and local government? According to the wags in the Commons tearoom, the only General Grant he knew of was a late nineteenth-century US president. His enemies were dismissive, his friends apprehensive. What credentials did this intellectual have to deal with housing and local government heavyweights?

No one will now ever know for certain what were the considerations which weighed most heavily with Harold Wilson in casting Crossman for Housing. For many years I believed what Harold Wilson himself told me in the spring of 1965, when I asked him the direct question. (Today it would stretch the imagination that an MP of less than three years' standing could ask the present Prime Minister why she appointed so-and-so to her Cabinet. Apart from my natural breeziness, or cheek, I imagined I knew my erstwhile Chairman of the Public Accounts Committee sufficiently well; only in later years did he stand on his dignity as Prime Minister, and did I have the sense to realize that once a friend had become Leader of the Party and Prime Minister, one's relationship with him was somewhat altered!)

In the spring of 1965, Wilson gave me a direct, and, I thought, frank answer. He would have sent Crossman to the Department of Education and Science, but for the fact that the tiny majority of three altered the entire scenario. Nothing could be achieved in the field of science in the necessarily short time before the inevitable next election, which might take place within months rather than years. Wilson told me that he was in a way very sorry, as I might think that all the work of eighteen months which I and others had done to cement the Labour Party's relations with scientists had been wasted. However, the paramount consideration for a prime minister was to notch up some achievement in the short term before going to the electorate. The sole area in which this could be done was housing. Therefore he chose to harness Crossman's great energy and willpower in the Ministry of Housing, where most impact for the political good of the government could be made expeditiously.

Years later, after Crossman's death, I learned of another set of circumstances which may have contributed to Crossman's despatch to Housing. I had been present when he had an idiotic row with a delegation of National Union of Teachers (NUT) members who had come to see him about the conditions of teachers in nursery schools. I thought he was clearly at fault, though he was tired at the fag-end of a frustrating day. It was one of those occasions when Crossman was embarrassingly rude to those who were in no position to answer back, and where his friends present could only cringe with embarrassment. To cap it all, ludicrously, after they had gone, he revealed that in general terms he accepted the case relating to the conditions of nursery teachers. But the damage was done. In sheer and understandable fury at the way they had been humiliated, the NUT representatives complained to their union hierarchy, who I discovered subsequently had descended on various sympathetic MPs, such as Ernest Popplewell, a powerful figure in the National Union of Railwaymen, and some members connected directly with the NUT itself. Surreptitiously, they in turn had gone to Harold Wilson and said: 'Don't land the teachers with that awful bully, Crossman. The NUT already hate him.' I believe Wilson heeded their advice. I also think there was another element in Wilson's decision – a simple desire to keep Crossman so occupied with a government Department that he would not stray into his old pastures of foreign affairs and defence where his views were so suspect to the Prime Minister.

In the event, disappointingly, Crossman did refrain from trying to demand collective Cabinet consideration of foreign and defence policy. On the other hand, in a way rare among Cabinet Ministers, he did fight for other spending departments, on the grounds that both equity and the success of the Labour Government in general were involved. For example, the first Minister of Pensions in the Wilson Government, Peggy Herbison, recently told me Crossman was a marvellous friend to the pensioners, when a normal Cabinet minister would simply have been concerned to get as large a share of the cake as possible for Housing.

After the Labour Government had been in office for a year, Dick Crossman and I were sitting in the Commons Smoking Room, when in came James Callaghan, the Chancellor of the Exchequer: looming over Crossman, Callaghan, half in fun and wholly earnest, muttered resignedly: 'You really are a pretty awful minister, Dick. Pity the poor Chancellor. You not only take most of the money for your own Housing Department, but then you come along to Cabinet, having won your own battles, and fight ferociously to get other ministers their money, too. That is not what most people do!'

After Callaghan had shuffled away, Crossman commented, 'It's true what he says. They don't. But are we not supposed to be a collective Labour Government?'

On entering the Ministry of Housing, what appalled him was not the Civil Service but our own Labour Party housing specialists. Whereas he had beavered hugely in the fields of education and science, and formulated policy documents, the housing cupboard was bare. The central task was to introduce a major measure reimposing rent control. Remember that the 1964 Election had been fought by the Labour Party on the issue of exploitation by slum landlords of tenants in the inner cities, and that it was precisely such urban areas that had produced for Harold Wilson the slimmest of parliamentary majorities. The short-hand name for such exploitation was Rachmanism: Peter Rachman had used and abused the provisions of the Conservatives 1957 Rent Act to flourish as a slum landlord in the area of Notting Hill and Paddington. This Act, introduced by Enoch Powell when he was Minister of Housing, freed from rent control over fifty per cent of the houses in England and Wales hitherto affected by rent-restriction legislation. Enoch Powell's Rent Act also created the conditions for raising the rent limits on most of those houses remaining subject to controls.

The Labour Party had created an enormous political hullabaloo about this situation. Yet, horror of horrors, all the incoming minister found from the files of Labour Party headquarters at Transport House was one small series of notes by the former Shadow Minister of Housing, Michael Stewart. Precious little work had been done by the party on how to replace the hated Powell Act or the means of redeeming much-trumpeted electoral promises. One evening in late October 1964, Crossman was launching a torrent of invective against the Labour Party for having been so idle on housing policy formation. I asked him the obvious question, as to what he had done as a member of the National Executive for a decade to make sure there *was* a housing policy. As often, lashing anger transformed itself into sombre reflection. 'I suppose I do have to take my share of the blame. I imagined Skeff [Arthur Skeffington, MP] and Ben [Ben Parkin, MP, who exposed Rachman] had done it in a working party. They hadn't! Nor had the Transport House research department.'

I've never admired a politician more than I do Dick Crossman for what he did in relation to legislation on rents, that autumn and winter of 1964–5. Just imagine the scenario. An incoming government with a majority so fragile that it could be forced into a general election at any time from the spring onwards. A major pledge on a populist issue, rent control, to be implemented. A civil service, uncertain as to whether their political masters the following summer would be those who had come in after a gap of thirteen years, or those whom they had served for those thirteen years, and on whose ideas, if they did not have a vested intellectual interest, at least they had sweated long and hard. Enoch Powell, Duncan Sandys, and Crossman's immediate predecessor, Keith Joseph, had been hard, if agreeable, taskmasters. Why should they exert themselves for incoming politicians who looked as though they might well be ephemeral?

Crossman did not throw in the towel. He was contemptuous of those who resorted to self-pity. Instead he turned to the wide range of his acquaintance, in particular to the shambling, 'vast orang-utan' figure of Arnold (later Lord) Goodman, senior partner in a firm of solicitors and much else. There was an almost thermo-nuclear reaction from Dame Evelyn Sharp, the long-serving and formidable Beatrice-Webb-like lady who was from 1955 to 1966 Permanent Secretary to the Ministry of Housing. (I write as one of Evelyn Sharp's admirers.) When she heard of the proposal to inject the thought and legal expertise of Mr Goodman, as he then was, into the legislation of her beloved ministry, Dame Evelyn declared throughout Whitehall that she had never, ever been so insulted in her life. But if Crossman had not gone to Goodman, and others, for help, no meaningful Rent Act would have reached the statute-book in 1965. It was not that the Ministry of Housing civil servants were not able. They were. So were their lawyers, like Mr Rogerson. Being present at meeting after meeting with Crossman and his officials, my impression was that they were sitting on the fence and procrastinating, not out of malice nor out of antipathy to a Labour Government, but rather out of concern that Crossman's ideas would cause confusion in the courts, and that they would be blamed for the shambles. In those days, preferment in the civil service was virtually assured, provided a civil servant did not accumulate black marks by incautious advice. Caution was the recipe for a successful career. It was Crossman's demonic energy that got a Rent Act on the statute-book at all, and created a real counterattack to the evils of Rachmanism.

Crossman understood that officials were resistant to outside advice. But he believed that it was an important part of the task of a minister to make sure that experts from relevant fields should be brought into the ministry on secondment, and that the vistas of civil servants should be widened. Blood should be pumped into their veins by people from outside who actually knew the realities which civil servants handled in such an abstract and aloof way.

Just as Macmillan as Minister of Housing had brought in Sir Percy Mills, and insisted on seeing him once a fortnight about building methods and housing figures, and just as Crossman himself in 1956–7 had brought in Brian Abel-Smith to aid him on pensions, Patrick Blackett and others to advise him on science policy, and now Goodman to assist him on the Rent Act, so for outside advice on building Crossman brought in Peter Lederer of Costain on secondment to help him develop a policy of encouraging local authorities to interest themselves in system building. Lederer was 'a sensible, extremely anglicized Czech Jew', who had worked his way up to become one of the top technical experts in the Costain empire. Crossman had known Lederer because he was responsible for constructing the jack-block building in Coventry, a technique, new in the 1960s, of jacking up each storey after it had been erected. The problem that faced Crossman, as an incoming minister, was that the ministry could do little itself to tackle the housing shortage. Everything had to be done through the local authorities; and there was a mosaic of hundreds of local authorities, all wanting 'to make each building just a little different and claim credit for it'.

116

At first Crossman thought that he was being allowed to see only those officials whom Dame Evelyn Sharp wanted him to see. This was galling for a curiosity-driven man of Crossman's temperament. After a time, relations dramatically improved, as a result of a very successful dinner party given by the Crossmans on 27 October 1964, at Number 9 Vincent Square, during which Dame Evelyn Sharp met Richard Llewelyn-Davies and his wife Patricia. He was a distinguished architect, he clicked with the Dame, and from that moment there was no resistance to Crossman's seeing the architect in the ministry, as well as other technical heavyweights like Jimmy James, the Chief Planner at the ministry itself, whose ideas Crossman came to admire.

However, it soon dawned on Crossman that there was a considerable esprit de corps in the ministry, and that what really mattered to civil servants was the MHLG line, the departmental view, as opposed to a ministerial view. The policy of the Department was paramount: Ministers came and went, but the Department remained. And every civil servant was infinitely more dependent on the goodwill of his professional colleagues, who could make or break his career, than on a Minister who could be here today and gone tomorrow. Loyalty and self-interest combined to give precedence to the Ministry, not the Minister, should there be a conflict. If Crossman wanted to challenge and try to direct the Ministry policy, there would be no formal tension at first, but a great deal of mulish resistance.

Often, in those early months of the Labour government, he would ask me anxiously: 'Do you think our ideas are getting across? How far are they being merely tolerated? And do you think that Dame Evelyn's existing departmental policies are being imposed on my own mind?'

If Crossman had succeeded in gaining Dame Evelyn's acquiescence in the introduction of Llewelyn-Davies and in establishing a direct relationship with Jimmy James, he had certainly not won her agreement to his questioning relatively junior members of the Ministry on what was actually going on. He thought Dame Evelyn almost relished crushing new ideas – she had been Permanent Secretary so long that she thought she knew the answer to everything. He believed he had to push her aside to get the junior members of the Ministry to talk freely. Dame Evelyn hated his interrogatory moods; the junior members of the upper echelons of the Ministry were scared of the process. But Dick Crossman's inquisitorial performances – for performances they certainly were – were neither showing off nor bombast. Sitting in bed late at night, surrounded by his red boxes, his nightshirt buttoned up to the neck, he would almost always call me into his bedroom as soon as I shut the front door, if Anne was not up for her day in the week. 'Unless I can get at the officials who are actually directly responsible for what is done in my name, how on earth can a Minister really grasp the issues which are involved in any problem?'

Trouble erupted in November 1964 over Stevenage. The MP for Stevenage was the daughter of George Catlin and Vera Brittain, newly-elected Mrs Shirley Williams, then wife of Bernard Williams, who had Crossman's old job as a philosophy don at New College, Oxford. She asked to see my boss pretty quickly, revealing that she wanted to give evidence at the public inquiry, arising out of a major proposal for the enlargement of the New Towns, Stevenage, Basildon and Harlow as a strategy for coping with the London overspill. Opposition in Basildon and Harlow had not been significant. But the outcry in Stevenage was of shocked horror that the town should be virtually doubled in size by the expedient of adding a twin-town, no less, on the far side of the motorway and railway track.

Crossman's instincts were that the protesters in Stevenage were right. Who in their right mind, he snorted – he often did snort going through official papers – would place the main London–Edinburgh railway and a motorway between two halves of a city? All Crossman's sympathies were with the people of Stevenage, which was, in his opinion, one of the very few New Towns in England which had achieved a genuine community civic sense. (Representing as part of my constituency a New Town, Livingston in West Lothian, I would agree.) Crossman's chagrin knew no bounds that the ministry of which he was the titular head was solemnly going to order Stevenage to accept an enlargement which, in the reckoning of the people who lived there, would destroy their whole unity as a town.

I arranged an urgent meeting between Crossman and Mrs Williams; and as soon as he heard her side of the story, he fixed up a seminar with all the officials involved, requiring the junior but directly involved officials to face his own questions. The Dame was as black as thunder, the tension electric. Crossman told me that part of the trouble was that Dame Evelyn regarded the New Towns as her children. She loved them, he said sardonically, because they had been created autocratically from above as Development Corporations. Crossman was convinced that it was high time that fully developed New Towns, like Hemel

Hempstead and Crawley, were handed over in toto to their local district councils rather than to the Commission for the New Towns. Labour Party policy was on his side; he knew that the NEC had stated in a policy document that New Towns should be transferred to the apropriate urban district council as soon as they were ready to take over, and as soon as a solution had been reached on the thorny problem of what was to happen to the assets.

About a fortnight later, I returned to Vincent Square after a minor but very late Commons vote on the night of 2–3 December. I opened the door and tiptoed upstairs, thinking Crossman had gone to sleep as he usually did after 1 a.m. Instead, the bedroom door was ajar, and he was pulsating with anger. I had never seen him so furious, and no wonder. The Private Office had tried a standard device to tame an inconvenient Minister, by piling into the night's three red boxes every kind of junk, in no particular order. I had heard Crossman on several occasions ask George Moseley, his Civil Service Private Secretary, to have the papers sorted into the categories of 'background' at the bottom of box three, 'less urgent' in box two and 'urgent and important' at the top of box one. On this particular evening, Wednesday 2 December 1964, Crossman had gone through a huge mass of 'urgent and important'. He had then come to the 'less urgent'. Spatchcocked into the less urgent there was a sheet on which the Assistant Private Secretary, Brian Ponsford, later to become a distinguished civil servant but then fresh from university, had scribbled: 'You might like to see what will be said on your behalf by the architect at the Stevenage inquiry.' Imagine Crossman's temper, in the middle of the night, when he saw to his consternation that the Ministry of Housing and Local Government architect was going to turn up at Stevenage that very morning in eight hours' time to make the strongest case possible for the doubling of the size of the town. Crossman, at the seminar on this very subject, had made it abundantly obvious to all of us present that he was not in any way going to commit himself to the departmental proposal to double the size of Stevenage; on the contrary, he was going to leave himself in a position to make up his own mind after the inquiry.

After the seminar, ministry officials had asked him if he wanted to cancel the inquiry. No, he said, because the inquiry would be a useful basis on which the whole case could be reconsidered; after that he could announce his decision, independently. In order to do what they wanted to Stevenage all along, it appeared to Crossman, the Ministry officials had slipped the Chief Architect's Stevenage statement into his box, to cover themselves for railroading him into doing something against his better judgement. He was beside himself with anger because the Ministry thought that by presenting him with a fait accompli, in the shape of a mere formality to be acted out within hours, they could override his expressed wishes.

The scene in the Ministry of Housing at 9.30 a.m., Crossman's normal time of arrival at his office, on the morning of Thursday 3 December 1964 was picturesque – but unfunny and indeed embarrassing at the time for all present. Mad with anger, Crossman rounded on George Moseley – later, deservedly to be Permanent Secretary at the Department of the Environment. A lady typist took to her heels and fled the office until the storm had subsided. Even I was embarrassed. Crossman virtually accused Moseley of conspiring against him: Ponsford was all but sent to Outer Mongolia on the spot. Eventually he calmed down, proposing that the following words should be inserted at the top of the draft statement: 'The paper which follows shows the Ministry policy as it was before the change of Government. It is not to be understood to prejudice the present Minister's views on the matter.' Moseley then said that the statement had already gone out to the press. It dawned on Crossman that in his box three had been what amounted to a snubbing *fait accompli*. He then reached a new crescendo of fury. Another future Permanent Secretary was summoned, James D. Jones, and was the recipient of a tongue-lashing the like of which I've never witnessed. The proposed statement was made at the inquiry. Later in the day, Dame Evelyn accepted full responsibility for the Stevenage debacle, coupled with an apology of that sulky variety for which a man would be hit physically or verbally, but which a high-minded, upper-middle-class lady can get away with – just.

As a result, sense prevailed at Stevenage. Years later, on a visit to Stevenage Labour Party, I was told by a veteran councillor that had Crossman not reacted as he did, it would have been a catastrophe for the New Town. One of Crossman's achievements, a lasting one, is that it caused the Ministry of Housing to take more notice in the course of their planning decisions, not only of the view of ministers, but more importantly, the views of local people, as channelled through their MPs like Shirley Williams.

It is a feature of Crossman's ministerial life that particular controversial cases should loom large. As we shall see later, when considering the role of the Ely Hospital in the wider issue of his mental health interests and campaigns for the subnormal, Crossman used concrete problems for wider purposes. Thus it was that the problem of 'Hartley' flowed through the rooms of 9 Vincent Square.

The Stevenage experience had focused his mind on a question that bothered him more and more in the run-up to Christmas 1964: how, as a minister, do I take my decisions? Ostensibly, every single planning decision was taken personally by the minister. In ninety-nine cases out of a hundred, the minister would know precious little about them. But if one was important enough for him to deal with, what should he do? Law and precedent were scarce. Decisions were taken on personal judgement. Therefore Crossman deduced that if he was required to take a big decision, such as whether to allow building in the green belt, he or one of the junior ministers should at the very least see the area for himself. I was present at a riveting and tension-filled discussion between Crossman, Dame Evelyn and James D. Jones. It took place against the background of the proposal by the Span Company for a model village at Hartley, in a scrubland area of northern Kent.

'If you are really asking me,' said Crossman, 'whether I should cause mayhem in the House of Commons, and bring a ton of coals on my head from Arthur Blenkinsop and every other do-gooder in the Labour Party by allowing building in the green belt, I'd bloody well better go and see the area for myself!'

J. D. Jones said firmly: 'Oh no Minister, you can't possibly do that – the Minister must judge without going to see for himself!'

This stretched Crossman's patience: 'But, that's judging without understanding. That means incompetent judgement.'

Unabashed, J. D. Jones said: 'Minister, do you propose that you visit every site of every major planning decision? If so, you'll have no time for Cabinet, the Rent Act, or anything else.'

Crossman: 'Don't spoil your case by exaggeration!'

Jones: 'Then there is a legal aspect. If you see a site, you might obtain new evidence, which was not available to the inspector, and that would require another public inquiry.'

Crossman, non-sequitive as often when confronted by an awkward argument: 'I know these Chancery lawyers. My father was one of them.'

This flummoxed the officials. Dame Evelyn: 'So, what do you want us to do?'

Crossman: 'I want a sane method of deciding what to do about this proposed model village in Kent. We'll send MacColl to see it for himself.'

James MacColl, MP for Widnes, Anglo-Catholic pillar of the Church, housing expert, and Parliamentary Secretary, was the most cautious of men. He went to Hartley. He took the view that we cannot preserve all the green belts intact. If the pressing problems of London overspill were to be confronted, MacColl had come to believe that ministers should allow planned incursions into the green belt in certain concentrated developments, with a New Town or model villages. The rest would then be kept truly green.

Crossman anticipated that there would be a row. None of us foresaw the extent of the sustained row that was unleashed by Hartley. I thought he was going to be crucified as a Labour Minister, the first to leave the Cabinet, on the altar of the green belt. Trouble, fomented by his old enemy, Norman Dodds, MP, rumbled on for weeks.

Years later, when we were friends and colleagues on the Labour delegation to the European Parliament, Lord Murray of Gravesend (who as Albert Murray, MP, had represented part of Kent) told me that the real trouble was that if Crossman gave to private developers the consent which had been denied to the local authority, the number of Conservative voters in Labour-held marginal parliamentary seats would increase. He was jeopardizing his colleagues' parliamentary future without consulting them, let alone the local authority. His defiance of his own inspector was a secondary consideration. Much of the undoubted antipathy to Crossman in the Parliamentary Labour Party arose from a certain cavalier naiveté towards the nitty-gritty of political life, which maddened those who saw him as living in the stratosphere of high office. While preparing this book, I talked to Sydney Irving, now Lord Irving of Dartford, in whose then constituency Hartley lay. Lord Irving thought that the real trouble was that the local authority was expected to provide facilities, without consultation, in an area which was far from their main developments. Lord Irving bears no ill-will, though his judgement, as Deputy Chief Whip at the time, that the Hartley decision did Crossman a lot of harm with his colleagues is surely correct. (The development was eventually built at Ash Green, but the Span Company later went into liquidation.)

Crossman felt that whenever he relaxed his guard, the civil service would try to reassert itself. They would do their utmost to get the departmental view adopted in spite of a clear directive from the minister.

It also riled Crossman that able officials like the Accountant General of the Ministry would refuse to provide information if they believed that his speech had a strong political content. Since the Labour government left office in 1979, the severe ethics about civil servants helping Ministers with highly political speeches seem to have been relaxed!

Legend has grown up that Crossman generally behaved badly to civil servants, and was rude to men who were not in a position to answer him back. The legend has a modicum of justification, yet it is so far from the whole truth as to amount to a distortion of it. Trouble started early in his ministerial life, and as his Sancho Panza at the time, attending most of the meetings in a listening capacity as his Parliamentary Private Secretary, I offer one view of the root of the difficulty. For once, it lay not with personalities and the jarring of human beings, but with the system. For Crossman, the first taste of office arrived when he was already fifty-seven years old – he had never served an apprenticeship as a junior minister, where any mistakes would hardly reverberate around the political cosmos. Catapulted at a late age into the heights of the Cabinet, he was far more nervous and less self-confident than his outward image of the brilliant Oxford don-cum-NEC politician suggested. Moreover, in being required to handle the major Rent Bill, he had on his plate the hottest domestic political potato in the government. Given a majority of three, and an election round the corner at any moment, there was a tremendous personal pressure not to make a mess of it.

Throughout the spring of 1965, the Rent Bill was being prepared. The catalytic moment came when Crossman first met Mr H. P. Rowe, the parliamentary draftsman, who like all his colleagues worked not in the ministry but in the Lord Chancellor's department. Now the critical importance of parliamentary draftsmen is not widely understood. They undertake an exceptionally skilled task, recondite even to most MPs, but vital. Shortage of parliamentary draftsmen is the most common reason for delay in legislation. The parliamentary draftsman has to put the minister's ideas in such a form that it will not only make sense to the courts of law who have to interpret what they put in an Act – not the speeches that Ministers make – but also prevent wicked and clever men from circumventing the law. This was especially relevant in the era of Rachmanism.

The straw that broke Crossman's camel's back emerged during the internal discussions at the Ministry of Clause 22, setting out the principle of 'fair rent', which Crossman wanted established by local assessment committees. He was deeply anxious about a situation in which his advisers on the Rent Bill were administrators who, he thought (rightly), knew little or nothing about the law. Only one of the Ministry's thirty-odd lawyers had been allocated to the Rent Bill, and here was the parliamentary draftsman quietly and politely exposing the whole shaky Rent Bill edifice.

Crossman's legendary bad relations with the civil service stemmed from what he perceived were the perils for a reforming Cabinet minister 'of relying entirely on the Department's advice for anything to do with the world outside Whitehall' (*Diaries*, I, 186).

Rather than keeping his driver hanging around, with her early start in the morning – he was more considerate than people thought – he would walk back to Vincent Square with me after a 10 p.m. vote. On several occasions in February and March 1965, he dwelt on the theme of trembling to think what the present-day equivalents of his father, the Chancery Judge, Mr Justice Crossman, would do about his Rent Bill in court. 'What on earth is a Minister of Housing to do? The Dame produces for me advisers on the Rent Bill who know nothing about the legal pitfalls. Then, on the housing side, literally nobody knows anything about building a house. That's why I have to bring in Peter [Lederer] as progress chaser on system building. No wonder we blunder along, no wonder we make mistakes. I think we'd better face up to it that we are inadequate as a ministry.' Crossman's quarrel was with the basic conviction of the civil service that assistant secretaries and principals are capable of dealing with any problem, including the preparation of a Rent Bill, even though they have no legal training. Both Crossman and I thought that the planning side of the ministry was much more formidable than the housing side, precisely because the professionals, such as Jimmy James, the Chief Planner, and Oliver Cox, the Deputy Chief Architect, were not only first rate but crucially on equal terms with the administrators.

Rather like Montgomery and the Eighth Army, Crossman wanted the officials at all grades to know whom they were working for. So the last day of March 1965, anyone in the ministry who wished to come was invited to attend a question-and-answer session at the Caxton Hall in Holborn. Six hundred came, others were locked out. I am not convinced that they appreciated being told how the staff looked to the minister – that they were like fish swimming about in a goldfish bowl, and the minister was the cat looking in from outside. However, he put a number of awkward questions, which should have the serious attention of a 'self-perpetuating hierarchy', and in turn a lot of the junior officials let it be known that they were immensely pleased that a minister had recognized that they might have views. Dame Evelyn's response to the Caxton Hall exercise was chilly to the point of being cryogenic. To be fair, I suspect her resentment was less to do with the approach to her 'underlings', and more to do with Crossman's irritating habit (which tempted me to walk out and leave him on several occasions) of butting in, intemperately, before one had got halfway through, let alone finished what one was going to say. On several occasions, notably in November 1965, Dame Evelyn took me aside and said plaintively, 'Can't you persuade him to give time to discuss such-and-such properly with us? Could he not give us just a couple of hours? He never seems to have time for us!'

If there was a sigh of relief amongst the highest echelons in the Ministry of Housing when Crossman left, it was above all because they hated his relentlessly applied pressure, which often made senior persons look foolish in front of their subordinates. I sympathized with them when they did not have the time nor the opportunity to state their case before interruption.

I did not tell Crossman that I was acting as Evelyn Sharp's messenger. But I agreed with her and put the substance of what she was saying. Crossman's side of the story was that he cut down time talking to his deputy and assistant secretaries because they did not have the kind of minds from which he could learn very much. Their contribution was, in his opinion, dry, better put down on paper than talked over. He could learn more from outsiders. This was resented until the day when Crossman left the Ministry. Crossman did not care for what he saw as the ministry's tradition of paternalism – for example, in relation to New Towns, though he conceded that autocracy might have been necessary in the first generation of New Towns. I accompanied Crossman on many of his ministerial visits to New Towns, where he would often chide the chairmen of the Development Corporations with being remote. Rather aggressively he would inquire precisely how they consulted public opinion – without listening too carefully to the answers, which I thought were frequently impressive.

It is impossible to exaggerate the importance which Crossman attached as Minister of Housing to regional visits. Curiously, a Minister of Housing was not in general regarded as an influential member of any Cabinet nationally — but in the regions his responsibilities made him almost the most influential member of the Cabinet. His power to affect peoples' lives was unequalled. Whenever Crossman sallied forth, his coverage by local press and television was so massive, that cumulatively he became a national figure more quickly than anybody, other than Wilson, Brown and Callaghan.

Of all his visits outside London, one was in retrospect to be of overwhelming consequence. On 13 January 1965, Crossman was welcomed in Leeds by the dapper, vibrant figure of Karl Cohen, who had given a decade of his life to the chairmanship of the Leeds Housing Committee. He was presiding over the physical transformation of the city of Leeds. The Leeds visit was a watershed because Manchester, Newcastle and a host of other towns and cities believed that they should raze their slum areas to the ground, and were boasting of their policy of total clearance, whereas Cohen argued the opposite case: he boasted about the Leeds policy of improving the old central areas wherever possible. Cohen derived pleasure in seeing how happy old people were when their eighteenth- and nineteenth-century slum houses were 'transformed by being given a bathroom and a skylight in the attic, and proper dry roofing and modern kitchens'. He won the battle for Crossman's mind against the Manchester school of thought and set Crossman on his way to being the most conservationist Labour figure since Dalton.

Four months later, another seminal event occurred. Crossman was told on his visit to the northeast that a beautiful area of magnificent Georgian Newcastle, Eldon Square, was to be destroyed in order to create a shopping centre. He was passionately opposed to this plan, fulminated against the regional staff of the ministry in Newcastle, and called them vandals for having given consent on his behalf. It was experiences such as Eldon Square that prompted Crossman to embrace the interest shown by Duncan Sandys (who by chance had come high up in the ballot for private members' bills) in a measure that dealt with townscapes — that is, groups of buildings — and not merely individual listed buildings. Sandys was Churchill's son-in-law and former holder (1954–7) of Crossman's job — his photograph adorned the outer office, along with those of all former Housing ministers — a hard-headed Tory ex-Cabinet minister who was also a founder (1956) of the Civic Trust and later (1969) of Europa Nostra. Crossman and Sandys were both

126

environmentalists, before the term became fashionable, and combined to overcome the resistance of officials who believed they could deal only with individual listed buildings, not groups.

Another of Crossman's special interests was the protection of the coastline. It was sparked off by Anne Crossman, who wanted him to freeze ribbon development on the coastline, just as he had been able to freeze office-building in London. I suspect that Crossman mishandled Lord Antrim when he gave him lunch, in June 1966, as Head of the National Trust – though, there may have been an endemic difficulty that if the Trust were to express an interest in purchase, prices of coastal land would have soared. Little progress was made. To Crossman the credit should go for making the nation conscious that there was an all-too-real problem of preserving the coastline from both erosion and ribbon development.

Crossman also saved Ullswater, arguably the most beautiful of the English lakes. For decades Manchester's water had come from the Lake District. A rising tide of justified anger had emanated from preservation groups; the trouble was that Manchester corporation had devastated Thirlmere, transforming an exquisitely attractive lake into an ugly reservoir. Crossman was confronted with proposals which would have meted out the same treatment to Windermere and Ullswater. I sensed he was terribly worried. Unlike many ministers, he would fuss about the rights and wrongs of issues *per se*, as opposed to the effect of the issues on the career of the politician involved. In his eightieth year, the eloquent advocate and former Lord Justice of Appeal, Norman, Baron Birkett of Ulverston, had made a passionate speech in the House of Lords ridiculing the Ministry's plans for Ullswater, with the result that the 1961–2 Bill had been rejected. Manchester Corporation had come back with a revised Bill which included a much more moderate proposal. The Ministry inspector had devised a plan for taking some of the water from Ullswater and some from Windermere, with the most elaborate series of controls to stop the water-level sinking. Crossman believed it to be sound, and was going to accept it, hook, line and sinker.

I was summoned to the Chief Whip. Scurrying along, I wondered which of my various possible misdemeanours on east-of-Suez issues had upset Ted Short. But the source of his considerable agitation was not my troublesome thoughts on the British presence in Singapore, but Ullswater. In politics, nothing stirs a man more greatly than his personal loves, even the most incorruptible of us. It transpired that the Chief

Whip's family had dwelt near Ullswater for several generations and that he himself, no less, was the leader of and driving force in the Ullswater preservation campaign. I told him I would not only get Crossman's diary cleared, but that I would get hold of, and give him, rightly or wrongly, the inspector's report. (The Dame, when she found out that I had slipped the inspector's report to my friend, was livid. I thought it was unnecessary secrecy, and the incident set me on a twenty-five-year crusade against gratuitous secrecy in Government!)

As a result, a proper compromise was devised to make sure that Manchester got the water it needed, mostly from Windermere, without too much scarring of the countryside. If anything, it was a solution that treated Manchester hard, by preserving all the amenities, and positively improving some of them. One of the reasons I would put Crossman in the first division of Housing Ministers is the infinite, painstaking trouble he took over Ullswater — which extended to himself answering an adjournment debate, instead of delegating the chore to a Parliamentary Secretary, at 7.30 a.m. on Tuesday 28 June, after an all-night sitting.

In politics, Ministers tend to trip up on the small issues, not the major, obvious ones. If Crossman's interest and assiduity in individual cases is the cause of considerable ministerial achievement, he did once nearly become unstuck. In February 1966 he became aware of what seemed to be a mere nuisance, Councillor Brack of Islington. He had been expelled from the Islington Labour Group on the grounds that he had violently opposed the pulling down of the flats at Packington to allow wholesale redevelopment of the area. He was one of 426 people who formally opposed the ministry planning decision. They claimed they had been misled by the references to improvements which Crossman himself had inserted in the letter of decision. They were then beside themselves with anger when Islington Council, backed by the Greater London Council and the Ministry of Housing, refused to wait for a second inquiry and went ahead on the basis of an improved version of their redevelopment plan. They had the wit, in their fury, to appeal to the Council on Tribunals. But a couple of days before the Council on Tribunals was due to sit and come to a decision, the Ministry of Housing whipped out a decision letter approving the redevelopment scheme. No wonder the Council on Tribunals felt that they had been insulted. Councillor Brack then came to tackle Crossman, who I thought dealt with him generously and in an adult way.

However, he was not deterred from going to the *Evening Standard*, who naturally made Crossman's treatment of the Council on Tribunals a front-page story. Crossman meanwhile went along to Dame Evelyn's room, telling me to come as a witness. Calmly he told her what Brack had said, adding acidly, 'The trouble is that as soon as you knew you were threatened with the Council on Tribunals, you expedited the second letter out, and simply infuriated the Council – without letting me know anything about it.' Her cool response stunned me. 'Of course we did,' she said, without a trace of contrition. 'We had to. If the press had got hold of it first, we should never have got our decision.' Crossman exploded. Why had she done it behind his back?

The Packington Debate on Wednessday 2 March, 1966 was the most uncomfortable that Crossman was ever to face in the House of Commons. The criticism was threefold – that Crossman had been grossly discourteous to the Council on Tribunals; that in his decision letter, he had given the opponents of the Packington scheme the strong impression that he would concede a second inquiry; and that the opponents of the scheme had been denied the right to see the second plan for redevelopment which the department had prepared in consultation with the GLC and Islington Council. Crossman told me that there was an uncomfortable amount of substance in each one of these complaints. However, Crossman of course eschewed getting out of it by saying that Dame Evelyn was to blame for doing it behind his back.

John Boyd Carpenter led for the Opposition. He had become chairman of the Public Accounts Committee on which I served, so I was in a position to know that he had taken enormous trouble with his prosecuting indictment. Instead of allowing Crossman to reply immediately, I had the nous to persuade three tough Labour lawyers MPs, Sam Silkin, QC, Ivor Richard, QC, and Tom Williams, QC, to speak in his defence. Then John Hobson, the Tory Shadow Attorney-General, made a waspish speech of the kind that the then House of Commons did not care for. Crossman took up his notes, and fought for his political life, fortunately saying unprompted that if he had been discourteous it was unintentional, and he regretted it. We scraped through by 290 votes to 285, and he had avoided passing the buck to the officials.

Where Crossman made me want to go under the floorboards with embarrassment was when he said, 'If this procedure is to work at all, the minister's decisions must be removed from party matters. He must try to do his job. He lives in a very difficult world surrounded by lawyers and a vast mythology of planning procedures.' Considering that the way he said 'lawyers' oozed hate, I had to go on my hands and knees to the three QCs who had come to the rescue. And I made Crossman pen abject letters of apology! Yet his Packington Speech was perhaps the finest, in a gutsy sense, that Crossman ever made in the House.

It was Harold Wilson, years later after Crossman's death, who answered for me the question of why Crossman got so much of his own way in Cabinet on housing and local government matters: 'In the Attlee Government, I served alongside men of real authority on matters of local government – Herbert Morrison, Chuter Ede, Nye Bevan; in my Cabinet there was not a single person of that quality of experience, and so Dick got away with murder.'

THIRTEEN

Lord President of the Council

Part of the job of Lord President of the Council is to preside over the government's relations with the Queen, and along with other ministers to attend the Queen for meetings of the Privy Council. The relationship could hardly have started more inauspiciously. His private office in the Ministry of Housing and Local Government had invariably organized ministerial visits in style – and indeed Crossman, because of Dame Evelyn's influence throughout the English counties, would often stay in the 'gorgeous' (a favourite Crossman word) judges' lodgings in some ancient city or county town. He adored the modern equivalent of a medieval royal progress.

However, calamity of calamities, having been spoiled by the Ministry of Housing, he found that on promotion to Lord President, his office had not even booked a room in a hotel so he could have a bath after the night sleeper. For a man dependent on his morning bath, an unfailing ritual, this was disaster. As usual, the Aberdeen hotels were chock-a-block. He complained bitterly that on promotion he was less well ministered to in his lordly isolation. So it was in a foul temper that Crossman was driven on the morning of Tuesday, 20 September 1966 from Aberdeen through Deeside in all its September colouring glory to Balmoral.

Crossman liked being stuffy about a place which Wilson, Bowden, and other senior Ministers had been delighted and entranced to visit. It was simply chosen by Albert because the weather conditions in summer and autumn were like those of Saxe-Coburg, and he liked hill-walking. It was an undistinguished (a term of great opprobrium in

131

Crossmanese) Scottish baronial house, looking as if it were put up ten years previously with a suburban rose garden. Only the palace staff played golf on the special golf course. Fortunately, he cooled off a bit after taking a walk with Sir Michael Adeane, for fifteen years Assistant Private Secretary to King George VI, and for an eventual total of nineteen years Private Secretary to the Queen herself.

As Lord President, Crossman had to go and see the Queen before the four other ministers who had accompanied him. He told me he chatted to her about Prince Albert, after which he was joined by his colleagues, so that he could read aloud some sixty titles of the Orders in Council. After a batch of half-a-dozen, he paused to draw breath, and allow Her Majesty to utter 'Agreed.' When he'd finished, he intoned the formula, 'So the business of the Council is concluded!' It had taken all of two and a half minutes flat!

Left-wing MP Emrys Hughes wrote a book on Parliamentary mumbo-jumbo: for Crossman the set-up of the Privy Council was mumbo-jumbo *in excelsis*! But it was less than funny. Five ministers of the Crown, all under pressure preparing for the Labour Party Conference, had had to take a night train, a day off, and a night-train back, simply to stand for two and a half minutes like a stage army.

Those who knew Crossman well could tell whether or not he had enjoyed an experience by the way in which he talked about it. Like many really interesting people, Crossman was a man of insatiable curiosity about other people, and he in turn interested them. One of the historical figures about whom he was so intensely curious was Albert – a German princeling, a scientific innovator, an entrepreneur who arranged the Great Exhibition of 1851, and a remarkably good husband to a difficult girl, woman and lady. Crossman enthused to me about the superb large painting, done on slate by Landseer and looking unfinished, which depicted Victoria riding back from a deer hunt with Albert tenderly bending over her. Albert was the kind of German he admired – a character from Wagner, in a Germany where the states of the Holy Roman Empire vied with one another in their patronage of Bach and his contemporary composers, and in the construction of elegant municipal buildings. Crossman told me at party conference in 1966, that he would like to write a biography of Prince Albert when he retired.

Later, when he had read what he considered the superb life of Lord Rosebery (1963) by Robert Rhodes James, future Conservative MP for

Cambridge from 1976, he demanded that I take him to see Barnbougle in my West Lothian constituency. Barnbougle is the extraordinary castle-fortress on the shore of the Forth, by Dalmeny, which the Foreign Secretary/Prime Minister used for his books, such as the annotated edition of Charles I's own prayer book, and to which he retreated when he got bored with his guests. After Eva, Marchioness of Rosebery, had spent two hours taking Crossman and me on a conducted tour, Crossman returned to the subject of Albert, and was quite definite about tackling a biography. But Crossman was not to be spared, and the task of writing a great book on Albert fell, oddly enough, to the author of *Rosebery*, Robert Rhodes James (*Albert, Prince Consort*, 1983).

I am told the Queen was rather tickled by Crossman's fascination with Albert, and in a strange way these two people, whose attitudes might have been assumed to be light years apart, got on rather well. Certainly, he was terribly, almost pathetically, concerned not to bore her. For him, she had a lovely laugh. He noticed that she laughed with her whole face. Because she was a very spontaneous person, she did not assume a mere smile. He thought that the Clerk of the Privy Council, Godfrey Agnew, was right when he told Crossman that the Queen found it difficult to suppress her emotions. When the Queen felt deeply about something and had to keep herself under control, she looked like an angry thundercloud. It was for this reason that on occasions when she had been genuinely moved by the applause of the crowd, the Queen looked somewhat ill-tempered.

Another topic on which Crossman got on to the same wavelength as the Queen was, he said, farming and forestry. Both felt strongly – before it became a cause made famous by the Council for the Preservation of Rural England, and Marion Shoard's *The Theft of the Countryside* – about the serried ranks of conifers replacing broad-leaved trees. Crossman, however, was given to understand that the Queen was not best pleased by his absence from a Privy Council meeting which took place during the 1966 Labour Party Conference. He told me that when he gave a half-apology, 'She didn't relent, she just listened.' But then Crossman never was a very convincing apologizer, and tended usually to give the impression that he continued to believe that he was justified. However, any frost was soon to thaw.

In January 1967, Crossman restored relations with a day at Sandringham, having taken the opportunity to have a tour of the city centre at King's Lynn in the early forenoon. He told me that the Queen knew that when he'd been Minister of Housing he had taken a detailed interest in the choice of model schemes to preserve the city centres of Bath, Chester, Chichester, King's Lynn and York and he was touchingly pleased at her sincere references to the way he continued his interest in areas of previous ministerial responsibility. He guessed that she had come to the conclusion over the years of her reign that politicians were not the sort of people who had a continuing interest in their area of previous responsibility for its own sake.

Crossman was exceedingly curious to see Sandringham. He told me it was an unexciting Edwardian baronial mansion. But inside he found Sandringham interesting and welcoming. The superb sepia photograph of Queen Victoria in the hall had taken his fancy. It was Crossman's and Ted Short's task to take the Queen copies of the new stamp design, and, as anticipated, she was satisfied: she had been horrified by the designs produced by Tony Wedgwood Benn when he had been Post-master General — and no wonder, added Crossman with a snort!

The Queen told Crossman that she felt 'a great deal more remote', oddly enough, from London, at Sandringham, than at Balmoral, and therefore more relaxed. Crossman divined that the royal family adored Edward VII's get-away estate because it had become a family house where they could begin to 'feel more like ordinary human beings'. He came out with one of those ill-thought-out, spur-of-the-moment ideas that a minute's reflection would have annihilated. Would it not be good if the Queen could commute from Sandringham and use Buckingham Palace as an office? Crossman was prone to make an idiot of himself with this kind of blurted-out notion. Sir Isaiah Berlin told me that when he had been at the British Embassy in Washington during the war, and Crossman had come to see the important OSS General 'Wild Bill' Donovan, he had suddenly said: 'Well, if we get out of India, you give us North Africa!' Donovan changed the subject. So did the Queen!

Crossman found the Queen extremely interested in his relations, and those of the Labour Party, with the civil service. 'She's read the Labour Party's evidence to the Fulton Committee, and that's more than 90 per cent of the PLP have bloody well bothered to do!' The Queen quizzed Crossman on how much the civil service concealed from ministers. He tended to the view that she genuinely imagined that civil servants were obedient, in the way that senior members of the Court would be honourable with her. Crossman admitted that he had begun to lecture her, and that she had the temerity to interrupt him — few people had when he was in full flow – and asked him how he knew. ' "Well," I said,' he told me, ' "Evelyn Sharp was my Permanent Secretary." ' He paused. 'She squashed me – but quite nicely. She said, "I like Evelyn Sharp very much!" ' Crossman added that he told the Queen that she had 'very good taste in people', and that she smiled warmly. As he could embellish a situation, I cannot vouch for what was actually said. Crossman was not a fantasist, but found it delicious to garnish a story in the telling.

Crossman was fascinated by the Queen's addiction to difficult jigsaws, and thought she ought to be painted by some latterday Vermeer, standing, talking to her visitors, her fingers gently fingering the cardboard pieces, while not turning her head. He was not in the least surprised she and Harold Wilson should like each other so much. 'Churchill was her Melbourne, Macmillan to some extent her Peel, Harold certainly her Disraeli, and if she gets Ted Heath, heaven help her, he will be as awful as Gladstone was to Victoria.'

After Sandringham, Crossman thought that the Queen liked him better as she got to know him – and indeed liked people in general better as she got used to them. Crossman was also getting to know the key court official, Sir Godfrey Agnew. At first sight, Sir Godfrey might have seemed a slightly stupid old buffer. Actually, on acquaintance, he turned out to be an extremely shrewd courtier, with a droll sense of humour which appealed to Crossman. As Clerk of the Privy Council, Sir Godfrey could have starred in a television series, possibly entitled *Yes, Mr Crossman*. On a memorable occasion in 70 Whitehall, I was transfixed with curiosity as to what Sir Godfrey would say, when Crossman said to him: 'Tell me, Godfrey, does the Queen prefer the Tory Ministers to us Labour Ministers, because they are our social superiors?' Agog, I waited for the answer. I took it down, and Crossman asked for the exact wording so he could put it in his diary (as he often did, quite legitimately, since I could take notes when he could not). 'I don't think so,' said Sir Godfrey softly and thoughtfully. 'The Queen does not make fine distinctions between politicians of different parties. They all roughly belong to the same social category in her view.' Crossman's considered judgement was that this was true.

I suspect Crossman was rather mild with the Queen, and when in the early spring of 1967, I asked him whether he had broached the awkward subject of Emrys Hughes's 'Abolition of Titles' ten-minutes-rule Bill, about which Harold Wilson was making a fuss, Crossman replied, 'My bump of irreverence does not get as far as the Palace.'

No apology. No explanation. Just the Crossman, no-nonsense, bald statement technique.

The following month, at Windsor, Crossman did raise the subject of Emrys Hughes's Bill after a debate had taken place. Hughes could not keep it going even for an hour: Crossman told the Queen that his PPS – I had been deputed to be an observer on the back-bench – had told him that the debate had been attended by half a dozen MPs out of 635. It was a sign of the changed times, for in 1945–50, such a debate would have packed the House of Commons. Emrys Hughes was simply regarded as a House of Commons jester, in a cruel place where men can play up to the caricature of themselves, and cheapen themselves by doing anything for a laugh. Crossman was incredulous that the Queen should have told him that she solemnly looked through the Saturday daily papers to see if she could spot any report, and found nothing. Crossman told her that there were actually a couple of brief reports, tucked away in *The Times* and the *Guardian*, commenting that the Hughes debate had turned out to be a fiasco. In an 'I told you so' voice, which he admitted had gone down like a lead balloon with the Queen, he pointed out to her that he and Roy Jenkins had predicted that if the Government were relaxed and did nothing, the whole episode would sink without trace. Crossman knew when he had boobed, because the Queen did not reply, and changed the subject.

The Queen was curious about Crossman's reforms of the House of Commons, and, in Crossman's retrospective view, had a shrewd grasp of the procedures of a place which constitutionally she can never visit. Crossman, by the spring of 1967, had become pretty tetchy on the question of morning sittings. He told me that the Queen had asked him about morning sittings of the House in rather the same tone of 'I told you so' as he had used to her ten minutes earlier about the fussing over the Emrys Hughes Bill. Crossman admitted that the Queen had touched a raw nerve, and that his expression had revealed his irritation. 'Being better mannered than I was to her, she said she was sorry and she wasn't really criticizing. But she was criticizing. And she bloody well knew I knew she was criticizing. And, damn it, I'm beginning to think she, and all the rest of you who think that morning sittings will never work, are right. In future, I might be better to stick to subjects like agriculture, and the dangers of Paraquat weedkiller, which is being used in parts of Windsor Great Park, and which concern her greatly.'

The Court functionaries, to their own amazement, took rather a liking to Crossman, as they found him cheerful and amusing, if sardonic. A senior official of the Palace, long retired, recalled only one of his traits 'really bugged us, and it certainly irritated the Queen on occasion'. This is what they saw as a Wykehamist trait of running down good efforts in a rather lofty way. For example, before the Queen went off to Canada for the Montreal World Fair at the end of June 1967, Crossman went to a Buckingham Palace Privy Council, and delivered a lecturette on how boring exhibitions were. The Queen, to be polite, observed that she was at a disadvantage being so small, because she found it difficult to see certain exhibits. Crossman then commiserated with her being traipsed around on miles of red carpet.

My own opinion is that he displayed on many occasions more than a trace of inverted snobbery. Cetainly he was in no position to disparage Expo '67, about which I discovered he knew nothing. A month later, when my wife Kathleen and I went to Montreal, and had lunch with the director of the British stand, General Sir William Oliver, he told me that the Queen had been thrilled – as we were. Crossman was often far too quick to dismiss other people's pleasures.

Where Crossman was extremely good with the Queen was in not placing her in a position where she was politically embarrassed. On Sunday, 19 November 1967, he was due to attend a Privy Council meeting at Windsor. It was the weekend of devaluation. Along with Gerald Gardiner, as Lord Chancellor, Patrick Gordon Walker, and Peter Shore, Crossman had gone to Windsor, and arranged to hold the 6 p.m. Privy Council meeting early so that both Queen and Ministers could see the Prime Minister's television broadcast. Having skedaddled (a favourite Crossman word meaning 'gone through helter-skelter') through the business, Crossman recounted to me that the Queen had told him to come along quick to the Windsor Castle TV room. Where-upon the Queen, a couple of brace of Privy Counsellors in tow, bounded along George III's long corridor like kangaroos, to witness Wilson on the box, in a sitting room with a glowing coal fire.

Crossman was asked to sit beside her on the sofa. Then he realized with a start that both the Queen and he were getting into an embar-rassing situation. How were they going to comment to each other when Harold faded out? Crossman saw from her twisting of her hands that she was becoming nervous, because anything she uttered was bound to be political, and any innocuous comment could well be interpreted as political criticism. As he anticipated, when Wilson stopped, there was

137

an interminable silence, broken eventually by the Queen's murmuring, 'Of course it's extraordinarily difficult to make that kind of speech!' Crossman told me he gave a polite grunt of assent to the proposition that it was extraordinarily difficult to make that kind of speech! Before he could get a word in edgeways, that bull-in-a-china-shop Patrick Gordon Walker, had enthused, 'Oh, a wonderful performance!' The Queen could not say 'Yes' and she could not say 'No', so Crossman immediately changed the subject to foot-and-mouth disease, at a time when upwards of sixty new cases a day were being confirmed.

In the autumn of 1967, Crossman's mind was more and more dominated by the issues involved in the reform of the House of Lords, which he took to Cabinet on Thursday, 12 October. From the beginning the Queen was exceedingly interested, and both pleased and amazed that he was obviously trying hard to get it by agreement with the other political parties. Crossman was 'chuffed' that the Queen should tell him that if he were to get Lords' reform by agreement, it would be a great feather in his cap. Crossman's motive was above all to get a settlement which had some chance of standing the test of time. In February 1968, when for a fleeting fortnight it looked as if Crossman might after all deliver agreed Lords' reform, he told me that the Queen had given him a sweet smile and observed, 'It's not something one expected of you!'

After Crossman ceased to be Lord President of the Council, he had little to do with the Palace, until June 1970 when he went to say farewell on the defeat of the Labour Government. He told me that she thanked him, to the full extent that it was proper for her to do so. Crossman asked if she objected to general elections. Artlessly, she said she did, since it meant her getting to know a number of new people. Crossman had come to the conclusion that she was genuinely neutral as between Labour and Conservative ministers.

Four years later, when he died, I understand she was very, very sorry. If she had not actually dreaded the relationship when he was appointed, and envisaged the possibility of having to meet what he ironically described as an anti-royalty, 'dangerous, left-wing republican', at least, she had not known what to expect. In the event, she recalled that Crossman had treated her very nicely indeed and often amused her. He, for his part, was at his best with women whom he liked – and the Queen was one such. Besides, it was by that time in his mind that he would like to be Labour leader in the Lords, and as such would have to have good relations with the Palace.

138

The reform of the House of Lords requires separate discussion from that on Crossman's performance as Leader of the House of Commons, for this was a task in which he continued to be chief negotiator while he was already installed as Secretary of State for the Social Services, long after he had left the leadership of the House of Commons.

It is a cautionary tale of a politician who accepts a brief because his party is pledged to 'do something about something', and then comes to believe with conviction in what he has been asked to do, only to find in the meantime that his colleagues have got cold feet. To make sense of what happened to Crossman, it is necessary to understand how he saw the background to the task he was handed, and the attitude and policy of the Labour party towards the House of Lords.

The Labour Party's manifesto for 1910 included the following statement:

'A general election is being forced upon the country by the action in the House of Lords rejecting the budget. *The great question you are to decide is whether the peers or the people are to rule this country* ... The time has come to put an end to their power to override the will of the Commons ... The Labour Party welcomes the opportunity to prove that 'the frugal age' is passed and that people are no longer willing to live on the sufferance of the Lords ...
The Lords must go.'

●The Labour Party did not take part in the Inter-Party Conference on the Reform of the House of Lords which preceded the passing of the first Parliament Act in 1911. They voted as a party against the preamble to the Parliament Bill on the grounds that abolition or a further curtailment of powers was preferable to any reform of composition.
●Their programme *Labour and the New Social Order*, produced in 1918, stated that no attempt by the Lords to control the people's representatives should be tolerated and envisaged a reform which would ensure that a Labour Government which obtained a majority in the Commons would not be a minority in the second House: no members of the upper House should hold their seats by virtue of hereditary rights or ex officio. The Labour party did not show any enthusiasm for any of the proposals for Lords reform which were brought forward from the centre and the right between the wars, but the two Labour Governments were able to survive their periods in office without any serious

crises between the two Houses. The manifesto for 1931 nevertheless stated that:

'This record was achieved under the intolerable restrictions of its minority position in the House of Commons. Frustrated by political intrigues under the class-conscious hostility of the Lords and undermined by the organised pressure of business interests it now asks the power to press forward rapidly for the fulfilment of its programme. In that endeavour it will tolerate no opposition from the House of Lords to the considered mandate of the People; and it will seek such emergency powers as are necessary for the full attainment of its objectives.'

• At the Labour Party Conference in 1933, Sir Stafford Cripps advocated the complete abolition of the House of Lords, but in the party's draft programme of July 1934 the proposed policy was to abolish the House of Lords only if it should interfere with the implementation of a Labour Government's policy. The manifesto for 1935 stated: 'Labour seeks a mandate to carry out this programme by constitutional and democratic means, and with this end in view it seeks power to abolish the House of Lords and improve the procedure of the House of Commons.'

• The manifesto for 1945 'Let Us Face The Future' stated that 'we give clear notice that we will not tolerate obstruction of the people's will by the House of Lords'. The decision to restrict further the powers of the Lords resulted in part from the fact that the then Labour Government found that it would not be able to nationalize the iron and steel industry until the session 1948–49, which meant that if the powers were left unchanged the Iron and Steel Bill could not be passed into law against Lords opposition during that parliament. A short account of the Parliament Bill, 1947–9, and of the 1948 Conference, is given Appendix I of the White Paper.

• When the Conservative Government introduced the Life Peerages Bill in 1957, the Labour Party opposed the measure on second reading on the general ground that this was 'tinkering not mending', but once the Bill had been passed into law, Mr Gaitskell co-operated with Mr Macmillan and proposed nominees for Labour life peerages on the strict understanding that Mr Macmillan would accept his recommendations. This is the basis of the convention to which references were made in the recent Lobby Conference and, more obliquely, in the White Paper.

In the Labour party's manifesto for 1964 *New Britain* it was stated

140

that 'we shall not permit effective action to be frustrated by the hereditary and non-elective Conservative majority in the House of Lords'; the manifesto for 1966 stated *'finally, legislation will be introduced to safeguard measures approved by the House of Commons from frustration by delay or defeat in the House of Lords.'*

Something had to be done. It could no longer be shelved. There was no excuse, as there had been in 1964–6 of a wafer-thin majority. The question was what?

It may seem to be a contradiction that I was a nonbeliever in Lords' reform from the beginning and pleaded with him not to touch it with the proverbial bargepole, but in the end I was very sorry for Crossman. He had worked hard and in good faith and had come up with a plan. Together with the assiduous and able Eddie Shackleton, the Labour negotiator for the Lords, Crossman and the Conservative Lords Carrington and Jellicoe became a 'band of brothers'.

The main feature of the proposals was to have been a two-tier House of Lords with voting members, entitled to speak and vote, and non-voting members entitled to speak but not generally to vote. Membership would, from 1969 onwards, be by creation as a life-peer alone: succession to a hereditary peerage would no longer carry the right to a seat. Existing members of the Lords – Crossman was solicitous about them – who sat by right of succession would be able to remain as non-voting members for the remainder of their lives; but only those members who had themselves been created hereditary peers or life peers would be able to exercise the right to vote. Crossman envisaged that some of the peers by succession who in recent times had been most active in the House of Lords would be granted life peerages, and so would become entitled to voting membership. Crossman also proposed that whoever was the government of the day would be entitled to secure for itself an adequate working majority over the opposition parties, although not a majority of the membership of the Lords as a whole, when those without party allegiance were included.

Crossman wanted in addition to reduce the powers of the Lords. On public bills, the Lords' one-year-delay powers of 1967 would be replaced by a power to impose a delay of six months from the date of disagreement between the House of Lords and the House of Commons. A disagreed Bill could be presented for Royal Assent in the ensuing session of parliament on a simple resolution of the House of Commons without having to be passed through all its stages. In regard to subordinate

141

legislation, the Lords would only have had a power sufficient to require the Commons to consider the matter again.

Crossman, partly influenced (I thought) by the Queen, came to the conclusion early on that a lot of his scheme would have to work by constitutional convention. This was because many of his proposals affected the use of the royal prerogative and matters of parliamentary procedure, which were not suitable for legislation. The most obvious example was the balance between the parties in the House of Lords, which everyone recognized was of cardinal importance to the work-ability of the whole scheme. Crossman's intention was that the government of the day should have a small majority of about ten per cent of the combined strength of the opposition parties. He intended that these figures should by convention be binding on the government, whatever its party. This was crucial. And Crossman trusted Lord Carrington to ensure that if and when the scheme came into operation, a Tory government would observe this convention. Crossman thought this undertaking to be a linchpin of the whole deal. It was also part of the answer to those who said that under the new scheme, the Prime Minister would have an increased power of patronage. He would not. Quite apart from the fact that the nominations for the other political parties were likely to be made by the leaders of those parties, the convention on members which Crossman proposed would have tended to impose a restriction on the number of new creations, of a kind which did not exist at that time.

Crossman proposed a watchdog committee, which would be there to give advice on the working of the reformed House, and to act as a forum for discussion on any points of difficulty which could have arisen. He guessed that the most suitable chairman of such a committee would be a Law Lord (*Sic tempora, sic mores!* His father would be laughing in his grave) or the quality of Lord Radcliffe or Lord Scarman. They would be able to draw attention to any abuse of patronage and also to any tendency which might appear for one interest or one point of view to get more or less than its fair representation in the House of Lords.

Crossman and I were on opposite sides of the fence on devolution: he was for it; I later (1977) wrote a book for Cape saying it would mean the break-up of Britain. But Crossman was practical and sincere in hoping a Radcliffe/Scarman Committee would have a particular concern for representation from — and the interests of — Scotland, Wales, Northern Ireland, and the regions of England itself. The committee would provide written reports, to be debated in both Houses of Parliament. Crossman thought this would give it teeth. He thought this committee would inhibit prime-ministerial patronage, though he also believed that the climate of opinion had changed so much by the 1960s that no future Prime Minister would outrageously pack the Lords. 'It's a very cynical view of our democracy,' he told me, 'to believe that any Prime Minister would want to do this, and it would insult those nominated. Wilson has deliberately put into the Lords men and women with independent views and strong minds.'

Crossman was in favour of the payment of peers by allowances, and the imposition of sanctions if the job of a voting peer was not done properly. He favoured a retirement age of eighty. He believed that joint committees of both Houses would be useful. In the 1980s, I have no hesitation in observing that the Lords' select committees often do a better job than their Commons counterparts.

Crossman had worked himself up into great enthusiasm. Why did he fail? Why did Lords' reform suddenly become friendless? In the crudest terms, once the political firmament was confronted with having to take a positive decision, it was clouded by an enveloping fog of 'Let ill alone!'

Once you start rationalizing the House of Lords and eliminating its anachronisms, by definition you create a rival to the House of Commons. And a serious rival to the House of Commons would have to reflect, in party terms, the will of the people at the previous general election. Months before he began to see it for himself, I and others repeatedly told Crossman that his dreams of being the man who reformed the House of Lords would never materialize and would end in tears. The Lords were basically content with their cosy arrangements, not least the hard-working Labour lords. The Commons collectively thought there were many other matters to which priority should be given, and anyway retaining the anachronisms protected the Commons position.

Besides, many opinion-formers in the Commons are delighted to be given the opportunity of keeping their links with their previous lifetime's incarnation by being given a peerage. Membership of the Lords is a life-prolonger for ex-MPs. My predecessor but four as MP for Linlithgow, Manny Shinwell, would not in his opinion, or mine, have stuck it out until he was 101 years old, unless he could have stumped along to keep in touch with his ennobled chums in the Lords on four afternoons a week. Many others are given the stimulus of a function in life by membership of the upper house. Crossman told me that he would very much have liked to have got to the Lords as Labour Leader in the Lords, a job with a place in the shadow Cabinet or Cabinet, which Lord Crossman of Cropredy would surely have done very well, and which he would have been offered by Harold Wilson in June 1974, had he lived.

All this was possible under the existing system. Those who might be affected were not at all sure that they would benefit under the Crossman proposals. Nor was Douglas Houghton, then current chairman of the PLP, any better disposed. I used to walk back in the direction of Marsham Street with him at nights after a vote. For good reason, he was content with the prospect of going to an unreformed House of Lords, where at over ninety he continues to do good work. Houghton would point out that 'your boss', as he referred to Crossman, was a product of his own past, and had argued for agreement rather than an imposed solution for the Lords, because 'he simply hates Hartley Shawcross' who was for ever associated with the 'We are the masters now' philosophy. At the party meeting on Wednesday, 13 November 1968, James Callaghan also attacked Shawcross for that remark which had done the Labour Party infinite harm, 'and for all the equally stupid things Shawcross has been saying ever since!'

For the first fortnight in June 1968, the Crossmans had been on holiday in Cyprus during the Whitsun recess. This did not help, as many of his colleagues had been working, and resented a man sunning himself in Cyprus. He came back to Britain to find that Roy Jenkins had made a widely-reported speech in Birmingham, threatening that the all-party talks on Lords' reform might break up if the Conservatives voted against the Rhodesia Sanctions Order. On Monday, 17 June, on his first full day back from Cyprus, Crossman went to see Harold Wilson. Wilson was vexed that the Chancellor had got all the headlines, and felt that Roy Jenkins was trying to get one up on him. There could be no question of any more talks. They had to be broken off, and a bill introduced taking away the powers of the Lords. Crossman wondered whether the Prime Minister had gone mad and was 'suffused with jealousy' of his Chancellor. Simply 'to outbid Roy in capturing the radical left', he thought Wilson 'had thrown away ... our negotiated settlement on Lords' reform'. [*Diaries* III, 97]

However, timing is everything in political life, and for Crossman, 18 June 1968 was Black Tuesday. The Lords chose this of all moments to vote down the Labour Government's sensitive Rhodesian Order by 193 votes to 184, where Ministers had the support of all the Liberals, ninety per cent of the Labour peers, eighteen Bishops and over thirty cross-bench peers. The Tory Whips had been reckless. Though the Tory built-in majority had nearly been defeated, and capitulated on 18 July, the damage had been done. Popular indignation against the House of Lords was rife. The Lords, the Labour Party was saying, deserved abolition. They were deaf when Crossman pointed out that one cannot destroy the powers of the Lords unless one deals with its composition. But it was not only in the Labour Party that trouble had been brewing.

There had been what Wilson had called to Crossman's face 'the cosy little world of all-Party conversations'. The Prime Minister had learned while Crossman had been away in Cyprus that a number of influential Conservatives were less than enamoured of what Lords Carrington and Jellicoe had been up to on their behalf. I later discovered that one of his sources was Reginald Maudling, who had been a half-in, half-out member of the Conservative negotiating team. The ringleader was Iain Macleod, who had no love either for a rationalized House of Lords or for Lord Carrington, the chief negotiator. Macleod persuaded Ted Heath and the shadow cabinet to authorize the three-line whip on Rhodesian sanctions, bringing in lame and halt backwoodsmen precisely with the purpose of stymying Lords' reform, as they foresaw the Labour reaction. However, it is also true that Carrington cared deeply about the Rhodesian sanctions issue, and took his share of the responsibility for imposing the whip.

To all intents and purposes Lords' reform perished with the Rhodesia Sanctions vote. Wilson pretended to be horrified at the amount of confidence Crossman had bestowed on Carrington, and, according to Crossman 'told me, that if I had that kind of bedwetting mania for compulsory communication, I got all I deserved!' Crossman was livid. He told me that he said to Wilson the less they saw of each other the better. Wilson had simply revealed again his own persecution mania, and how obsessed he was by suspicions of an inner conspiracy. My judgement is that the row about Lords' reform was more than a tiff. It had lasting consequences. Wilson thought it too dangerous to ask his henchman to leave the Government. On the other hand, I don't think Crossman was ever again in the inner Wilson circle.

Crossman, for his part, never brought himself to forgive Wilson for throwing away, as he saw it, sensible Lords' reform. In the spring of 1969, having easily got through the Lords, the Parliament Bill went to the Commons where it met a slow death from the hounds in the form of the Conservatives' Enoch Powell, Labour's Michael Foot and Robert Sheldon, and other skilled parliamentarians. As Crossman bitterly pointed out, the Government was paying the price for breaking off the talks.

Foot saw it as a way of maintaining the traditions of Parliament, and the seventeenth-century MPs who put Cromwell in power, and abolished the House of Lords. (Foot conveniently omitted to recall that his hero, Cromwell, set up a new Upper House, a Lords of his own, in order to reward his friends!) Foot also saw it as a heaven-sent opportunity to make life difficult for Jim Callaghan, Home Secretary.

Gradually, the Parliament Bill accumulated what Enoch Powell was to call the 'smell of death about this measure'. It became a lost cause. And truth to tell, Crossman himself had lost interest by September 1968. He found it difficult to concentrate on a topic unless he himself was actively and ministerially trying to do something about it.

Without co-operation on timetabling, no such measure can get through the Commons – as I learned to my advantage, and bore in mind ten years later in using forty-seven days on the floor of the House to oppose the Scotland and Wales Bills on Devolution. Doubtless Crossman was revolving in his grave in his impatience with me on that occasion, as he was (romantically) in favour of devolution.

My friends and his friends were astonished that Crossman and I should have borne each other such a long time. My friends said, 'How can you stick that man so long?' Some of his friends thought and said he would be better off without a PPS who was one of only two Old Etonians in the Parliamentary Labour Party. Our mutual friends marvelled at how the relationship had worked. I am a placid fellow who can laugh at bombastic insult. Crossman never bore grudges and was good at letting bygones be bygones. In ten years we had three gargantuan rows, and the most gargantuan is worth description.

I used, except on Wednesdays, when Anne was at Vincent Square, to cook his two poached eggs, make toast and do coffee for him, and then call him away from his boxes, whereupon he would descend in pyjamas and dressing gown to the basement dining room. We then read *The Times* and the *Guardian*, and commented to each other on them. Crossman was the most methodical reader of newspapers I ever saw – he devoured them.

On this occasion (27 February 1969), I drew his attention to an article by the Political Editor of *The Times* entitled 'Fight to the Death for Bill Nobody Wants'. In this article, David Wood wrote, 'Yet it is a Bill that nobody at all, with the possible exception of Mr Crossman who fathered it, now really wants or believes in. Luckless Mr Callagham, who as Home Secretary has been unwillingly saddled with the job of piloting it through the House, has gone sour on it and resents the fact that his Cabinet colleagues have stopped pretending that they think the Bill worth the effort it is costing.'

I told Crossman that he'd better cut his losses, and drop the bill. He launched into a diatribe that it was late in the day to come out with 'such ignorant nonense'. I reminded him that I had been against his tampering with the Lords. With some justice, he reminded me of the manifesto of 1966, on which we'd all been elected. Tired, since we'd been up till 3 a.m., I retorted that he should then bring in a short Bill to abolish powers.

'Don't be frivolous!' he bawled at me.

'In that case, guillotine your Bill – only you won't get the guillotine.'

At this he blew his top. I told him he would have forty-five Labour MPs against the Bill, and another twenty who would not vote for slamming a guillotine on a constitutional Bill. And quite right too, I added. Crossman's rage knew no bounds. Nor did I improve matters by saying at that moment that Michael Foot and Robert Sheldon, architects of the demise of the Parliament Bill, were among the MPs whom I liked most and admired most in the Commons.

Crossman was so angry because he believed he knew more about the subject than anyone else in the Commons. Heavyweight peers like Eddie Shackleton had told him that he was the only person in the Commons who really appreciated the work done by the Lords. Crossman developed an intellectual vested interest in Lords' reform which, after he had lost interest in the autumn of 1968, he came to see as simply a personal issue.

On 17 April 1969, Harold Wilson announced that his government had 'decided not to proceed at this time with the Parliament Bill'. Amidst wry smiles and ribald laughter, the Prime Minister told the Commons that our programme was unexpectedly full with other busines. The Secretary of State for the Social Services did not share in the mirth. He had worked far too hard for that, and he hoped that Lords' reform could be a kind for memorial to his leadership of the

Commons when he retired from the post. His behaviour on Lords' reform gives credibility to criticisms of Crossman made by two very clever, very different men. Harold Wilson complained separately to Judith Hart and me, during the time that Crossman was Leader of the House, that just because he now had time to read the Cabinet papers, 'he knows all about a subject when he doesn't'.

In one of the best-written and most vividly shrewd books by a politician which I have ever read, Ian Mikardo writes:

> Dick, as I have said, enjoyed the game for its own sake, and revelled in his ability to dribble round opponents. He was always ready, if he couldn't get in a shot, to pass the ball to a colleague, and if that didn't result in a goal he was prepared to wait for the next breakaway and the next opportunity. But Harold Wilson was quite different: he had eyes for nothing but the goal, and his goal was to become Leader of the Party and then Prime Minister; every thought and action, every word he said or wrote, every contact he made was all directed singlemindedly to that end.
>
> (*Back-Bencher*, p. 152)

FOURTEEN
Leader of the House of Commons

In twenty-seven years in Westminster, I do not recollect anything to parallel the amused incredulity among the older and more senior denizens of the palace – elected Members and clerks of the House of Commons alike – with which the appointment of Crossman as Lord President of the Council and Leader of the House of Commons was received. In politics, it is not unusual for poachers to become gamekeepers. Sometimes the rebel, Macmillan or Bevan, becomes an effective Minister; more often not. But to appoint this particular turbulent stirrer-upper to the leadership of the House, where hitherto the chief qualification had been the emollience of an experienced House of Commons man and popularity in all parts of the House, was a novel departure! After all was said and done, the fellow – and it was by no means only crusty knights of the shire who employed the term – had never once sat on a standing committee of a Bill in nineteen years as a backbencher. And they'd hardly seen him. Some of Attlee's former junior ministers, gone grey during thirteen years of Conservative rule, spluttered at the insult to their *amour propre*.

This was understandable on both sides. True, Crossman had not been a good 'House of Commons man', and had shown not even token willingness to do any of the necessary slog (or donkeywork) of Parliament. He had lived his political life in Smith Square, at Transport House. Attlee's ex-Ministers remembered against Crossman that when he had come to the Shadow Cabinet as spokesman on pensions, he had not bothered to conceal his feelings. Loudly he let it be known that he thought that the Shadow Cabinet was aptly named. He saw men behaving like Shadow Ministers in an alternative Government, with a lot of parliamentary pomp and circumstance, and acting, as he saw them, self-consciously and ostentatiously as Westminster characters. In Parliament, memories are long, and forgettories are not in good repair; older Labour MPs remembered: in particular, Emmanuel Shinwell, the Chairman of the Parliamentary Labour Party, whose autobiography, *Conflict Without Malice* (1955), bears the most inappropriate title ever chosen by an author. Politicians, I believe, on the whole show a good grace towards those of their parliamentary colleagues who are given preferment; we are at least a good deal less catty about one another than academics, for example. Appointed to a job where the goodwill of the House is a sine qua non, Crossman inherited unprecedented illwill from the established members.

I'd better confess I myself was apprehensive in the extreme and thought that Wilson, by his casting of Crossman as the successor to the leaders of the House I had known – the wily Rab Butler, the circumspect Iain Macleod, the charming, disarming Selwyn Lloyd, and the ramrodly cautious Herbert Bowden – was going to be riding a tiger from which he might find it difficult to dismount. But Wilson had his reasons. And in the context of August 1966, those reasons made sense. What were they?

The first was simply that Wilson believed that playing the game of Cabinet ministerial musical chairs was healthy for a Government. Ministers might go stale, or become too cosy with their civil servants. Among those who profoundly disagreed was Crossman's friend, the architect and planner Lord Esher, who pointed out that among the serious, professional, uncommitted people of this country, constant chopping and changing served to give the impression that the government was not serious about tackling Britain's long-term problems.

The second was rather personal. Wilson increasingly valued his Tuesday evening sessions and other contacts with the Queen. In a nice way, he was becoming increasingly fond of her, and wanted to impress her with the calibre of people in the Wilson Cabinet. He had the impression that the martinet Herbert Bowden had been only a qualified success with her, and she might like someone more communicative. 'My Dick,' thought the Prime Minister, would fit this particular bill.

The third reason in Wilson's mind for appointing Crossman was the most important and the political imperative. First in 1964 but much more dramatically in 1966, the new intake of MPs had transformed the

150

Mr Justice Crossman.

Richard Crossman (centre) when he was a pupil and scholar at Winchester College, 1926.

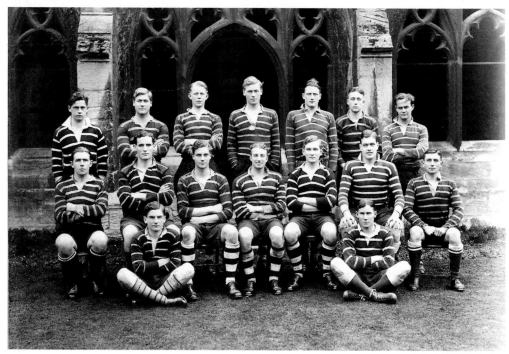

Above: H. A. L. Fisher, Warden of New College (Oxford), Lloyd-George's Education Minister, and author of *The History of Europe*.

Campaigning in Oxford, 1938, for the Oxford By-Election, which was the first since the Munich Agreement.

Left: Crossman (seated, far left) in the Rugby team when he was an Oxford undergraduate at New College.

Right: Speaking to Coventry businessmen, trade union officials and Civic representatives at a meeting to discuss the City's business interests, 1945.

Below: Labour Member of Parliament for Coventry East at the Party Conference, Scarborough, May 1948.

Right: A delegation came from Coventry City Council to the Home Secretary Sir David Maxwell in 1954 to discuss the future of Civil Defence in relation to the Hydrogen Bomb. George Hodgkinson is second to left.

Below right: Jenny Lee, James Callaghan and Richard Crossman at the Labour Party Conference, Brighton, 1964.

Left: Reading on the terrace of the House of Commons.

Below: Marriage to Miss Anne Patricia McDougall in 1954.

Right: Working quietly at home, 1968.

Below right: Opening Greenwich District Hospital, 1969.

Left: Attending the first Cabinet meeting of the new Wilson Government, October 1964, with James Griffiths, Secretary of State for Wales.

Below: The Ministerial team appointed in 1968 to head the newly formed Department of Health and Social Security. *Left to right:* Stephen Swingler, Richard Crossman, David Ennals.

Crossman with his wife and children, Patrick and Virginia, at Prescote, his country home, in 1970.

Labour lost the General Election of 1970 but Crossman retained Coventry East with a reduced majority.

Parliamentary Labour Party. A taste of what was to come had been provided by by-elections of the previous couple of years when Bill Rodgers was elected in Stockton-on-Tees, Dick Taverne in Lincoln, Jeremy Bray in Middlesbrough West, I myself in West Lothian, Guy Barnett in Dorset South, and Neil Carmichael in Glasgow Woodside. In the general election of 1964, the newcomers included Stan Orme and Eric Heffer, whom Crossman respected and liked.

In 1966, something different occurred. A number of candidates whom no one, least of all themselves, expected to win suddenly found they were Members of the House of Commons. Having got over their surprise, they did not expect to remain more than one parliament. They wanted to have their fling, or to make their mark in a seat they would probably lose in a 1970 or 1971 general election, so that at the following general election – or better still in a safe-seat by-election – they would be adopted. This meant high-profile Socialist politicians. It also meant that Herbert Bowden, for all his virtues in running the old, disciplined, trade-union-dominated PLP, ought to be shifted. The newcomers were clamouring for reform within weeks of arriving. Wilson confided in his own former philosophy tutor at Jesus College, Oxford, Sir Malcolm Knox, by then Principal of St Andrew's University, who told me some years later that the only men able to take on the new lecturers in Parliament, from polytechnic or university, were 'my Oxford dons'. Patrick Gordon Walker, by that time, could not cope. C. A. R. Crosland was generally considered, and thought by Wilson, to be too abrasive – and, too much of a crown prince and rival for the premiership, if the economic situation went sour. That left the Great Educator himself, R. H. S. Crossman. Above all, in an era when the leader of the Labour Party was elected by MPs alone, the Leader of the House of Commons was in a unique position to create a dangerous following, so Wilson deemed it wise to choose a Cabinet colleague who was not a contender for his own job in Downing Street.

What the new generation of Labour MPs demanded was reform of Parliament. Yet the instrument for reform was to be the senior MP, let alone Minister, who had shown no interest whatsoever in parliamentary procedure. Hitherto he had regarded it as profoundly unimportant and boring. Crossman made no bones about the fact that he was as ignorant about the mechanics of parliamentary reform as he had been about housing policy, some twenty months earlier, when he went into the Ministry of Housing for the first time. Parliamentary reform does not provide the kind of issue that brings crowds to the streets.

Trouble was not long in coming. The Prices and Incomes legislation was exceedingly contentious. Crossman had to deal with the elected members of the Parliamentary Labour Party Liaison Committee, Manny Shinwell, Willie Hamilton and Malcolm MacPherson, and they were bombastically threatening to resign, unless Crossman and the new Chief Whip, John Silkin, 'did something' about twenty-eight MPs who had defied the Whip. It is one of the worst habits of politicians to explode about 'doing something about...': when the same persons are asked 'Do what about?' they tend to shrug their shoulders.

The plain fact was that the experienced clerks anticipated the problems that any Leader of the House will encounter, if he allows Government business to be slowed down. They also knew from experience how angry his colleagues would become if they could not get time for their measures, and that the Parliamentary Party would become exasperated. Crossman was warned how quickly the House of Commons can move from sympathy for its leader to hostility.

Crossman had reflected on his own past as a back-bench Member of Parliament and was determined to protect the right to criticize, even if it did mean that trouble would ensue. But, first and foremost, Crossman faced party dificulties, rather than parliamentary institutional difficulties. 'What really astonished them was that I should actually want to make my job more difficult for myself and my Cabinet colleagues.'

The first hint of things to come emerged in September 1966. Crossman was good at using the parliamentary recess to tackle the strategic problems with which he was likely to be faced. So, using the Garrick Club, that gorgeous candle-lit dining room within walking distance of the House of Commons, he invited certain clerks in the House of Commons and Freddy Warren, the medium-grade civil servant who was the 'usual channels' between Government and Opposition to dinner. Crossman phoned me on another matter, and then poured out, as he sometimes would, what he thought about his interesting evening. The senior clerks and Freddy Warren had started off the evening on the assumption that like every other Leader of the House of Commons whom they had known, Crossman simply wanted to get the government's business through the House as expeditiously as possible. Then he warmed to the exquisite pleasure he had derived from shocking them: one of his weaknesses was that he liked to shock people sometimes for the sake of it. He expressed his interest in the right, and indeed the duty, of the House of Commons to criticize the Executive seriously and properly. The concept of the influence of back-bench MPs on the Government side became fashionable.

As on some other occasions, Crossman turned 180 degrees. He became not only a champion, but a militant, passionate champion, not only of parliamentary reform, but of the rights and position of the House of Commons. Within weeks of Crossman's becoming Leader of the House, Lord Stow Hill (formerly Sir Frank Soskice, Wilson's first Home Secretary) commented to me with a smirk, 'Isn't it wonderful to behold how once a man finds himself in a position in politics he had regarded as inconsequential, he suddenly preaches the importance of the job he himself has been given!'

The pressing demand for reform was the main reason for the casting of Crossman in the role of the Leader of the House. This clamour had to be satisfied by action. And, it so happened that one new member, above all others, was going to have to be satisfied – a new member who had unexpectedly defeated the former chairman of Ways and Means, the current chairman of the 1922 Committee, Sir William Anstruther Gray, in the predominantly rural community of Berwick and East Lothian. The late Professor John P. Mackintosh was the most brilliant and stimulating university lecturer to be elected to the House of Commons since Crossman himself took his seat in 1945. He was, even more importantly, a man of enormous seriousness of purpose and of demonic energy. (Had John Mackintosh not died of cancer in 1978, before he was 50, he would probably have prevailed on Roy Jenkins, David Owen, Bill Rodgers, and Shirley Williams – and others, like David Marquand – not to leave the Labour Party, and the whole British political scene would have been different.)

Mackintosh was the author of *The British Cabinet* (1962). And he articulated more forcefully than anyone else what the new MPs thought was wrong with Parliament. In particular, he sold Crossman the concept of prime-ministerial government. Now, timing is all-important in politics. Ever since the strike in May–June 1966 by the National Union of Seamen, on the heels of Labour's general-election victory, Crossman had had mounting reservations about Wilson's style as Prime Minister.

The row over Party discipline and Prices and Incomes legislation turned out to be a watershed in Crossman's career. The issue was whether or not members elected to the House of Commons had the right to challenge their own Government and abstain conscientiously –

provided that conscience could be reasonably shown to be individual, not collective, and not organized by a faction.

In later years, long after Crossman and John Silkin had both died, some members of the PLP tried to remind me, somewhat tartly, that 'the discipline rot in the PLP set in with your mates Crossman and Silkin!' Some MPs even today would try to heap most of the current problems of the opposition on to their deceased shoulders.

With all the conviction that I can command, I will say to anyone who was not a member of the PLP in 1966–70 that the political cauldron of the Left would have boiled over, had not some development along the lines of the Crossman–Silkin reforms taken place. Had there not been a couple of stubborn, liberal (rather than libertarian) senior ministers in the key positions of Leader of the House and Goverment Chief Whip, the second Wilson government would have been blown apart over the East-of-Suez policy and Prices and Incomes legislation.

Crossman and Silkin believed that while the final decision on discipline would be taken on a one-person one-vote basis at the Parliamentary Labour Party, the crucial initiative for recommending disciplinary action rested with the Government Chief Whip. The Chief Whip and the Leader of the House would decide whether they would reprimand members or recommend the party to withdraw the whip. In order to run a modern left-wing party, one had to assume that every member of the party might well, on occasion, have to conscientiously abstain. Conscientious abstention would not in future be limited to pacifists and to teetotallers, but would have to be accepted in future as a right of every member of the Parliamentary Labour Party. Furthermore, Crossman with his Transport House rather than Westminster background, emphasized that when a Labour Cabinet proposed measures which were deeply controversial and were not to be found in the Labour Party Manifesto, then Labour MPs had every actual and moral right to challenge the Government.

In the autumn of 1966, I believe Crossman saved the Labour Government by striding across to Michael Foot, Eric Heffer, John Mendelson and other leaders of the Left, and conducting two-hour 'teach-ins' as he put it. You cannot, in politics, be really and bitterly angry with a colleague who comes to talk to you for hours, however violent the disagreement on the issue.

Crossman's real critics were on the sullen old right of the party. It was partly resentment that, having borne the heat of the day in the

1950s and early 1960s, many of them were without Government posts. It was partly that Crossman did not quite understand what these colleagues were increasingly having to put up with in their constituencies. For an MP in difficulty with his constituency Party, the excuse or fact of the Whip's categorical imperative for blindly voting the way the Government wanted on a three-line whip could be a life-saver.

As the loyalists (mostly but not exclusively moderate or right-wing) saw it, some people were allowed to have consciences at the expense of others. For a Labour MP, there is nothing more sensitive than his relations with his own Constituency Labour Party. Therefore when they went to their own power-base and found that frequently they were being vilified for not rebelling against the Labour government on the Prices and Incomes issue, the loyalist MPs were beside themselves with rage.

If Crossman had displeased the moderates and right-wing of the PLP by the Crossman–Silkin liberal discipline reforms, he displeased their spokesmen in the Cabinet even more with his proposals for specialist Select Committees. Now we take Select Committees for granted as part of the Westminster scene. However, the birth of Select Committees was a 'close run thing'.

The key date was Thursday, 17 November, 1966, which happened to be my wife's twenty-ninth birthday. Crossman gave us a nightcap, and talked to us late into the night about all that had happened to him that morning. I sensed that it was a day of decision and took even more voluminous notes than usual. In retrospect, the 17 November 1966 Cabinet was a Battle of Salamis for the House of Commons. Had Crossman lost – and he won by the closest of margins – there would have been no new-style specialist Select Committes that year – which would, *de facto*, have meant in that parliament, because given the troubles to come in 1967 and 1968, the Cabinet would not have countenanced any reform which would add to their burdens. By 1969, it was the fag-end of the parliament, and there was no steam left for embarking on reform.

The Heath Government was rather inflexible, whatever Ted Heath's 1980s image, and would not have turned its attention to Select Committee innovation. Nor, in my opinion, would the 1974–9 Labour Governments, with their wafer-thin majorities and day-to-day precarious existence. Besides the composition of the Parliamentary Labour Party was by then far less radical and reform-concious than a decade earlier. Nor would the establishment of potentially critical Select Committees have been one of Margaret Thatcher's interests.

The only opportunity was to be found in a time-window in 1966, and only Crossman could have done it – and Wilfred-of-Ivanhoe-like, he would have failed, had it not been for the Black Knight riding to his rescue in the shape of Harold Wilson.

A digression.   I had an unusual relationship with Harold Wilson. He, I always felt, liked me very much; I certainly always liked him. I know I exasperated him on occasion. But he would chat to me very freely, even at the height of his premiership, about a number of subjects, one of which was Select Committees. This was because in 1962, he had, when chairman of the Public Accounts Committee, put me on his committee. From a conversation I had with him before Christmas 1966, Harold Wilson believed that he had helped Crossman overcome insuperable odds to get experimental Select Committees. Do not suppose that the argument was between fuddy-duddies and reactionaries led by Michael Stewart versus progressives and reformers led by Crossman. As invariably with Michael Stewart, there was a powerful and respectable case to be considered.

The Cabinet had opened with an inordinately prolonged discussion of Crossman's proposals for the reform of parliamentary procedure. (Later he was to discover to his fury that the minutes simply recorded the contents of the brief which he took with him from his office, rather than his opening comments, which he changed at the last moment, when he said he realized how inappropriate the brief was for that particular meeting. He said the minutes bore little relation to what actually happened.) Crossman put the case for morning sittings of the House of Commons, more frequent use of the Standing Order Number 9 (now the Standing Order Number 20) emergency debate procedure, and the setting up of Specialist Select Committees.

Michael Stewart had opposed the reforms, root and branch. He did not want morning debates in the House, where, even if there were no votes, Ministers would be tied up on the House of Commons front bench, dragged away from the work of their departments. Nor did it appeal to the Cabinet when Crossman pointed out that such debates would get a great deal of press coverage, since they would have taken place at a time during the day when newspapers would not have to alter their early editions in order to cover parliamentary proceedings. (Ironically, as technology in the newspaper industry improves, deadlines become even earlier.)

The idea of more topical emergency Commons debates went down like the proverbial lead balloon. Emergency debates, always dangerous for Ministers since, by definition, preparation can be lacking, was the last thing that the Foreign Secretary, George Brown, wanted. Emergency debates often relate to Foreign Office responsibilities. Since the whole idea of morning sittings had been concocted to please eager backbenchers from the Parliamentary Labour Party, Crossman's case was not helped by the fact that the octogenarian Manny Shinwell, Chairman of the Parliamentary Labour Party was vehemently against the reform. 'With Manny,' Crossman commented sardonically, 'I have learned that it takes just one to have a row!' But it was Crossman's proposals for the Specialist Select Committees which raised the hackles of his Cabinet colleagues. Why should they be burdened with more and more work by the House of Commons? Should not backbenchers be thankful that as a Socialist Government, the Cabinet wanted to keep the Executive strong? Back-bench MPs had perfectly satisfactory full-time jobs to do, and there was no reason why Crossman should imagine that the Government had to create work for them, in order to keep them happy. Now that they themselves were sitting round the Cabinet table, any former enthusiasm for parliamentary control had simply evaporated. Yet they were all part of a Government which was pledged to fundamental change.

Crossman asked himself and his colleagues about the role of a Socialist party, and a Socialist Parliamentary Party, under a Socialist government. There was a creeping suspicion that some Cabinet Ministers were beginning to imply that our Party was of little consequence under our Labour Government. Not surprisingly, Crossman fumed to me that he had only been supported by one minister, apart from Harold Wilson – Barbara Castle. The two of them had spent nineteen years apiece (1945–64) on the back benches, and knew what it was like: Michael Stewart, George Brown, and Jim Callaghan had hardly been backbenchers at any time over the same period and were either junior Ministers in the Attlee Government, or Shadow Ministers. But because, as I commented to him, there was more than an element of truth in it, which did not improve his temper, Crossman was stung by Jim Callaghan's acerbic comment, which I told him not to omit from his diary: 'We've got to be careful of our Lord President now he has transferred his attention from boosting housing to boosting the House of Commons. Just as he knew nothing about housing before he went to the Ministry this fellow was never there when he was a back-bencher. Now he's boosting the Commons with all the strength and power he gave to his housing programme and we've got to resist him in the same way.'

On balance, and looking back over twenty-plus years, I think Crossman's anger was more justified on this issue than that of his critics. Part of the reason for the Labour government's being elected in 1964 and its enhanced mandate in 1966 was that people wanted reform. This was being rather conveniently forgotten, by Ministers who seemed to Crossman and me to have lost contact with the parliamentary rank-and-file and were hardly ever there in the Palace of Westminster except for votes. They were doing their boxes of departmental papers, participating in ministerial committees, outside London on official visits, and increasingly, with a few notable exceptions, divorced from Westminster life. He who wrote the introduction to Walter Bagehot's *The English Constitution* in 1963 was uneasy that the executive in Britain should be on a pedestal, and give the impression of not wanting to be bothered with the legislature. As to Commons Select Committees, they can never aspire to the power or status of the US Congressional Committee. Crucially, they don't have the power of veto over cash. An American committee can actually stop government money from being used. British committees can only talk, examine and write reports, which the executive may not deign even to have discussed on the floor in Parliament, let alone acted upon.

The basis of this geological fault – Bagehot saw it more clearly than Crossman – is that the Congress and the White House executive are divided by the Montesquieu-inspired separation of powers in the Constitution; and, critically, a senator or a congressman in Washington sees preferment as dependent upon the esteem of his fellow senators and congressmen. The ladder for a legislator in Congress depends on his or her peers, not on the President of the United States and his acolytes.

The House of Commons is geologically different. An MP is dependent on his Party, his Whips, and above all the Leader of his Party, who may be the Prime Minister too. Any youngish MP on a Select Committee who is too awkward towards Ministers or his party's policy is not going to help him/herself become a junior Minister or a Shadow Minister. The pressure on a young MP to keep one's political nose clean is obvious and potent. Few MPs are going to make the Select Committee, for its own sake, go wheresoever the investigation may lead; they are not inhibited physically (Select Committees go everywhere from China and Nepal to Timbuktu!) but politically. Certainly great store is set by the unanimous, all-party support. But, when, as in the Westlands affair, there is a really crunch issue, British MPs flinch from embarrassing their Party. Americans go the whole hog. Nor do ex-Ministers show greater independence than their young colleagues. They tend to want something – that knighthood, for instance, which is important to the Constituency Conservative Association. Chairmen of Select Committees are *papabile* for elevation to the House of Lords – provided that they behave within the accepted parameters. Crossman did not fully comprehend the power of patronage, about which he himself had written on so many occasions. He did not identify Party and patronage as the stumbling block on which his Plato-like dream of powerful, fearless, investigative scrutiny committees of the Commons would founder. Only, in my opinion, towards the very end of his Cabinet career did Crossman find the sensitivity to realize that few politicians had the outside interest that he had in Prescote (or Tam Dalyell had in his National Trust home at The Binns), if things went disastrously wrong politically. In personal terms neither of us was in a moral position to chide our Parliamentary colleagues for overdependency on the Party. Nor, truth to tell, was Crossman himself consistent when it came to personal involvement in really wanting Select Committees.

If I was unhappy about Crossman's reasons for taking the job of Leader of the House in August 1966, I was no less unhappy about his leaving the job in April 1968. It was a pity. He should have stayed on. He would certainly have wished and been able to continue the experiment in radio broadcasts of proceedings. He believed in broadcasting, and it would have arrived fifteen years before it eventually did. Moreover, given the composition of the 1966–70 House of Commons and the mood of optimism of the time, the broadcasting experiment would have led to the televising of the British Parliament, like other Parliaments: 1966–70 was the window of opportunity for the TV producers in a way the Labour Government of 1974–9 never was. The chemistry was right in 1966–70, and Crossman would have presided over the completion of the experiment. Crossman would have kept going the Specialist Committees, which his successor, Fred Peart, distrusted. Peart would be blowed if he was going to allow any development to prosper, if it was going to make the task of Labour Ministers any more difficult!

Ironically, Peart was an ideal House of Commons man – good

159

relationships, bonhomie and disarming emollience. It was Crossman the apostate who, once he was in charge, wanted to make the institutions of parliament actually work effectively. It was Crossman the apostate who was leading the drive to get the House to control the Executive. Peart the supposed parliamentarian was absolutely opposed to Parliament's doing anything meaningful to hamper the Labour government. It was Crossman who was championing the notion that the House should discuss more private business – in other words, giving members of the House of Commons more than the mere charade of a say in topical issues as and when they arose. When his personality was beginning to count, Crossman allowed himself to walk out of the central job of Leader of the House. It was the key political, parliamentary and Government perch.

When Fred Peart succeeded Crossman, his total lack of interest in, let alone drive for, encouraging parliamentary criticism of the Executive, his equally total opposition to Crossman's enthusiasm for broadcasting and televising the proceedings of the Commons, and his straight and narrow loyalty to government Ministers, to the extent of muffling justified criticism, made all the difference. Had Crossman stayed ... is one of the big ifs of the history of parliamentary reform. But as it was, Fred Peart did extremely well in terms of House of Commons Labour traditionalists and Tories. He developed a line in keeping with previous obliging Leaders of the House, and in Crossman's repeated laughing-cum-rueful belly laugh could not have been more different from 'the arrogant, high-handed intellectual Dick Crossman'. For Crossman, who saw him as an easygoing, pleasant, nonprogressive, sensible man, he became a friend. (Crossman also had an increasing regard for him as Minister of Agriculture in 1964–8.)

The House of Commons is a very inward-looking place, rather like a village. And never underestimate the effect on politics and public life of simple logistical matters of convenience to MPs – particularly when assessing the ups and downs of individual Ministers. Woe betide the Minister who, through incompetence or what is perceived as a cock-up, requires his colleagues to stay after midnight or return to Westminster, when they think they ought to be away. Crossman's sin – and he, not Peart, rightly had to accept the odium – had been in piloting the reform whereby large sections of the Finance Bills are discussed not on the floor of the House but in Committee Room 10 upstairs. What this meant actually is that the Treasury Ministers and officials get a more serious going-over in regard to detail than would ever be possible from the whole House of Commons. But it did mean infinitely more work for Opposition MPs and Treasury Ministers, and dutiful silent patience from Government backbenchers on the committee for many hours in sweaty June and July.

Any assessment of Crossman as Leader of the House must be a matter of *'chacun à son goût'*. If the assessor judges him by the smooth running of the House of Commons and skill with the flattering emollient fluff, then he will be near but not at the bottom of the postwar league. If, on the other hand, the assessor judges according to change actually brought about, then Crossman must be at the top of the league, put there by points gained on the establishment of Select Committees and changes in ways of dealing with the Finance Bill which would not then and probably never would have happened without him. In recent times, only John Biffen, a non-innovative Leader of the House, has been equally concerned to protect the rights of critics and dissenters.

Perhaps the most eloquent testimony to the conflicting view was given in *The Times* of March 1967. Within a week, Crossman was described as 'possibly the worst Leader of the House for a generation', and then, by the then *Times* columnist Ian Trethowan, later (1977–82) Director-General of the BBC, as 'probably the best Leader of the House since Herbert Morrison'.

No picture of Crossman as Leader of the House of Commons would be complete without reference to his weekly meetings with the Lobby, which took place, unattributably, in the upstairs turret of the upper corridor of the House of Commons. He was sparkling, witty, good-natured and perilously candid. To give a flavour of the occasions, I quote the following:

30 November 1967
David Wood (*The Times*): Mr Crossman, don't you think it might be misunderstood by the public outside if at this time the House of Commons was to spend Wednesday debating procedure?
Mr Crossman: (Laughing) There is no danger of it being misunderstood because you people will see that it isn't reported to the public.
David Wood: In answering Tom Price do you think you were convincing when he made the point that most people will wonder why Parliament should use this time to talk about procedure?
Mr Crossman: Parliament must continue its routine work, and anyhow

our debate on procedure does have some relevance – more than you think – to what we, the Government, can do about prices. It is not so irrelevant to the Transport Bill as you imagine.

David Wood: You cannot say that it is a matter of carrying on routine work because we don't normally have devaluation.

John Silkin: Devaluation doesn't alter the procedure on Questions.

David Wood: I still say it will be misunderstood outside.

Mr Crossman: I know how difficult it is in a paper of your kind David (*The Times*) to put this sort of thing over. (Laughter)

Victor Knight (*Daily Mirror*): When are we going to hear about wigs and gowns?

Mr Crossman: Well there really is an issue that we can all put over.

FIFTEEN
DHSS: Pensions

Had the prime minister, Harold Wilson, been able to foretell that Crossman would row with the National Union of Teachers, excluding himself from the position of Secretary of State for Education and Science, and had he been able to foretell in October 1964 that there would be a Labour majority of 100 in 1966, he would have given Crossman responsibility for pensions with a seat in the Cabinet. Soon after I started working for him, Crossman told me of a conversation which he had with Wilson on 19 February 1963. The leader of the opposition then said that he wanted Crossman beside himself on the front bench, to apply Socialist planning to higher education and science – what was to become the 'White Heat of the Technological Revolution'. Wilson had added that if he insisted on doing pensions, he could not deny him the portfolio. And Wilson said that he could not promise him the job of Minister for Science. (At that moment, he had Pat Blackett in mind.) Crossman did tell Wilson that he wanted to be Minister of Social Security, saying, 'Harold, it is by far the most important thing we have to push through.' Wilson demurred, 'I should have thought you wanted something more important than that!'

Crossman candidly admitted to me that he did not know quite how to take Wilson. To Crossman's credit, he was not a job-conscious politician, forever concerned about his place on the Opposition front-bench, and calculating his every move – he was always more interested in doing a job which was a meaningful task than simply occupying a prestigious ministerial position. On the other hand, could Wilson possibly have in mind for him the post in which he thought he could be

163

most effective, the Foreign Office? He told me all this at the time, as my own life was affected — I knew a lot about science and higher education policy, and little about pension policy. Only later did we discover that the slightest possibility of Crossman going to the Foreign Office in any administration headed by Harold Wilson was a pipe-dream. Bar the Foreign Office, or defence, it was pensions that Crossman would have opted for and the whole history of the first two Wilson Governments might have been different, since from the outset a clear pensions strategy would have been evident. Serious trouble started within weeks of the 1964 General Election, at a rancid party meeting in the sepulchral Westminster Hall — never underestimate the effect of physical surroundings on the content of the party meetings — where platform and members were suddenly ranged against one another. Subject: pensions!

Had Labour won the 1959 General Election, Gaitskell would have made Crossman Minister of Pensions, though possibly not with a Cabinet seat. The position could then hardly have been denied to him. He was the Pensioneer. (Whether, had there been a Gaitskell government in 1964, Crossman would have been given a post is a different question. Much political water had flowed under the bridge!)

As a twenty-six-year-old Labour candidate in Roxburgh, Selkirk, and Peebles in 1958–9, I cannot fully convey, thirty years later, the importance of National Superannuation. In the prosperous tweed-manufacturing Scottish Borders, it was the best plank for arguing Labour's cause on the domestic front. Labour Parties up and down the country were deeply grateful to Crossman. Why? Basically, because he had been grinding away for five years, since he had written a seminal article for the *New Statesman* in 1954 on National Insurance.

As an issue politician myself, I can say that one of the nice things about the Labour movement is that it warms to its marathon runners. As I found over the *Belgrano*, over Westlands, or over kidney transplants, or the need to protect the ecology of Aldabra atoll, if one goes on long enough, and one's facts are sustained as true, the Labour movement can give heart-warming support. That's why Crossman got on National Superannuation. But he worked for it!

By contact with Sir Alfred Roberts, the Chairman of the TUC Social Services Committee 1947–57, and for over a quarter of a century General Secretary of the National Association of Card, Blowing and Ring Room Operatives, at an early stage in 1955, Crossman made certain that his reply at the Bournemouth Labour Party Conference that year would be welcomed by the trade unions. He was, when I saw him in action, far more skilful than any of his ministerial contemporaries, other than James Callaghan, at handling the top trade union leaders. He treated them as equals and took them into his confidence.

When Crossman was given a job or task, he was extremely good at picking other people's brains and experiences. For example, on the potentially sticky issue of trade-union pension schemes, he talked to Arthur Horner, the Communist general secretary of the then National Union of Mineworkers, a pivotally important part of the Labour movement. Horner gave Crossman the idea that a Labour Government should negotiate the takeover of schemes such as those of the NUM, so that they could concentrate on fringe benefits. I knew Arthur Horner ever since I had been alongside him in a Cambridge Union Debate in 1955, and he confirmed this to me. So did Abe Moffatt of the Scottish Miners, the only man (when he came to the Elephant and Castle on behalf of the Scottish, Merseyside and South Wales pensioners) whom I ever saw out-argue Crossman on aspects of pensions policy. As we have seen, Crossman was an excellent picker of people to help him on science policy. He had done the same on social security, choosing the late Professor Richard Titmuss, Brian Abel-Smith and Peter Townsend. An ascetic, soft-spoken, gaunt man, Titmuss was Professor of Social Administration at the London School of Economics (LSE) from 1950 until his premature death in 1973. He was a believer in an integrated social policy, and in the last five years of his life he was deputy chairman of the Supplementary Benefits Commission. His opinion mattered to Crossman, who thought he was a modern saint – if, politically, sometimes a little unrealistic.

A more direct influence was Brian Abel-Smith, in 1957 a lecturer at the LSE and subsequently Professor of Social Administration. A decade after they started working together, Crossman brought him into the Department as a senior adviser. From my personal observation of countless ministerial meetings, Abel-Smith was superb – and, astonishingly (since advisers were resented) popular with the civil servants, who rightly judged that he had a lot to contribute. Abel-Smith's many books, which include *A History of the Nursing Profession* (1960), *The Hospitals, 1800–1948* (1964), and *Value for Money in Health Services* (1976), are in my opinion required reading for anyone seriously interested in the field. It was an indication of his success that the 1974–9

Labour Government asked him to return as senior adviser.

The third member of this expert, imaginative and dedicated triumvirate was Peter Townsend, a lecturer at the LSE in the same department and then from 1963 Professor of Sociology in the University of Essex. In 1957 he had published his famous study of *The Family Life of Old People* (in Bethnal Green), a book that influenced Crossman (and me) greatly. He brought home to Crossman the problem of inner-city poverty, of a type that did not exist in Coventry.

In May 1957, Crossman sold his National Superannuation Scheme to the Parliamentary Labour Party. The PLP, few of whose meetings I have missed in twenty-seven years, is a most sceptical body, and quite extraordinarily difficult to impress. Crossman got a wonderful reception, not least because he had been open about how the scheme had to be paid for. When the legendary Tom Williams, Attlee's successful miner–Minister of Agriculture, got up and said that Crossman's was the best scheme that the Labour party had ever put forward in his whole memory of Party history, Crossman knew that he was safe.

Crossman believed that the supreme test of the welfare state was the provision it made for old age. By this test, Crossman pointed out that we in Britain lagged behind Canada, Australia, New Zealand, France, Germany and Holland. Twelve years earlier, the Germans had been defeated in war and Europe overrun with armies, so we in Britain could not be proud of ourselves.

Crossman said that in the Britain of 1957, grinding poverty was still the rule and not the exception among retired workers with no superannuation or private insurance. This had to be put right. The full-employment policies of the 1945–51 Labour Government had abolished poverty among those of working age. A Labour Government in 1959 had to abolish poverty among old people too. This objective was to be achieved through National Superannuation – which Crossman defined as the provision to every employed worker of the benefits currently enjoyed by the privileged minority who were members of sound occupational pension schemes. Crossman was a leveller-up rather than down: only the best was good enough for the workers. To illustrate his point, he would tell a story about Simon Marks, one of the founders of Marks & Spencer. Marks would identify the best product in any line he could find which was bought by discerning and discriminating people. Marks, Sieff and their colleagues then applied their minds as to how the same excellent product for the privileged could be brought within the range of everyone. Crossman wanted to do the same for pensioners. His proposals would have brought immediate relief to existing pensions by raising the basic rate to £3 per week (1957 prices!), while those reaching pensionable age after the introduction of the scheme would get, in addition, a new wage-related benefit in return for a novel wage-related contribution. In due course such a scheme would have ensured that the average wage-earner received a pension equivalent to half-pay at 65.

Crossman lost no opportunity to emphasize that the much more generous provision for old age which the Labour Party proposed would demand both self-restraint and hard work from the rest of the community. If the old were enabled to spend more, the rest of the British people would have less to spend, unless they made up the loss by increased national production.

Collectively – and here was the Coventry shop-steward influence coming out – we had to be ready to see national consumption held back, and the necessary savings built up in Labour's new National Pensions Fund – which itself would be one of the instruments for investment, modernization, and development of industry. The contributions, claimed Crossman credibly, for National Superannuation would increase the growth of national income and so enable us to pay the constantly increasing bill in the 1960s and 1970s for old-age pensions. Crossman, as ever cussedly determined to make people understand the price of his proposals, was brutally candid with the 1957 Labour Party Conference, where he unveiled the final scheme. The blunt fact was that an adequate subsistence pension for all could only be financed by increased taxation, or by increased insurance contributions, or else by a sensible balance between the two. The foolish and completely gratuitous pledge given by Gaitskell, the weekend before polling day, that a Labour government would not increase taxation, damaged belief in Crossman's scheme. The electors were sceptical about financial matters including pensions from that point on, and many were diverted from their intention to vote Labour. I remember going round Galashiels the day after Gaitskell had committed his gaffe, and being asked, 'How do you finance National Superannuation now?' The whole crux of the argument was that National Superannuation – with its graduated contributions from employer and employee and its Exchequer grant – enabled just such a fair balance to be struck.

It helped enormously that National Superanuation was launched in one of the most memorable, in some ways THE most memorable speech of its kind ever given by anybody at any Labour Party conference before or since. The venue was the old ice-rink at Brighton – far removed from the modern anaesthetized, soulless Conference Centre, which kills emotion and drama. We were all – delegates and visitors alike – getting our feet frozen because the insulation from the ice had not been properly fixed. (Many delegates were to go home with incipient pneumonia.) The Conference was getting into a foul temper. The Left were dismayed at Nye Bevan's intellectual and emotional somersaults on the H-bomb. Brighton was expensive and uncomfortable. Besides, Crossman's mind was very much with his wife Anne, who was giving birth to his first child, in London. Instead of going home on the Monday night, Crossman remained in Brighton for his Tuesday speech – but got into an absurd argument with Bill Connor ('Cassandra') and other *Daily Mirror* colleagues, and did no work on his speech. Then on Tuesday morning, dropping a huge number of votes, he just scraped back on to the NEC.

He therefore suggested that he would simply wind up the debate, rather than introducing the policy document. (Besides he was not keen on a second executive speaker on National Superannuation, and thought the atmosphere would be better if more precious time went to floor speakers.) As Crossman anticipated, the floor speeches covered practically all the sensible and important questions he had been asked during the dozen conferences which he had held at forums up and down Britain. He ticked off each question as it arose. His speech consisted of three minutes of thanks to the Party and Abel-Smith, Titmuss and Townsend at the beginning, factual answers, and a couple of minutes of a pep talk at the end.

But only a politician immersed in the subject would dare to take the risk. He opened, after thanks, by saying that in view of the excellence of the debate, he would merely answer it. Crossman gave a tutorial and addressed it to Frank Cousins in the middle of the ice-rink, 'the ideal WEA three-year class member – a long, not very intelligent face, which nods when it's got it at last'. Years later, I heard Crossman use these words to Frank Cousins's face, who to his breathtaking credit took it, and laughed heartily. Few others would have got away with it! Curiously, it had helped that in his passionate advocacy of his pension scheme, his hair flopped over his face throughout his speech. The reason was simple – it was not so much enthusiastic belief in what he was saying (though this was genuine) but because he had had to shampoo his hair to get rid of dandruff. What Crossman had done was to give the Labour

Party conference a moral justification for liking a new idea. Crossman believed that the British Labour Party, unlike the continental labour parties, had a fear and suspicion of new ideas, and of the intellectuals who produce them. In that matter-of-fact tone of voice which suggested that reasonable men should expect little else, Crossman took it for granted aloud that intellectuals were potential traitors; therefore the new ideas which they put forward were always, by their very nature, assumed to be anti-Socialist – until it could be demonstrated that they were nothing of the kind. His surprising achievement at Brighton, made possible by his evangelizing up and down the country at regional conferences on pensions, was to convince the Labour Movement that a really practical workable scheme was compatible with the Socialist conscience. He had achieved it by applying his mind to the myriad of questions, mostly legitimate, which were thrown at him, and conscientiously dealing with any serious objection.

[**A digression.** Other politicians – not many – have been better than Crossman at answering questions on television, where there is a snappy time limit. Other politicians, such as James Callaghan and Tony Benn, have been better presenters of the official or unofficial Labour case. Other politicians, such as Roy Jenkins, Iain Macleod and Enoch Powell, have been superior in answering interruptions in the House of Commons. No one – but no one – in my experience has come within shouting distance of Crossman in his ability to answer questions at a medium-sized or small political meeting. It was partly that what Ian Mikardo was to call his 'towering intellect' was allowed full play; it was partly a combination of charm and brutal candour, which made even hostile questioners, who disagreed with the content of the answer, feel that they were treated to a special dissection of the issue.]

Having shamed the Conservatives into bringing forward superannuation proposals of their own, he called them 'The Tory Swindle' so repeatedly that it stuck. Crossman never indulged in pointless namecalling and was careful to make sure that his attack was mounted on solid ground. In this case, it cetainly was. Under the Conservative scheme, the additional pension was strictly related to the additional contribution, on an actuarial basis in terms of cash. Crossman could then point out up and down the country that on any reasonable assumption about inflation, contributors would certainly receive in real terms less out of the scheme than they had contributed. Crossman claimed that his proposals were dynamic and inflation-proofed, and that the

Conservative proposals, for which John Boyd-Carpenter was responsible, were neither. (However, it should be said that in his fascinating autobiography, *Way of Life* (1980), Boyd-Carpenter writes: 'Basically, it was the financial soundness to which Crossman objected, although I think he also felt that by taking the first step, however short, in the direction of graduation, I had stolen some of his clothes.' But, unlike in this decade, those were the days when an Opposition could influence the actions of Government!)

After 1959 and the general election defeat, Crossman went into a huff on pensions. He, almost alone, was not thanked by the Executive — and he was ignored by Gaitskell, with whom he thought (rightly) he was suffering guilt by association. As Peter Shore told him, 'After all, you did work out for them their only good policy. You were personally responsible for their only two successful propaganda pamphlets and you ran their campaign. But you are the only person, they have deliberately not thanked. That's fairly tough.'

Let us now advance over twelve eventful years to a November afternoon in the House of Commons in 1969 when Crossman introduced the second reading of his bill on National Superannuation. As his Parliamentary Private Secretary, sitting behind him, I was handed his text from which he spoke at the Commons despatch box. Somehow I forgot to hand it back to the civil servants in the box of the Commons, to the left of Mr Speaker's chair as one looks from the visitors' gallery. It got mislaid! I kept it, because I am a magpie with political documents which could one day be interesting. I quote only one brief section dealing with poverty in old age:

> ...the greatest social problem of our domestic politics in the second half of the twentieth century [is] how to abolish poverty in old age, that poverty which drives 2 million of our fellow citizens to apply for supplementary benefit under a means test, and which should increasingly irk our conscience as society grows more and more affluent. Poverty in the 1930s was infinitely more widespread than now but it was also shared by whole communities in the distressed areas. It was mass poverty in a society dominated by mass unemployment. But today it is poverty in the midst of plenty. A poverty from which the working population, even in what were once the distressed areas, is largely excluded; poverty concentrated indeed among those who are the weakest and least able to protect themselves in the community, the chronic sick, the widows and deserted wives and unmarried mothers, and above all the 14 per cent of

the population who are over pension age.

In the 50s and 60s the standard of living of those at work in this country rose far, far faster than in any previous epoch of history. When Harold Macmillan remarked 'You have never had it so good', he coined a platitude, since in this period of technological change every industrial nation has almost automatically a higher standard of living this year than in the preceding year. Modern science, modern technology, modern management have indeed solved the problem of poverty in the sense that they have made it possible for nations equipped with these techniques to increase the national wealth year by year. What these techniques have not done is to ensure that this wealth is fairly shared between those who are fit and able to look after themselves and those who are too weak, too sick or too old to fight for a fair share of the wealth of the affluent society. And one of the tests by which I suggest that this government and its Tory predecessor should be compared is to ask what precisely each has done to assure to our old people, our sick and our widows their fair share of rising national prosperity.

Crossman was at his best in forcing himself to get to grips with and understand appallingly difficult subjects. He had never really understood the negotiations between his Department and the Life Assurance Officer on the vital topic of 'contracting out'. Yet I saw him struggle with a problem that comes more easily to the numerate than to the literate throughout April 1969. The way that he dealt with the technical difficulties of National Superannuation was individual. He invited an Assistant Secretary at DHSS, the late Herbert Lewin, to breakfast from time to time. As the maker of the breakfast, I was transfixed. Crossman had a rather special relationship with Lewin. He had given Lewin dinner, on a train to Newcastle in August 1968, soon after becoming Secretary of State. Soon he discovered Lewin's background, a 'pertinacious Russian Jew', a scholarly musicologist, who had done a year's PPE prewar at Oxford, had a 'good war' and returned to another year at Oxford before joining the civil service. Crossman, a good judge of intellect, rated Lewin a potential Fellow of All Souls. The way he cross-examined Lewin was superb – and Lewin loved his vigour, and being taken notice of. When Herbert Lewin took his own life in November 1970 – maybe, partly on account of his work on National Superannuation being, as he thought, wasted by the premature election – Crossman was deeply, deeply upset; so was I.

In the area of social security, one of Crossman's other achievements –

171

though many Labour MPs did not thank him for it — was to tighten up on supplementary-benefit payments. This may be thought to be a pre-Thatcherite tendency. In fact, the problem was brought to Crossman's attention by his Minister of State for Pensions, a man of impeccable left-wing credentials, the late Stephen Swingler. Since 1964, in five years, the number of letters being sent by MPs to local DHSS offices had actually doubled. Crossman confided to me that he was driven to the conclusion that a number of our parliamentary colleagues had discovered that social security discretionary payments could be a pork-barrel for their constituents. Just because a person went to their MP, it should not mean that he gets something, while the person in an exactly similar situation who does not go to their MP is worse off. If the public tumbled to it that applicants got better treatment through ministers and MPs, there would be real trouble, in terms of both taxpayers' money and political consequences. Crossman took the view that the abuse of supplementary benefits was bringing the entire Government into disrepute, and that the money would be better spent on constant attendance for the sick and disabled who were the subject of Alfred Morris's important Private Member's Bill dealing with the handicapped. From the spring of 1969, almost every speech he made, as Secretary of State, stressed his object of combining humanity with efficient severity.

SIXTEEN

DHSS: Health

If Crossman was appointed to head the vast new combined and reorganized Ministry of Health and Social Security (separated again, rightly in my view, by Mrs Thatcher in 1988) on account of his background in social security, it was understandably health which took up more of his time and energy as Secretary of State.

Health in those days was rather a remote ministry in terms of Whitehall. Every Tuesday, Wednesday and Thursday morning, and some Monday and Friday mornings, I would hop into the back of Crossman's ministerial car at 9 Vincent Square at 9.15 a.m. and accompany him for a normally eleven-minute drive over Lambeth Bridge, past the Imperial War Museum's battleship guns to the Elephant and Castle. Having been next to the Treasury and Cabinet office at Housing, having been in the Cabinet office at 70 Whitehall during the leadership of the House, we felt as if we were exiled – and maybe in retrospect I realize that Wilson by November 1968 wanted Crossman to be exiled. It was no longer so easy for him to pop round to see the Prime Minister or the Cabinet Secretary, although he did still have a co-ordinating office in 70 Whitehall, to co-ordinate Health at the Elephant and Castle and Pensions at John Adam Street, near Charing Cross.

Alexander Fleming House was an ugly and shoddily-built sky-scraper over Elephant and Castle tube station. The Secretary of State had a suite of offices on the seventh floor. Crossman would joke edgily and testily that he found himself not in an ivory tower but in a steel one with double glazing to give absolute silence, so far up above the world as it went about its business that nothing seemed to relate to him. His first difficulty was that the Private Office of the Department of Health was not used to having a senior Cabinet minister at all. It was a galvanic struggle for Crossman to get them to work at the pace necessary to service a Cabinet minister.

Then I was indirectly responsible for landing Crossman in a time-consuming and awkward row. He was due to come to Scotland the weekend after he had stepped into the Elephant and Castle. After his Fabian School, I arranged for him to go to dinner to the house of my old friends, Michael and Tess Swann, daughter of the famous art master R. M. Y. Gleadowe, and then to meet a group of surgeons and doctors. He was tackled, as I warned him he would be, on the subject of merit awards, than which there is little more sensitive in the medical world. The question that lit the fire of Crossman's concern was, 'Why should not even the chairmen of the Regional Hospital Board finance committees have a right to know the names of the doctors who receive merit awards?' Well, indeed, why not?

From his own association with Aneurin Bevan, Crossman knew the stark truth. The system of merit awards was the carrot through which Bevan was able to get the consultants to back his proposals for a National Health Service, so that he could argue with Dr Cockshut and Dr Dain and other leaders of the British Medical Association from the firm ground of the consultants' agreement. The undertaking to provide merit awards tipped the balance in the ranks of the consultants in favour of acquiescing in the National Health Service. The proviso was that though the total sums and subjects were published, the names of the recipients were kept secret. Crossman reckoned that merit awards had too often become a sort of old-boy arrangement, designed to the advantage of the older consultants. And he was certainly correct in supposing that merit awards created deep resentments among young consultants, no less than among general practitioners. To start his second week, Crossman returned to the Elephant and Castle, full of enthusiasm, straight from Scotland, to deal with this pernicious (as he saw it), corrupting system. I will never forget the look of alarm on the face of Sir George Godber, the distinguished and long-serving Chief Medical Officer, when Crossman announced that he was determined either to end the system of merit awards altogether, or at least to publish the names of recipients and the amount of money which each received. Godber envisaged an unholy row with the Royal Colleges, and the leading consultants. Aware of what I might be letting him in for, I pleaded with Crossman to be cautious, since an early quarrel on this ground would endanger his whole relationship with the medical profession. Thankfully, he checked his instinct to tackle merit awards head on. Had he not done so, he would not have been able to get support on tackling other more important issues.

To understand Crossman's attitudes and priorities in the Health Service, it is necessary to mention two very personal events which helped to shape them – the circumstances of the death of his mother, which I have already mentioned, and the death of his second wife, Zita.

His mother had spent some time before she died in a not-very-clean and sometimes squalid nursing home. Crossman felt guilty – and angry. He came to hold passionately the view that people should be allowed to die with dignity. For example, he became a champion of the smallish village or cottage hospitals, which might not have had the latest equipment or been cost-effective – but where there were usually caring people to tend the sick and the patients might be among people they knew.

It was, however, the circumstances of the death of Zita that brought home to him the delicate problems of discrimination in the Health Service. First of all, after Zita's stroke in July 1952, at the Lambeth Children's Hospital, where she was a voluntary helper, she was taken to Westminster Hospital. Crossman was then pressurized to decide if she should go into a private ward. She could have a bed in a private room for three weeks at £15 per week, and he was told that the specialist would cost about £80 for the first five weeks. However, the question did not need an immediate response, since one of the young doctors, sympathetic to Crossman, said to him quietly that Zita was in no fit state to be moved at all.

After Zita had died, Crossman mentioned this to his own friendly GP, who explained to him that Zita had only been accepted into Westminster Hospital because he had told the specialist that if he could just get her into the casualty ward, Crossman would agree to her being a private patient.

Crossman often repeated, as Secretary of State, what he had said to the GP of whom he was very fond. 'You mean Zita would have been left to die here at 9 Vincent Square, if the specialist had not had the impression that she was going to be a private patient.' The GP replied that this was indeed the situation, unless she could have been got into some small hospital away from the centre of London.

That was the moment when Crossman realized that the notion that the Attlee government and Nye Bevan had succeeded in removing the money element from sickness was pie-in-the-sky. He did not blame the Westminster Hospital of the day. It was simply a result of the system of having alongside one another, in the same building, public and private wards. Given human nature, and the sacrifices he had to make for years in his own training, he could not really point the finger of criticism at the specialist. If Crossman, a relatively high earner then aged forty-four, had insisted on his rights to have his wife in public care, the specialist would have got nothing. Yet had Zita survived some weeks, Crossman imagined that he would have been blackmailed into deciding that she should go private; the specialist would then, and only then, get his substantial fee. The whole position was quite unacceptable, and left on him an indelible mark. The National Health Service had to provide meaningful health care, and not simply the trappings, for those who could not afford it.

But it was, in my opinion, the circumstances of his mother's death that generated Crossman's greatest service to Health. Mrs Crossman had eventually died in a dingy nursing home in wartime Britain.

As men grow older, it may be that they reflect more on their childhood and deceased parents. All I know for sure is that in 1968–9, Crossman himself, with whom I stayed when in London, suddenly aged and certainly mellowed (rather attractively). Whenever he had to deal with psychiatric illness or mental handicap, he spoke, I felt, from the heart. I know his mother's suffering increasingly preyed on his mind.

To digress for a moment, I believe Crossman's three wives each contributed in different ways to his passionate concern about the psychiatrically ill.

Erika Landau (or Glück, her second name by her previous marriage) was amost certainly herself unbalanced. It was not only a question of dancing on the table at college occasions, screaming, 'Ich bin kleine Erika' – which, as Isaiah Berlin commented to me – was a little much even for Oxford of the early 1930s. Even after she had gone off with at least one other man in Oxford (as Mrs Mary Bennett, H. A. L. Fisher's daughter, told me), Crossman tried to retrieve the situation. Mrs Bennet is in a position to know, since Dick and Erika Crossman were married from her father's lodgings in New College. Later, Crossman was to traverse Europe in search of this lady, who he thought had lost her reason. George Weidenfeld describes Erika as 'flamboyant'.

Zita (Inezita Davis), married to the zoologist John Baker, was altogether a different kettle of fish. It was characteristic of her that she had been on an expedition to Borneo, where the anthropologist Tom Harrison was doing his early research. Harrison believed in the concept of access to common property – which included women. It was this and other problems, rather than Crossman, in the first instance, that broke up John Baker's marriage. Since I was Dick and Anne Crossman's lodger, I did not like to ask too much about Zita, who had lived in Vincent Square. Sufficient to say that she had strong views, which mattered to Crossman, and one of them was that society had to do something to the mentally handicapped.

Of Anne McDougall, who still lives at Prescote, and who remains a warm friend to my wife and me, I simply say that living ten years in her house, my observation was that she was an absolutely marvellous wife to Crossman. Anne was not an interfering wife. But I thought she was a powerful and benign influence. Certainly on a number of subjects, she made her views known, and one of those views was that the Labour government in general, and the Secretary of State for the Social Services in particular, should jolly well do something for the mentally ill. Politicians (I am another) who have wives with a fierce sense of right and wrong had better take those views into account. Anne thought that the mentally ill deserved special consideration, partly because they had no clout politically.

It was against this background, that Crossman chose, as one of his first ministerial visits, to go to an old-fashioned, old-building, big psychiatric hospital. The Department offered Friern Barnet. Now I had at that time in my West Lothian constituency, Old Bangour Village Hospital, so I was as familiar with the problems as most MPs. At Friern Barnet, I was appalled. Not by the staff, most of whom seemed to be angels struggling to do their best, but by the conditions under which they were expected to work, as a result of the shortage of resources and investment. I never saw Crossman so subdued or shaken, by the stench and the soaking walls, and the consequent treatment of the helpless, incontinent, and usually relationless patients. In his car on the way back to the Elephant and Castle, he repeated, 'I am responsible for running the worst kind of Dickensian, Victorian loony bin.' From that moment on, the issue of the mentally ill was at the top of his mental and ministerial in-tray.

The problem was that, quite brutally, the cause of the mentally was not, at that or any time, a political priority. Is it too cynical to recall that lunatics have no vote? And that relations generally visited less often and had less concern for the mentally ill than for the physically ill? So the first thing Crossman had to do was to raise public awareness and public sympathy for the cause. If he did nothing else – though I'd dispute that – while he had the opportunity as Health supremo, he certainly altered the political ethos towards the mentally ill. I beg leave to doubt whether anybody else in top politics would have acted in quite the same way, or achieved the same results in putting the mentally ill on the political agenda. How did he do it? The answer is the story of Ely Hospital, which I tell in essential if necessarily truncated form.

In the summer of 1967, there had been alarming newspaper reports about pilfering and cruelty by staff at the Ely Mental Hospital in Cardiff. Quite properly, Kenneth Robinson, then the well-respected Health Minister outside the Cabinet, set up an inquiry in September 1967. It took a year. But there was no apology from the chairman of the inquiry. He was a young and (in Crossman's opinion) extremely able Conservative lawyer, Geoffrey Howe. The report was no less than 83,000 words long. Both Crossman and I read it, and agreed it was a most formidable and well-written document. The Department of Health officials wanted a confidential report in full for their use, and a short version for publication. Howe was not having that. He insisted that 'I must get out the essential facts.' His report had, indeed, completely substantiated the newspaper allegations.

Crossman saw his chance. Rather than play down Ely and treat it as an embarrassment to the Government, he would use a concrete example to put the national spotlight on a disgrace. At breakfast on the morning of Wednesday, 12 March 1969, he told me that he was going to use Ely, in the cause of the psychiatrically ill. 'An actual case will galvanize Whitehall and Westminster more than any number of pious speeches.' The morning meeting that raged on over lunchtime was memorable. The officials came in force. Also present was Lady (Bea) Serota, the new Minister of State for health, a life peer whose appointment from the Lords had got Crossman criticized in the Commons. Crossman opened. Everyone in Alexander Fleming House had better face up to it that the Howe Report was an indictment not only of the Ely Hospital, but also of the Hospital Management Committee which had failed lamentably to find out about what was happening, and of the Regional Hospital Board, and added Crossman, looking at every one of us in the room, 'of ourselves, because we as a Ministry are responsible for our agents in Cardiff in the Health Service!' You could have heard a pin drop in the embarrassment. Terrible things had been allowed to go on at Ely over a period of years. How was it that the Department of Health had apparently not even known that two nurses at Ely had been sacked from their posts, simply because they had attempted to expose the scandals?

It became clear to me that the officials of the Ministry intended Crossman to do what almost every other Minister I knew would have done – publish the report, or preferably an abbreviated version, along with a press statement simply deploring what had taken place. Crossman was having none of that. Besides, had he followed their advice, he told them that there would be a whole panoply of investigations into psychiatric hospitals throughout Britain. All of us had better understand that what we were dealing with was no less than a national crisis. Crossman said that there were at least one quarter of a million 'souls' – the word I record him as having used – in long-stay, sub-normal psychiatric and geriatric hospitals; they were 'cooped up' in Georgian or Victorian public assistance buildings and poorhouses, with no proper system of inspection whatsoever. Crossman asserted that Ely was not a one-off situation, at which some, not all, of the officials visibly dissented. (South Ockendon was one among a number of cases in 1969 and 1970 which were to prove him right.) Crossman's peroration demanded a system of inspection.

The officials started putting all sorts of obstacles in the way of a system of inspection. The doctors would not co-operate unless their affairs were inspected only by doctors. At this, Crossman unusually used dirty language. Making sure that a little trouble was taken to see that mental patients were given back their own false teeth, rather than just anyone's pair of false teeth, did not require a doctor inspecting other doctors.

Well past the normal lunch hour, Crossman made a reference to the Department not knowing anything about the situation at Ely. I was electrified when suddenly Lady Serota, who had been a powerful figure in the LCC where she represented Brixton for eleven years, and on the GLC, chipped in, 'Didn't we just? Secretary of State, you'd better ask the Chief Nursing Officer what she knows about it.' The walls of the departmental Jericho crumbled. Everyone looked at Dame Kathleen Raven, a former matron of Leeds General Infirmary, and from 1958 to

179

1972 the Chief Nursing Officer of the Ministry of Health and then the DHSS.

'Oh yes,' said Dame Kathleen nervously, 'we used to have people going down to Ely, regularly visiting.'

'Did they report?' quizzed Crossman.

'Yes.'

'When was the last report?'

'Three or four years ago.'

'Have you got it?' asked Crossman.

Lady Serota had it. She threw it across the table at him. It was a really frightful report. It admitted bad nursing, deplorable and indeed inexcusable conditions, and gave credence to all the worst of the newspaper revelations that the Howe Report had confirmed. Naturally Crossman demanded to know what had happened to it when it came to the Ministry of Health. All the officials would say to Crossman was that it had gone on file.

Crossman was deeply upset that evening. He reckoned that the Department knew perfectly well what had happened at Ely. The easy way out had been to set up an inquiry. If they had been honest, they would not have wasted Geoffrey Howe's time and a lot of other people's.

For my part, ever since Ely, I have been profoundly sceptical of some inquiries set up by Ministers. For example, when Mrs Thatcher set up an inquiry into the leaked law officer's letter in the Westland affair, it had nothing to do with finding the truth, and everything to do with calming Sir Michael Havers, who was so angry that he is alleged to have threatened to have Scotland Yard detectives at the door of 10 Downing Street, unless an inquiry was set up.

Crossman also began to suspect unfairly that the senior officials of the Department, the chief Medical Officers, Sir George Godber and Dr (lately Sir Henry) Yellowlees, and Dame Kathleen were not being straight with him, and that they had a shrewd idea that there were a host of long-stay psychiatric hospitals in Britain where the set-up was like that of Ely. Old buildings were one thing – pilfering from patients, cruelty and occasional torture were quite another. Nonetheless, staff did get completely demoralized by old buildings, facilities ill maintained, lack of domestic help, staff shortages, and hopelessly inadequate pay.

Crossman then brought the meeting to a dramatic finale. He would see the Secretary of State for Wales the following day, and tell him, as a matter of courtesy, that he was going to publish Howe in its entirety. He would not, even then, follow official advice, and simply put a copy in the Commons Library and give a copy to the press. He would publish it as a White Paper. He was determined to bring the whole issue out into the open, and he asked for a draft statement which he could submit to the Social Services Committee of the Cabinet. Then, in a casual and matter-of-fact voice, almost contrived, he added as a throwaway, 'I have talked to the Prime Minister already about Ely – he agrees to a White Paper!' Had he not done so, my impression at the time is that the department would have tried to scupper a White Paper, through the Cabinet Office grapevine. I have never witnessed officials troop out of a meeting so flustered.

But the department did set up a system of inspectors, the Advisory Service, which required relatively limited amounts of manpower and money. The Director of the Advisory Service was made directly responsible to the Secretary of State. But the real costs in meeting the actual problem were substantial. In 1969, the cost per patient in round figures was £12–14 per week in long-stay psychiatric hospitals, compared to £40–80 in district hospitals. Some extra money was forthcoming from the Treasury, and there were reallocations in favour of the mentally ill within the departmental budget. Far more important, Crossman's White Paper inspired a lot more activity on behalf of the mentally ill, and changed the climate of opinion in Britain towards mental illness. Later it led to the White Paper on Mental Handicap, which paved the way for the legislation of the 1970s.

Before leaving the saga of Ely, which Crossman held to his dying day meant a great deal to him, I must add two postscripts – one agreeable, the other rather disagreeable.

First, the agreeable. On Monday, 24 March 1969, I was present at a pleasant interview over glasses of dry sherry with, as Crossman put, 'all the appurtenances of old-fashioned parliamentary life' between Crossman, in his Secretary of State's Room in the Elephant, and Geoffrey Howe, QC, then the adopted candidate for the blue-chip Conservative constituency of Reigate. The meeting encapsulated important questions about the nature of public inquiries, a topic that increasingly interested Crossman. Crossman suggested to Howe that both of them should go on television together and discuss the whole issue. Crossman was surprised that Howe refused. I was not. Howe responded, quite rightly in my opinion, that he was keen to maintain his position as chairman of an impartial committee, and the last thing he wanted was to compromise the report by finding himself pushed into political statements. His tone was of serious, judicious impartiality. Howe impressed Crossman and me precisely because he was emphatically not a young Tory lawyer on the make, seeking Party advantage, but genuinely interested in the committee's findings. Howe did seem a little apprehensive about what this inquiry might do to his career. He had certainly taken a risk in making himself unpopular – not only possible in his political circles, but also in legal circles, which have a say in what kind of jobs Queen's Counsels get. The Government law officers, and the Lord Chancellor's office had made it abundantly clear that QCs must keep any inquiry to which they were appointed extremely narrow, and on no account should they stray into wider issues arising from their inquiry. Howe had defied this ruling, regardless of consequences to himself and his future, because he felt so strongly about the issue. He had felt duty-bound to take the inquiry beyond Ely to the Hospital Management Committee, Regional Hospital Board, and Ministry level. Crossman admired Howe for making the report not simply a report on Ely, but a document which pointed to a genuine defect in the structure of the Health Service. My impression was that Howe was astonished, but delighted that the report was to be published in full. I don't think he realized that Crossman had been told until the last minute that the Department were trying to get an abridged version published. Howe was also pleased to find a minister who meant to do far more about his recommendations than mere polite acceptance.

After Geoffrey Howe had left the room, Crossman said, 'Well, there goes a future Lord Chancellor.' I replied, 'But maybe a future leader of the opposition or prime minister.' His behaviour on Ely had been impeccable.

Some twenty years later, I asked Howe, then Foreign Secretary, about his view on Crossman. 'He was wholly honourable with me,' he said.

A working party was to be set up, the members external to DHSS being Eileen Skellern, Superintendent of Nursing at the Royal Bethlem and Maudsley Hospitals, Gerald O'Gorman, Physician Superintendent for the Borocourt Hospital near Reading, Professor Peter Townsend of Essex University and Geoffrey Howe himself. One of their first tasks was to work out how money for research into subnormality should be spent. It caused terrible ructions in the department. Miss Hilda Hedley, the Under-Secretary in charge of the Hospital Section, and Sir George

Godber had no enthusiasm, in Crossman's opinion, for a joint working party of outsiders and insiders. At best, he felt, they were both exceedingly indiscreet about what they thought of their Secretary of State, and of Lady Serota. Besides the Consultants' Committee wanted either a statutory inspectorate run by themselves, or preferably nothing at all. Fortunately, the cause of the mentally ill had gathered such a head of political steam that no one could shut the Pandora's box which Crossman had intentionally opened.

My second postcript is that after the Ely meeting on 12 March 1969, I don't think that Crossman ever fully trusted the DHSS officials again. Though I understood why, this was a pity. There are, as with everything concerning Crossman, two sides to the story. It certainly appeared to me that they had not been candid with him as to how much they knew as a department about Ely. He told me that he thought the civil servants were trying to sweep the problems, and certainly the unfavourable reflections on the Ministry of Health, under the carpet. When I stuck up for the department, as I did, he was at his intolerant worst.

On the other side of the coin, by the spring of 1969, one of Crossman's bad habits had become worse. He had always made it difficult for someone who had to present a coherent argument to get through to the end with it. He would interrupt in the rudest way, having alighted on a point or two at the start of the presentation of a person's case. Most civil servants would not dream of answering a Secretary of State back in kind. Crossman used quite often to complete their sentences for them, and get it wrong in doing so. His interruptions, implying incompetence, made it wellnigh impossible for civil servants to defend themselves, and sometimes, when he ought to have seen they were at a disadvantage, he exploited the relationship. This habit developed to an intolerable extent when he had his leg up on a chair, suffering intermittent pain from phlebitis, which he bore bravely and uncomplainingly. After he had interrupted, it was sometimes difficult for civil servants to get a word in edgeways. I could see how some highly intelligent men would just give up trying to put their point over. Crossman would fly off at some tangent of his own, and then come to a conclusion which he might well not have reached if he had bothered to listen just a couple of minutes longer.

Until he went to Social Security and Health, I thought Crossman had been a relatively good ministerial listener – indeed excellent when he was Shadow Minister of Higher Education and Science. It may have

183

been a combination of age, creeping ministerial weariness, and more frequent bouts of pain that transformed him into a bad listener. (In my experience, the first-class senior ministerial listeners were Hugh Gaitskell, James Callaghan Reginald Maudling, Alec Douglas-Home, Iain Macleod, and Michael Foot.) Whatever the causes, the fact is that the civil servants of the Department of Health and Social Security found it difficult to have a discussion with him. Nor was it clever of Crossman to be extremely rough on certain individuals if he wanted to get the best out of them. I rebuked him in his own bullying style for his treatment of Dame Kathleen Raven, the Chief Nursing Offier, after Ely. His answer was unexpectedly disarming: 'Of course, I was mad to say that to her.' And, the following week I noticed he made her a half-apology. The damage was done. If Crossman had listened more gently to what his officials were saying, my view at the time was that they would have been more forthcoming about what they did and did not know about Ely, and this rankling suspicion would not have developed.

Years after Crossman had died, I asked Kathleen Raven for her version of events. 'Crossman got a bit of the wrong end of the stick, when he thought I was trying to keep something back from him. I remember the meeting well. It was one of the best days of my life. My predecessor as Chief Nursing Officer had appointed two mental nursing officers to do a complete survey of all mental hospitals. Many of the worst things they reported on had been acted on as soon as possible, but we just did not have the necessary money. That's why I made sure Lady Serota had the report. I was thrilled when he said he had to do something about mental hospitals. It was the highlight of my career, because we had got the Secretary of State on our side.'

With the benefit of hindsight, I realize that if Crossman had been less of a conspirator himself, he might not have been so quick on the draw in so often attributing conspiratorial motives to others. Kathleen Raven was an artless, good, able lady, a successful matron doing her best in the stratosphere of Whitehall. Yet, to be fair to Crossman, I myself had the impression at the time that he was not being told the whole truth. Curiously enough, Crossman quite often used the phrase – and on one occasion much to my chagrin, to my face, about something I had said to George Wigg – 'economical with the truth', twenty years before Sir Robert Armstrong was to make it famous in an Australian court during the *Spycatcher* fiasco.

The rankling suspicion was perhaps beginning to be exorcized when something else happened that was to take up an inordinate amount of Crossman's time and mental energy. It is often matters affecting individual colleagues or senior civil servants, things which never get into the newspapers, that consume a disproportionate number of a Cabinet Minister's waking hours, and create more worry and tension than any number of public issues. This was one such.

In November 1969, the Senior Permanent Secretary of the DHSS, Sir Clifford Jarrett, sent Crossman a top-secret letter, to be opened personally, saying that when he retired he wanted to be given leave to accept a job he had been offered as President of the Society of Pension Consultants. This was due to become vacant in the following autumn. Sir Clifford Jarrett had a letter from Sir William, later Lord, Armstrong, then Head of the Civil Service Department, stating that if Crossman would agree, such an appointment would technically be perfectly respectable. (Years later, when I went to lunch with Lord Armstrong at the Midland Bank, I asked him about this letter. He replied, 'It was a particularly awkward case because there were conflicting interests, potentially. However, how could I deny Clifford Jarrett, when we all do it? Here I am as Chairman of the Midland Bank! Do you want our expertise as Permanent Secretaries used for the country or put on the scrapheap?')

Crossman asked me what I thought he should do. I wasn't sure. On the one hand, civil servants had a right to earn what they could, when political ministers were uninhibited about sailing off to the City pretty promptly after leaving office. On the other hand, the Clifford Jarrett situation was immensely awkward, and could let all hell loose in the Labour Party. In the autumn of 1969, Crossman was involved in a tremendous tussle with the private pension interests, the Society of Pension Consultants. It they were not the enemy, they were at least entrenched opponents of governmental and departmental policy. And, lo and behold, the Permanent Secretary had been talking to them about a retirement job. Crossman did not say to me that Jarrett was being dishonest or underhand. Crossman, being a spender himself, accepted that he might need the money to visit his daughter in America regularly on his retirement. Yet here were the private pension giants approaching the Permanent Secretary while he was still in the DHSS, presumably because they judged that Jarrett's expertise would be really valuable to them in the early 1970s. It looked than as if the National Superannuation

Act would be on the statute-book by autumn 1970 – in the event, it fell on account of Harold Wilson's opportunistic and idiotic decision to call a general election in June 1970.

Back in 1969, Harold Wilson was also extremely concerned, and gave up some valuable prime-ministerial time to Sir Clifford Jarrett's future. There was talk of having to change the rules if Jarrett went ahead. But as it turned out, Jarrett was still in place when the Labour government fell. However, this whole business, I thought, gnawed away at the impetus in the department – and had it not occurred, Crossman's National Superannuation Act might have been on the statute-book. Had it got that far, I doubt if the Heath government would have tried to unscramble that particular Act.

I also think that Crossman's attempt to put a spoke in Sir Clifford Jarrett's plans on retirement is one of the reasons why Crossman has posthumously been harshly treated by Jarrett himself, Sir Richard Powell, and some other permanent secretaries.

There were other issues and causes which Crossman championed. First among them was the treatment of drug addiction, a far less serious problem twenty years ago than it is today. The sight of heroin-stricken, incontinent fifteen- and sixteen-year-old boys, unable to control their limbs, mooning around the drug addiction unit of the London Hospital in Whitechapel, appalled Crossman during his visit of 18 November 1968. He promised to, and did, take action to try to ensure that sufficient nursing staff should be made available for day patients and inpatients. He forecast to me that drug-related illness would be a major problem of the Health Service when I reached his age – which I have, and it is!

Another of Crossman's causes was that of democracy in the Health Service. During this same ministerial visit to the London Hospital, as on other occasions, Crossman would quiz people in charge about their democracy – often to their bewilderment! In a conversation with Sir Hubert Ashton, celebrated cricketer, ex-Conservative MP, Hugh Gaitskell's brother-in-law, and deputy chairman of the board of governors – and a friend of Crossman's – he voiced his concerns. Was the setup too oligarchical? Why was the patient unrepresented and the public excluded? Why were the doctors in control and the chairman and members of the board of governors so remote and detached? Hubert Ashton, with whom I was friendly and had paired in the House, took me aside: 'Dick does ask interesting questions! But has he much idea of how anyone has to run an organization like this?' Ashton was a civilized, decent, concerned man. Like many MPs, Crossman had never himself actually *managed* anything. If he had, he would not have put such questions, often legitimate, quite so aggressively!

Another of his causes was the creation of new residential homes by local authorities. Crossman felt that, as a matter of right, people were entitled to a dignified, decent old age, in places very different from the old workhouse-type set-up – though he was the first to praise the staff at such places, where they performed miracles with what little was available to them. In presenting the case for nice residential homes Crossman's basic philosophy was that political action should be taken to transfer the privileges of the few into the rights of the many.

No account of Crossman's stewardship of the DHSS would be complete without reference to his gaffe of gaffes. For politicians are remembered in the public mind, if at all – and certainly by their own colleagues – for their gaffes rather than good deeds or constructive work. It was May 1969. And still I feel guilty twenty years later. Against Crossman's wishes, I had been selected as a member of the Inter-Parliamentary Union visit to Indonesia, with which I had special links, and Japan. (The only such visit I have ever gone on, other than leading the first IPU delegation to Brazil ten years later.) Over the weekend of 3–4 May, at the bottom of his fourth red box, there was a trivial regularization relating to charges for NHS teeth and spectacles.

Without thinking, he okayed it automatically, only to find banner headlines in the *Evening Standard* of the Monday. He had forgotten that there were local elections on the Thursday. He was, he said in his diary, 'a broken idol'. He was in the Cabinet doghouse. He was reviled by the press. It was his 'worst clanger', he felt, since he had written in the *Mirror* of 5 July 1957, that only four trade-union MPs were fit for office.

When I returned from Jakarta, I realized that he minded the indignity terribly and was sensitive to this kind of mental pain. His Party unpopularity affected his authority in the DHSS. Before May, he had been on the up-and-up. Indeed, for about two months in the spring of 1969, Crossman was being talked of as a possible future Prime Minister in the Parliamentary Party (whose votes alone at that time chose the Leader of the Party). Such a prospect, if it ever existed, vanished after the teeth and specs debacle. By the summer recess of 1969. Crossman was saying to me that he felt instinctively that Harold Wilson now saw him as an old friend who was beginning to be a ruddy nuisance. Wilson might feel entitled to get rid of him on grounds of dodderiness or failure. A politician who is thought not to have a future has not got much of a present either! To approaching journalists, Crossman would clap one hand to his brow and ward them off with the other: 'Don't tell me. I know my trousers have fallen down. I can see them lying there between my ankles!'

It was a quality of his that in 'unmitigated disaster' – one of his own oft-used phrases – his resilience did not desert him.

SEVENTEEN

In Cabinet

In one of the most heavyweight autobiographies of recent times, *Time and Chance* (1987) James Callaghan writes:

> Dick Crossman, who had an inventive mind, even affected to believe at one moment that I was in league with some unnamed group in the City of London to bring about a national government under my leadership. If the suggestion had come from anyone else I would have been insulted but Crossman's diaries reveal his obsessional search for hidden motives behind the most transparent actions of his colleagues. This trait was a singular weakness in a powerful intellect, and the passion for conspiratorial politics which he shared with George Wigg and some others had a divisive and weakening effect on Cabinet unity.

Was Crossman a conspirator? His enemies and many of his friends would give a firm yes. Personally, I doubt if he revelled in conspiratorial politics any more than most denizens of Westminster. It was subtler. Crossman prided himself, as ex-don and psychological warrior, in being *au fait* with the real motives of those with whom he was dealing. As a result he could be extraordinarily clumsy in personal relations.

Relations with Jim Callaghan were unique, and like relations with no other colleague. Firstly, Callaghan was Chancellor of the Exchequer, and a Minister in charge of a big spending Department is dependent on his relations with the Treasury for success or failure, inside or outside his department. Secondly, for Crossman, Callaghan was the only alternative to Wilson, at any rate so long as Wilson's own hat was in the ring. On the first page of his autobiography, James Callaghan makes a valid and important point about a political diarist's totality of relationship with his colleagues:

Historians of the future will certainly know more, thanks to the inde-fatigable energy of Dick Crossman, Barbara Castle, and perhaps Tony Benn, when his voluminous records appear. But the weakness of diaries is that they are written in haste and therefore lack perspective about the totality of the writer's relationship with his colleagues. I have myself reproduced verbatim extracts from a few conversations, but am generally cautious about diaries. In general, diary extracts, even when correctly reported, rarely catch either the inflexion of voice or the gesture that modifies the spoken word. Nor does such conversation when written down convey the notion that sometimes a man talking with his colleagues may be arguing as much with himself as with them, modifying his own views in the very process of exposing them.

Dick Crossman had a particularly emphatic way of expressing himself and would never have admitted such a possibility. His reputation for changing his mind came not only from his own intellectual flightiness but also because in the course of argument, at the very moment that he was engaged in destroying the other's case, he consciously or unconsciously absorbed what his oponent was saying. A week later, the listener might well be astonished to hear Crossman repeat as his own opinion the very argument that he had demolished with such ferocity at their previous encounter. It was this trait that instilled in me a mistrust of Crossman's judgement – and this within a month of our first meeting in the Smoking Room of the House of Commons after the great General Election of 1945, where the excitement of hearing that powerful mind at work had at first carried me away.

I am reinforced in this by an undated letter from Crossman which I found recently among my papers. It ran as follows:

Dear James
I made a thorough exhibition of myself talking to you and Hugh last night. Please accept my regrets and also my assurance that I am NOT as bad as that!! If you can't forget what I said, at least don't hold my remarks against me as settled convictions.
                                                                    Dick Crossman

To be candid, I cannot remember the occasion, the subject, or whether Hugh Dalton or Hugh Gaitskell was the third person present. But it was because of this spontaneous and characteristic response and contrition of

Dick's that we always remained on friendly terms, and I found stimulation in his company, even if I was not always convinced that he was expressing his 'settled convictions'. And his weekly diaries should be read accordingly. (pp. 19–20)

My view of Crossman's settled conviction about James Callaghan is that it was grudgingly friendly and admiring. He thought Callaghan almost always superb on television and a considerable vote-winner for the Labour Party. (Others can be superb and vote-losers!) He commanded the House of Commons with greater authority in speeches, statements and questions than anyone in senior ministerial office in my time, with the exception of pre-Profumo Macmillan and Iain Macleod.

For Crossman, Callaghan was an extremely interesting example of how important image was in modern politics. He had a good public image outside Parliament, his presence in Parliament was exactly right, and he had a good image inside the Treasury, and subsequently the Home Office in the sense that they liked him.

Where Crossman got exasperated with him was in Cabinet where, on occasion, he would return to his office and complain about the weak, vacillating and self-commiserating Chancellor. The same adjectives were not used in my hearing about him as the Home Secretary, though Crossman thought that, like himself, Callaghan was a little reactionary on some Home Office topics. Even when he was annoyed with Callaghan, and his alleged self-pity, he would end up by confessing that Callaghan had a very considerable grasp of his subject and a really remarkable power of putting it over.

Callaghan had good cause to get exasperated with Crossman. He had the bad habit of changing his mind on undertakings either because he persuaded himself that circumstances had changed, or else that the end justified the means. For instance, there was the father-and-mother of a row about the housing figures a couple of months after the April 1966 election victory. The number of housing starts was falling. Crossman, alarmed, went to the Treasury. When Crossman told the Cabinet that the Labour Government would face a major crisis in 1967, Callaghan replied: 'How do you know? My confident belief is that the private sector will start building suddenly this autumn, and we shall find ourselves with too many houses started.'

Crossman told me that he had responded that he would have to apply the regulator to the public sector. He then added that he had given his word to the Chancellor that if the private housing sector did suddenly get going, he would curb the public sector in the autumn or in the spring of 1968. 'So what did Jim say?' I asked. Oh, laughed Crossman, he said he knew the Minister of Housing well enough to tell the Cabinet that he would get out of doing anything of the kind when the time came. Crossman recounted to me that he showed a good deal of moral indignation – he was at his least attractive when he was showing moral indignation. I bet him that the moral indignation would sound a little synthetic to the Labour Cabinet. 'Well,' said Crossman, with breathtaking effrontery, 'yes, of course what Jim said was true. I would not dream of ever cutting back public housing. I was only having the row which every effective housing minister has had with his Chancellor!' 'But were you proper,' I said, 'in giving Jim Callaghan an undertaking, if you believe all this?' Crossman addressed me as an innocent, naive child. These battles had been going on since 1945. Nye Bevan fought the Treasury. Macmillan fought the Treasury. Now Crossman was fighting the Treasury. Crossman's justification of his behaviour was that Chancellors are bound to consider housing inflationary and to try to throttle back on housing Ministers. Housing Ministers, by their very nature, were bound to be regarded as hoggers getting more than their share of the national cake. But unless they did hog, they would simply be defeated by an alliance of the Chancellor and the other social service Ministers.

This conversation took place in the early hours of a June morning when the dawn was coming in. I expressed my opinion that Crossman's behaviour did not help the Labour Government, and made to go upstairs. I was recalled with a bellow. He wanted me to know he was jolly pleased that he had won a reputation in Cabinet as a bully and a thug, and that this was really to his credit. I'd better understand that a minister who did less then he did would be squeezed and pounded into subjection. I was not a member of that (or any other) Cabinet but I don't think Crossman was fair to them. He too easily found excuses for unjustified behaviour, to get his own way. An official of the Cabinet office, long since retired, told me that in his opinion Callaghan had every right to be aggrieved.

The officials in the Cabinet Office were wary of Crossman, and discreetly hostile. There were several reasons. The first was that when Crossman first became a Minister, he found minute-writing very difficult. Of course he was used to writing articles. But all his business he had done by word of mouth. He started writing minutes in longhand but the officials complained that they found his Greek-influenced, very unusual, angular handwriting, illegible. So he dictated minutes, and became increasingly aware of their importance. If he contented himself with merely saying things to officials, or phoning them, they could conveniently forget to pass on messages on which they did not want to take action. But the typed minute, dictated and signed by a senior minister, had got to be circularized. My impression is that central areas of the senior civil service were offended that Crossman did not trust them, and offended, too that he often gave the impression that anything the civil service wanted must *ipso facto* be wrong. Isaiah Berlin told me that ever since the 1920s Crossman had been quite unreasonable in his dislike of the civil service. In the presence of civil servants, I heard him quite often warn any historian who came to see him how little he could trust the Cabinet minutes to tell what really went on. All that minutes revealed was what went on according to the officials and official briefs. Curiously, Crossman's relations with his Cabinet colleagues improved after the summer of 1966, and in my opinion for a strange reason. He ceased in his own mind to be Harold Wilson's henchman. Partly, he grew in confidence, and had enough material for his books, if the worst came to the worst. But the cause in change of attitude was the Prime Minister's behaviour on the Seaman's strike of 1966, which Crossman found nauseating. Crossman thought that it was ridiculous to get into a fight with the seamen, who obviously had genuine grievances, and worse still if the Labour Government were to find itself fighting an open conflict with the seamen, against the protests of the TUC, and all for the sake of a prices and incomes policy which had fallen to pieces before the strike began.

Crossman was shocked to realize that Harold Wilson was hellbent on smashing the Seamen's Union. At a time when a Labour Government had just given huge concessions to doctors, judges and higher civil servants, Crossman thought that it was 'an ironical interpretation of a socialist incomes policy'. Crossman had the uncomfortable feeling that going down to the House of Commons and threatening to name Communists in the National Union of Seamen smacked altogether too much of the techniques of the late Senator Joseph McCarthy. From June 1966, Crossman's reservations about Wilson grew quietly and privately. After all, he did not believe in Leaderolatry, and saw the Leader and Prime Minister as emerging from the husk of an ordinary politician.

193

From the time of the seamen's strike, I could not help noticing that the length and frequency of the early, sometimes interminable morning telephone calls between 9 Vincent Square and 10 Downing Street declined – albeit Crossman was still to be appointed to the close position of Leader of the House. Crossman was fond of adumbrating the qualities required in a prime minister. Eleven years before anyone contemplated Mrs Thatcher in Number 10, Crossman was saying publicly (for example, at the Norwich Labour Party, 18 October 1968) that the qualities required for a prime minister are more often held by women than by men.

It was in the summer of 1966 that Crossman reconciled himself to the fact that Wilson would never give him the Foreign Office or Defence, areas in which he believed he was far more suited than the incumbents. I remember Crossman seizing on a malicious and probably apocryphal story that on being appointed to the Foreign Office early in 1965, Michael Stewart had turned to his wife, the distinguished Fabian pamphleteer and later life peer, and said, 'Well, Mary, we will now have to read those items of foreign news in the papers which we have never thought it necessary to read before.' Frankly, Crossman was jealous of Michael Stewart's reward, and the fact that Wilson appointed him as a safe pair of hands. (He disliked Patrick Gordon Walker, Wilson's initial choice, from Oxford days.) Curiously enough, though he had had a physical fight with George Brown in the Commons lobby in 1957, he approved of his appointment in 1966 as Foreign Secretary.

Of Denis Healey as Defence Secretary, Crossman was deeply critical and not only, in my opinion, because he thought he would have done the job better. He conceded his qualification as the brave beach-master at Anzio. He conceded also that Healey was heavyweight, 'and if Callaghan gets too old might be your best choice as successor to Wilson.' Crossman admired Healey's qualities as a thug and bruiser, and would have liked to see them deployed in a home ministry such as Education or Min Tech. What Crossman could not stand was Healey's penchant, as he saw it, for trying to be the British equivalent of the US Defence Secretary Robert McNamara – the guy 'who is briefed on all the top-level secrets, and who can mock and deride any thoughts put forward by his amateur colleagues'. Crossman observed that the supercilious, sneering expert would always be in danger in a British Cabinet – and Denis Healey got his deserts when the Cabinet decided to cancel the British purchase of F-111 aircraft from the USA in 1968. Crossman was incensed that the Cabinet had originally been persuaded to endorse the purchase, because it was essential to our position east of Suez, and then, in 1968, after the decision to withdraw from east of Suez, it suddenly became essential for the defence of Europe. Unlike most other people, Crossman thought that Healey was putty in the hands of the Chiefs of Staff.

Crossman ascribed his exclusion from the Foreign Office or Defence to his Israeli past. He regarded it as a decision of fate, and the truth was that he rather liked having difficult decisions made for him by fate.

The massive briefing provided to Defence and Foreign Office ministers by their departments and the Chiefs of Staff was part of a wider problem. Crossman had increasing doubts whether the massive briefing that ministers now got for Cabinet led to good government. In the days before copying machines, and certainly before typewriters, ministers did a lot more for themselves in the way of thinking. Apart from a handful of Chequers conferences, no thinking sessions took place in the first four years of the Labour Government. It was because Ministers had become so 'ministerial' that Crossman thought that they had appallingly ineffective discussion of great social issues.

Crossman always found time for wide political reading. Perusing the second volume (1967) of Churchill's biography, covering his period as Home Secretary in the Asquith government, Crossman realized that the 'marvellous thing then was how much Ministers normally thought out their own policy, talked things out among themselves and wrote their own state papers'. In the Cabinet in which he sat, Crossman said that he and his colleagues did not have the time because they were 'so overweighted with departmental responsibilities', and with parroting aloud drafts prepared for them by civil servants. As a result, Crossman came to believe that the 'policy-making functions' of ministers were 'virtually eliminated'. One of Crossman's remedies was that the Cabinet should have some social life. I shall never forget his consternation when I told him one evening on returning to 9 Vincent Square in February 1968 that Colin Jackson, MP, and I had organized a dinner for a score of MPs under forty, at which we had entertained Harold Wilson for two and a half hours in the St Stephen's Tavern upper room, opposite the House of Commons. 'If he can (expletive) find the time to dine with you and your friends, why can't he find an evening for the Cabinet?' The following day he complained to Roy Jenkins and others about prime-ministerial priorities. Crossman realized that friendship at the top was difficult, given the patronage aspect of British government — but he also believed that Cabinet government required some lubrication.

With Roy Jenkins, he did value his relations; and his settled conviction was, I believe, one of genuine regard. In moments of frustration with the Chancellor, he saw Jenkins as really a literary man, sometimes an indolent man, who was overconcerned with his own image. But then Crossman thought that by 1969, members of the Cabinet had become too tired, too absorbed in their own interests, to feel any great collective responsibility. I noticed that with Roy Jenkins, Crossman would often put on the air of being reasonableness itself. Yet, as he himself recognized, when he was reasonableness itself, he could be at his most maddening.

In the last year of his membership of the Cabinet, Crossman wondered aloud to me whether he really ought not to resign. His life at Prescote, the farm, the books he had to write, and his son and daughter, Patrick and Virginia, all combined to keep him aware of the possibility of resigning from the Cabinet. He said that he acknowledged that his feelings about politics were becoming remote from those of most members of the Coventry Labour Party, who worked hard to make him an MP. With their desire to see the Labour Party doing well and their natural partisanship, Crossman felt that many party members would be put off by his relish for being in the Cabinet and his simultaneous detachment. He pondered on how much of the emotions and ideals of the Party he still felt after five to six years in a British Cabinet. Crossman was sensitive to this sort of question being asked by Labour Party members: 'What has Dick Crossman got for us? Are we sure that he is still in the Labour Party? He is rich by our standards. He lives in a beautiful house in a lovely part of Oxfordshire. He has a swimming pool. He gets expensive and elegant new furniture made. Has he floated away from the Labour Party? Isn't he in the Cabinet as a professional politician? Is there only a vestigial remnant of former Socialist fire in that man's belly?'

I remember telling him that he had a duty to put these worrying questions into his diary quite openly — which he did. His reply to me to his nagging questions was that he knew he was near the end but that he was no more detached than Roy Jenkins or Tony Crosland. He said to me that intellectually he continued to share the emotions of the Left. The problem was that it was in his personality that he was getting more comfortable and more detached, and that was what put people off in

196

the Labour Party, particularly in the milieu of young careerist MPs and their research assistants. 'When they meet me,' he said to me sadly, 'I am frightening and argumentative, yet remote and disconcerting.'

Personally, I do not think Crossman's self-doubts on this score were necessary. What is true is that with age and a troublsome phlebitis-ridden leg, he became more subdued about the whole gamut of Labour policy. But he set himself certain goals in the social services which would have engaged the enthusiasm of many Labour people.

If the election had been called in October 1970 or March 1971, Crossman's achievement would have been the more considerable. He never really forgave Wilson for calling the election, not even taking time to consider the all-but-finished measures in the Department of Health and Social Security, most of which would not, had they been on the statute book, have been unscrambled by the incoming Conservative government. It is with a certain sadness that I address the essential process of Crossman's deteriorating relationship with Wilson. James Callaghan writes, in *Time and Chance*, on the occasion of Harold Wilson's retiral from the premiership in April 1976:

> Except for our differences over Barbara Castle's proposals for trade union reform, he and I had worked closely together since 1964, and during my early days as Chancellor of the Exchequer when sterling was under great strain he was a considerable strength and comfort.
>
> When we were in difficulties his sagacity and sangfroid were beyond doubt, as was his kindliness to his colleagues. There had been a period when he allowed Barbara Castle, Dick Crossman and George Wigg, all of whom suffered from the belief that politics was a conspiracy, to influence him too much, but in later years he had broken free from them and I suddenly realised how much I had got used to him being there to shoulder the final responsibility, to feeling able to turn to him naturally for a second opinion and for well-informed advice. Now in a short time he would be gone, and the era that had begun in the 1960s with the triumvirate of Harold Wilson, George Brown and myself would be at an end. Only I would be left. Three weeks later, on the day I became Prime Minister, my first impulse was to sit down in the study which had been Harold's and write him a letter of appreciation and grateful thanks.

James Callaghan does not pinpoint any exact moment when Crossman's influence began to wane. The trouble started, I think, back in the summer of 1965, when Crossman was dismayed to find that Wilson did

197

not see his job as actually launching a strategy so much as carrying out a manifesto. Out of seventy-three or some such number, he would tick off the number of things which Labour was doing. As my witty and astringent roommate, Ray Fletcher, MP for Ilkeston, used to put it: 'This Government is being mercilessly flayed not for the abandonment of pledges but for carrying them out.'

Crossman believed that from the point of view of the British electorate, technical promise-keeping was quite unimportant. What mattered was strategy. Yet, Crossman told me, he was on the horns of a dilemma. If he did try to intervene in order to get a strategy to meet people's needs, involving an incomes guarantee, proper housing policies and a central coherent drive, he would be accused of splitting the Cabinet and his effort would be seen as anti-Wilson. The only avenue of avoiding being anti-Wilson was to go to him privately and let him either take or reject advice. If Crossman took an open initiative in Cabinet, it would have been seen as challenging his leadership. That was one of the eternal problems of the Labour Party. It is difficult to put any views strongly without being accused of factional strife. Then for another three years relations with Wilson remained close, if dented by the seamen's strike. It was as a member of the Overseas Policy and Defence Committee of the Cabinet that Crossman became terribly dissatisfied. He knew he was often behaving frivolously, and that his stock contribution consisted of macabre jokes.

Harold Wilson, Crossman thought, had one of the most unphilosophical minds in the world. But much more serious was Harold Wilson's changing attitude towards the Labour Party and the trade unions. Do you think we have to worry about the Trades Union Congress? Don't you think we can safely disregard the TUC? The Government's standing with the public will not be affected by the TUC, will it, Dick? – these were the prime-ministerial thoughts that really bothered Crossman.

In 1968, Crossman realized with a shudder that Wilson did not any longer really feel himself representing the Labour Movement. Unlike the Harold of old, he no longer really cared about the feelings of the trade-union leaders. Crossman began to wonder about his loyalty to the party. He had become 'de-partied', an occupant of 10 Downing Street who merely wanted to run things well. He had come to care about being Prime Minister, about politics, about power; he had leftist loyalties, but they had been battered by his relations within the party. Crossman said to a number of people – indiscreetly – that Wilson was in danger of becoming a Lloyd-George figure, detached from the party, feeling not much loyalty or affection for the organization, but deeply resenting the nuisance it caused him. For Crossman, there was nothing left of Wilson as a leader or a leftist. He was simply just a figure posturing there in the middle, with no strategy, except to stay as Prime Minister for as long as possible.

I myself did not go along with all these strictures on Wilson. Where I did think that Crossman was right was in observing that being cocooned in Downing Street, living above the shop, did Wilson no favours. In his 1974–6 tenure, after Crossman's death, Wilson was, to my agreeable surprise, a much better, more relaxed prime minister than he had been in 1967–70. Perhaps it was partly because Mary Wilson got her way and cajoled Harold Wilson into living in Lord North Street, and going into Number 10 as an office.

By the spring of 1969, Crossman thought that there were only two members who could stand up to Wilson – himself, because his loyalty was not in dispute, and James Callaghan, precisely because his loyalty was in dispute. In Crossman's view he himself had an utterly independent position, downright and outspoken. I had grave doubts, and thought he had been marginalized from central decisions and left to rule his roost at the Elephant and Castle. Wilson wanted to run a foreign policy, in Crossman's view, in Nigeria and elsewhere, the main purpose of which was to intervene, to make Britain look active, and above all to enable the Prime Minister himself to shine as a negotiator. Since Crossman was sympathetic, during the Nigerian civil war of 1967–70, to the separatist Ibos of Biafra, and I supported Wilson and Stewart who believed in maintaining the integrity of Nigeria, it is perhaps not surprising that I should feel Crossman was being unduly harsh on Wilson.

By the autumn of 1969, Crossman had despaired of Wilson. He thought the Government was sustained only by good departmental ministers such as Barbara Castle, Jim Callaghan, Denis Healey, Tony Crosland, and himself. As for Wilson, he had revealed that he was interested only in his own personal success, and Crossman expressed doubts as to whether he was ever a natural Cabinet minister. Crossman always did think that Wilson had not been much good as Attlee's President of the Board of Trade (1947–51). Crossman told me that if Wilson had not resigned with Nye Bevan and John Freeman over health charges, he would have been moved out of the Labour Cabinet to a lesser government post. Whether it is true that Attlee would have done this, I do not know. The point is Crossman believed it.

EIGHTEEN

The Wider World

In 1957, Crossman was interested in relations with Italy, and as a member of the International Committee of the NEC was involved, following on from the 1947 split in the Italian Socialist party, in attempts to back the left-wing Nenni Socialists and Nye Bevan against the right-wing Saragat Socialists and Hugh Gaitskell. When the situation became tense, he poured water on the fires by appealing to his colleagues not to split the British Labour Party over the issue of how to unify the Italians.

In August 1958, Crossman went on an extended solo visit to Russia and China. One of his memories was the discovery that there was a reason for the shortage of fruit in large areas of the Soviet Union. Stalin had imposed a tax on fruit trees. The consequence was that millions of peasants had simply burned their fruit trees as firewood rather than pay the tax. Crossman learned that one of Khruschev's first acts was to remit this tax and thereby to make it possible for fruit to be grown widely in Russia. Another memory was of being informed that the average Russian read twenty times as much English literature as the average Englishman, and that between the 1917 Revolution and 1952, forty-five billion translations of English books had been sold in Russia (nearly one book per adult per month throughout, on average). For Crossman, the paramount fact about Russia was that between 1941 and 1945 they had lost twenty-five million dead, had sustained the siege of Leningrad and much else, and would never trust the West in the light of German rearmament. He also took the line, in relation to human rights, that we could not possibly lecture Mother Russia on what to do with her own nationals.

There was a tough streak in Crossman about life and death. All right, Harold Macmillan and Thomas Brimelow may have had a shrewd suspicion that their decision to return Cossacks from Italy and Yugoslavia at the end of the war might have been sending them to their death. But these same Cossacks had co-operated with the Germans, and deserved what they got.

His five weeks in China were a source of tremendous exhilaration. The experience made him more interested and excited about life in general. Thirteen years later, when he was editing the *New Statesman* in 1971, Crossman was pathetically pleased when I was able to report, after I returned from Mao's China, where I had been accompanying a Scottish Council for Trade and Industry delegation, that Chum-wen-Chin, head of the American and European Section of the Chinese Foreign Office remembered his visit well, though the Culture Revolution had intervened.

In August 1960, Harold Wilson, not then likely to be leader, expressed the view that Crossman should go to the Presidency of the Board of Trade in a Labour government, as his talents suited Common-Market negotiating. Crossman was deeply sceptical about Harold Macmillan's attempt to enter the Common Market. He believed entry was a gamble and an unjustified gamble, though 'the old gambler' had been right once before. In Algiers in 1943, Crossman along with Colonel James Bowes-Lyon, had been sitting in Macmillan's office. A telegram had arrived from Churchill, ordering Macmillan to alter tactics in an important area of his responsibilities in North Africa. This would, in effect, have negated months of successful work. Crossman and Bowes-Lyon anticipated that Macmillan would obey the telegram from the Prime Minister. Not one bit of it. With the wry comment, 'He was wrong about Gallipoli,' Macmillan crunched up the telegram, and consigned it to the waste-paper basket, and continued the discussion. Crossman and Bowes-Lyon were hugely impressed. Crossman's reiterated feeling was that a man who can do that to Churchill at the height of his wartime power might even get the better of General de Gaulle.

Crossman thought that the day-to-day negotiator, Ted Heath in his prime, burbled along in his reports to the Commons like the most bromidic kind of junior Foreign Office Minister.

By the end of the 1960s and Wilson's ill-fated attempt to join the

European Community, Crossman believed that Britain should work out its terms, soberly and objectively, on agriculture, the sugar interests, Australia and New Zealand, and on the balance of payments and assistance which would come from the EEC. In 1960–1 he was for the policy of standing aside, and waiting for the Government to commit itself on the Common Market, instead of embarking on the kind of self-rending discussion in which the Labour Party was indulging itself on nuclear weapons. Indeed, since April 1958 Crossman's life, like that of many other people in the Labour Party, had been gyrating around nuclear weapons. He recognized that it was the greatest single issue facing the country but equally one to which, in his view, the Labour Party tended to commit itself with an extraordinary combination of irresponsibility and prejudice. Crossman's attitude revealed itself in his frequent choice of the word 'palaver' to describe the row on nuclear weapons. In December 1960, Crossman was one of the ringleading abstentionists among sixty-eight Labour MPs who defied the party whip, and expressed opposition to the establishment of a US Polaris submarine base at Holy Loch in the Firth of Clyde, north of Dunoon.

Another abiding interest was Germany. Ever since its foundation in 1949, Crossman had been an active member of the Deutsch-Englische Gesellschaft. He was a favourite of its ebullient secretary, Lilo Milch-sack, who was, partly on Crossman's initiative, created a DCMG in 1972 for her services to Anglo-German understanding.

Crossman's main contribution to the thinking of Keep Left, the party pressure group founded in 1947, had been in the analysis of the problems created by German rearmament. He took enormous trouble over getting to know the members of the Foreign Press Association in London, and in particular, those from papers such as the *Frankfurter Allgemeine Zeitung* and the *Süddeutscher Zeitung*. Crossman also made a point of knowing successive ambassadors of the Communist German Democratic Republic. Poland, too, was a continuing interest, ever since he had been interested in Polish planning ideas by the distinguished economist Oscar Lange in 1956.

As I have pointed out elsewhere, I found it difficult to focus Crossman's mind on taking any Cabinet action on East-of-Suez policy before the 1966 general election – or on any other aspect of foreign affairs. However, there was one area in which Crossman became more and more curious and suspicious, though he deemed it wise not to be indiscreetly inquisitive. He was simply raging before Christmas 1966 on the extent to which he thought Wilson had got himself 'in hock to LBJ'. His view was that Wilson, above all, wanted to be esteemed in Washington, and simply adored hearing 'Hail to the Chief' played for him on the White House lawn. 'Wilson has simply given L.B.J. every damn commitment he is asking for!' In the cold light of the following morning, Crossman forbade me to refer to the subject to anyone. Reliance on President Lyndon Johnson was a peculiarly Wilsonian touch. Crossman believed that Wilson and James Callaghan had committed us, head over heels, to the Americans, and more deeply than any previous British government of any colour. Furthermore, he was told by his friend, the *New York Times* columnist James Reston, that Wilson as shadow foreign secretary in 1961 had made pledges to President John Kennedy about maintaining British bases east of Suez. In my opinion, it is all very well for Harold Wilson, James Callaghan and assorted commentators to tag Crossman with the label of conspirator, when in a real sense others conspired clandestinely to ensure that Britain remained a major power and played a role in the Far East which we as a country had long ceased to be able to afford.

During these early years in government, Crossman shuttled between criticism of the Wilson–Brown–Callaghan foreign policy access, and loyalty. We had a bitter row in early February 1967. It was the occasion of the visit of Soviet Prime Minister Alexi Kosygin. He addressed both Houses in the Princes' Chamber of the House of Lords, and was critical of British policy on Vietnam.

That evening, I returned to Vincent Square in a bad temper with Crossman who had missed important votes, and told him that it was bad manners sitting next to Kosygin and grimacing during his speech. And warming to my subject, 'I'd better tell you that on this Vietnam issue most of us backbenchers are much more on the side of the Russian Prime Minister, than on that of the British Prime Minister.'

Crossman blew his top. 'What on earth can you mean? You can't be on Kosygin's side. He's a totalitarian apparatchik and his aim is to divide Britain and cause trouble. Apart from that, he's not going to give us a single inch. He will only gain from the propaganda storm he makes because it will undermine party resistance and extract a softer line from Harold Wilson and George Brown!'

I told him he did not understand the impact of white troops in Asia. He was even more angry. So was I. In such circumstances, the only thing to do was to go upstairs, put on my track suit and go running round Vincent Square. I forgot my key, and Crossman relented – just – to the extent of opening the door, which saved me from going back and dossing down somewhere in the House of Commons. The following morning nothing was said. The following week he apologized and said that an MP, independent of me, had confirmed what I said about Vietnam. From February 1967, ever-increasing doubts about LBJ and Wilson on Vietnam set it.

On 28 June 1967, I arranged for Singapore PM Lee Kuan Yew to see Crossman. He was almost spoiling for an argument, not least because he had heard so much about Lee Kuan Yew and his Cambridge double-first in law from Harold Wilson. Crossman suspected that he ran rings round British Foreign Office ministers, and 'persuaded them that we must stay much longer in Singapore than we would naturally do and that our withdrawal must be extended over a decade'. It was received wisdom in the upper echelons of the Labour Party that Harry Lee was 'the only social-democratic Prime Minister East of Suez', and that we could not let him down. Crossman let him talk, and soon the clash of arms came. 'These speeches,' Crossman mildly observed, 'you've made to my colleagues have made an immense impression on them!' Lee Kuan Yew purred with pleasure. It was true. Then my heart went into my mouth. 'I personally am concerned to resist your moral blackmail and look after the concerns of this country. It is in the interest of Great Britain to get out of the Far East as fast as we possibly can. Our presence may be useful to you but it isn't useful to us. We mustn't have a strategy beyond our economic strength.' Even Lee Kuan Yew did not know what was hitting him. No Englishman had ever spoken to him like that before, he stammered out, as Crossman got into his most forensic stride. Eventually Lee said: 'How can you talk like that? How can you create that kind of damage in our part of the world?' Crossman responded, 'What's the minimum time we need to get out?' 'Five years,' said Harry Lee. Like a Chicago attorney, Crossman said, 'Thank you. That's what I wanted to learn from you – your view on our withdrawal!' Lee Kuan Yew was obviously kicking himself for having conceded a five-year deadline. He obviously thought that clever bastard Crossman had lured him into saying it, and that he had delivered himself to the devil. At this precise point, there was a Commons division along the passage from the then Leader of the House's room. I returned after voting but before Crossman, who was waylaid by an MP in the lobby. Harry Lee was very, very perturbed. How could I work for so aggressive a man?

'Well,' I said, 'he's rather like you are, yourself!' He laughed – wanly. Crossman returned. 'Of course, we should try to avoid hurting friends like you abroad, but what we really need is a rapid, ruthless withdrawal.' Thereupon Crossman took my breath away by extolling the virtues of Attlee's getting out of India and Ernie Bevin's getting the troops out of Greece and Turkey at the end of the war – examples which, coming from Crossman, were pretty rich! He seriously believed (and rightly in my view) that the only big withdrawals which really worked were those that were sudden and abrupt.

[**A digression.** When he knew that he was dying, just before Christmas 1973, Crossman said to me, 'England will never get troops out of Ireland in your lifetime unless there is a big, sudden abrupt withdrawal!']

Lee Kuan Yew told Crossman several times, 'Well, please, whatever you do, do not announce the date for withdrawal.' 'Yes,' said Crossman, 'but in that case, Britain ought to leave much quicker, not much slower.' When I gave Lee Kuan Yew dinner that evening to meet four of my contemporary MPs, he clearly realized that there were people in the Cabinet who were not as soft and pliable in his hands as Harold Wilson and George Brown. Lee Kuan Yew told us with force that from his perception the British people did not want to surrender their world rule; and that if the Crossman attitude prevailed, it would be harder, not easier, for a Labour Government to be re-elected!

But the truth is that whatever he said in the *New Statesman* after 1970, Crossman did not try very hard at all on changing East-of-Suez policy. Withdrawal from Lee Kuan Yew's Singapore was not popular in the Cabinet, and still less popular in its Overseas Policy and Defence subcommittee. Nor did he do very much about cutting down on the hugely expensive Malta Mediterranean naval base. Nor should we pretend that the *'End of Empire'* thesis, propounded in a book of that title in 1959 by John Strachey was universally popular in the Parliamentary Labour Party of the day. They simply did not want what Strachey (borrowing a phrase from Trotsky) called the 'Belgianization of Britain' – that is to say, becoming a country which turns its back on a world role and devotes herself to narrow commercial prosperity. I vividly remember the bitterness against the East-of-Suez rebels by some of my trade-union Scottish colleagues. It took the form of Tom Steele, right-wing Labour MP for West Dumbartonshire, telling Crossman on 28 February 1967 that even some of the loyalists in the Parliamentary

Party would abstain along with the left-wingers on defence to teach him a lesson for allowing indiscipline – and they did.

My diary for 7 March 1967 records that Crossman told me that he had participated in a 'sensible discussion' at the Overseas Policy and Defence (OPD) committee of the Cabinet on what on earth to do about the fag-ends of Empire, such as Hong Kong, Gibraltar, Gan (in the Maldives) and the Falkland Islands. He had tried to get some idea of the net costs but figures were not forthcoming. He said there was no point in his making a fuss since no one present, least of all the Prime Minister, showed any inclination to want to pull out. Hong Kong could be very ugly, once the Chinese had come together after the Cultural Revolution, and they were free to deal with outside issues. Wilson was not going down in history as the Lord North who gave up Gibraltar. Healey said Gan (which was eventually given up in 1976) was essential, and there were no problems of natives. But there was no reason for keeping the Falkland Islands, and Crossman imagined that an agreement would soon be reached with Argentina to share costs. Yes, the problem seemed to be about money. But Crossman's mind had not been on Port Stanley, but on the altogether more pressing issue of Manny Shinwell, George Wigg, and the liberalization of party discipline. If the minds of OPD that day had been concentrated on their business rather than on other political preoccupations ... that must be one of the great 'Ifs' of history! No Falklands War!

The Overseas Policy and Defence Committee of the Cabinet returned to the subject on 29 May 1968. This time Crossman's mind was on Hong Kong, and in particular the prospect of mass immigration from Hong Kong to the UK. In that I-jolly-well-won't-let-you-forget-what-you've-done mood, he said to me aggressively – 'As a result of the great triumph of Barnett, Heffer, Sheldon, yourself and company, in getting us out of Singapore, we are now putting another couple of battalions of troops into Hong Kong, plus fighter aircraft, frigates, minelayers, minesweepers, an entire bloody fleet, because as a result of your hard work, Hong Kong has got to be able to defend itself in its isolation!' I was annoyed, and asked him what any of these luminaries in the Overseas Policy and Defence Committee actually proposed to do if military action were taken by a thousand million Chinese. 'Oh,' said Crossman, 'I asked them, "You may or may not have a justifiable short-term policy, but what are you going to do about our long-term policy for withdrawal?"' That had flummoxed them, he claimed. Michael

Stewart, as Foreign Secretary, had told him that there was a long-term policy for withdrawal and a special Hong Kong Committee was at work on it. Crossman complained to me that something really important was being discussed not at the official Cabinet Committee but in a Special Committee which he knew nothing about, as Leader of the House, Lord President of the Council, and Chairman of the Legislation Committee of the Cabinet.

I was rather critical of Crossman at the time about his attitude to these issues, as I thought he had got into a rather infantile, silly sulk, and the frame of mind which says 'You bloody well won't allow me near the Foreign Office, so you can stew in your own juice and make your own mistakes!' In retrospect, I am even more critical. He could perfectly easily have talked seriously to Michael Stewart and other colleagues. On foreign policy, in my personal opinion, having been snubbed in an area of genuine expertise, Crossman was far too quick to leap on to a high horse – to the detriment of posterity!

I wish to heaven in May 1968 that he had given his mind to the second item that was on the OPD agenda – a paper prepared by officials on what we were to do about Ascension Island, Easter Island, the Falkland Islands, Gibraltar and the Seychelles. Crossman told me he was exasperated. The document purported to deal with each case, one by one, providing apparently incontrovertible reasons for remaining in each place, and increasing the amount of facilities and the number of troops available for action in case of emergency. I would have had more sympathy with Crossman's exasperation if he had given any indication that he had fought his corner. Instead he lamented that there was no recommendation to wind up our involvement. By 1968 he was too inclined to wring his hands about foreign-policy issues where he was (justifiably) unhappy! I have never been in government myself, and therefore can be chided with not knowing how awkward it can be for even a roving Lord President, let alone a departmental Minister, to meddle in foreign affairs. It is not only with hindsight that I believe Crossman should have applied himself more seriously.

Just before Christmas 1967, Harold Holt, the Australian Prime Minister, was drowned. Harold Wilson went to one of those new international working funerals and got his three-quarters-of-an-hour interview with Lyndon Johnson. However, LBJ's main concern was to talk to the Pope about mediation in Vietnam. This confirmed Crossman in his view that there was no role for Wilson or Brown as mediators.

I used to keep Crossman informed about what transpired at the Foreign Affairs Group of the Parliamentary Labour Party, and reported to him that a great parliamentarian, John Mendelson, had made a speech asking why Britain did not back U Thant and the United Nations rather than uncritically backing the United States. I was curious as to what George Brown, the Foreign Secretary, would say, so I had pen at the ready. In his stentorian boom, he told his back-bench colleagues: 'I have an understanding in Moscow so that any moment when we can get a breakthrough I can act as intermediary. The only basis on which I can stay in play is if the communists in Peking and Hanoi believe that I can deliver the Americans. The US trusts me not to deliver them unless I can get something suitable in return. I could deliver Johnson in two minutes flat from here if I could get something from Hanoi. I am the one chap who has influence with the Americans. The communists do not ask me to cut myself off from the Americans; the Russians ask me to keep in contact with the United States and keep our association. It is only nice chaps like you who want us to dissociate.' Open-mouthed with wonderment, I told Crossman what had exactly been said at the Foreign Affairs group. Grief! Crossman shook his head – he had always known that George Brown indulged in poetic licence when he was talking off the record at Labour Party groups. But this 'preposterous tripe' was out of *Alice in Wonderland*. The mind boggled at the picture encapsulated by the notion of George Brown delivering L.B.J. in two minutes – flat, no less!

Czechoslovakia, too, was one of Crossman's special interests. In August 1968, he was thrilled to make a Hyde Park mass rally speech in support of Mr Dubček, switching back to Czechoslovakia as a subject he knew very well, a country he knew quite well, and a part of the world he had been thinking about for years. With a touch of bitterness which was not characteristic of him, by 1969 Crossman was ruefully regretting that he had said to himself for over four years, 'I must leave foreign affairs to Harold Wilson, Michael Stewart, George Brown and Jim Callaghan, as they know all about it.' In Crossman's later view, 1969–70, when his influence on Wilson had waned, they knew nothing about it. He confided to me that there was a feeling of resentment about being kept out of foreign affairs, growing in him, which he had long suppressed. What really annoyed him was the priggish response, as he saw it, of Wilson and Stewart to De Gaulle's overtures on meaningful

West European co-operation, in the face of what was taking place in Eastern Europe.

There was a particular and rather bizarre event which sparked off Crossman's most deep-seated anger at his exclusion from foreign affairs. This was the occasion of the visit on 25 February 1969 of President Nixon. Crossman described to me what occurred. Piqued at not being one of those invited to dinner, Crossman arrived at Number 10 at 9.30 p.m. and after an hour or so there was a sort of pseudo-Cabinet meeting. Crossman said he started by being embarrassed beyond belief by this movie-Cabinet. Wilson asked Nixon to hold forth on the problems of youth and race, and in Crossman's view he was surprisingly good on the theme of idealism. There was nothing novel about it, but Crossman judged that Nixon was hugely more impressive than his television image. He was more vigorous and fresher, even after a tiring day, than the picture Crossman had of him.

Above all, he made a far better impression on Crossman than a liberal like ex-Vice-President Hubert Humphrey, who had recently harangued him for three-quarters of an hour on the need to support Lyndon Johnson over Vietnam. Crossman heaved a sigh of relief that Nixon did not appear to have the doctrinaire ideology of the anti-Communist crusading Democrats like Dean Acheson or Walter Rostow – whom I met in his White House basement office in 1967, and whom Crossman found it particularly hard to take. Like Wilson, Crossman said he took a fancy to Nixon for his 'lack of doctrinaireness' and his evident pragmatism. Wilson called on various members of the Cabinet who had not been invited to dinner to speak. After contributions from James Callaghan, Ted Short and Dick Marsh, as the youngest member of the Cabinet, Crossman as the oldest member was asked to give a philosophical wind-up. All I talked to later, friend and foe, who were present, told me that Crossman absolutely excelled himself, and was at his superb best. Crossman told me he opened his contribution by describing how so many people talked endlessly about youth and revolution; of course, we had to discover a philosophy to satisfy youth – this was, according to Crossman, the conventional wisdom. But he then told Nixon and his colleagues why he was an old sceptic: the actual numbers of youth in revolt were in actual fact 'a tiny minority of university students', with precious little philosophy; they indulged themselves by wallowing in an anti-philosophy. The important point about the students of the late 1960s was that they were 'sentimentalists with no understanding of power'. In this, Crossman pointed out, they differed from their predecessors in previous generations of students, who seized all too clearly that politics was about power; many of them had not only read, but had grasped what Marx was all about. The 1960s students had neither read Marx nor understood him. They were under the delusion that politics was simply about protest, and that was why they were deep-down so toothless. Crossman then told me how suddenly an analogy occurred to him – 1968 was 1848 all over again. It was 'the year of unsuccessful revolutions', when the Establishments, staggering from body-blow after body-blow, hit back. I told Crossman to put on paper at once what he had actually said to Nixon. He wrote down: 'It was the crushing of Czechoslovakian modern liberal communism which was the really characteristic event of last year. Possibly de Gaulle's crushing of student revolt in particular, and liberalism in general, in France, was almost as important. In the United States, if I may say so bluntly, Mr President, the East Coast Establishment rose up, and you took it over.' Coming from many people, the last sentence would have jarred, and bordered on rudeness to a guest. Crossman in full academic flight was a phenomenon which did not give great offence.

Crossman concluded on the theme that even in Britain and America, the central problem of the hour was the achievement of a delicate balance combining the general growth of liberty with, on the other hand, the authority and the efficiency of the executive. Crossman then expatiated on the British attempts to strike this balance of the Select Committees and Government, and pointed out to Mr Nixon how the 'Members of the Congressional committees could not care very much about you, as their present and futures depend on their fellow congressmen, while government members of Select Committees in Britain depend on him [with a nod towards Harold Wilson] for their futures in politics.' Crossman warmed to his theme. 'Even so, our Select Committees are turning against us!' At this there was the general ribald merriment that Crossman often sparked off. Nixon was entranced, and said with charm, 'I'll swap you my Professor Marcuse any day of the week, if you will exchange me your Professor Crossman!'

(Professor Herbert Marcuse was well known to Nixon as a professor of philosophy at the San Diego branch of the University of his native California. He was educated at the Universities of Berlin and Freiberg and went to America in 1934, later to become a professor at Brandeis University. His books *Reason and Revolution* (1941), *One-Dimensional*

211

Man (1965, a title which suggests near-total innumeracy), and *The Ethics of Revolution* (1966), had won him a considerable following. Leszek Kolakowski has described him as 'the ideologist of obscurantism'.)

Crossman said that he thought that his Cabinet colleagues had been rather proud of him, as he had helped put on a good show, even if it was a bit of an Oxford turn, to gratify the Prime Minister's desire to head a Cabinet of some real intellectual distinction.

The following Monday evening, I found Crossman purring with pleasure. He had been to the farewell party for the US Ambassador, David Bruce, and his wife Evangeline. That 'tall woodland creature' Evangeline Bruce had heaped praise on him for the impression he had made on her guest, Richard Nixon. Her husband, a stiff New England banker and veteran American Ambassador to Bonn and Paris as well as London, took Crossman aside: 'You are the most popular man in the Cabinet with Nixon. The President could talk of nothing except you and what you said at that famous late-night Cabinet. My congratulations! You can go and visit him in the White House whenever you want.'

Crossman felt sad and deprived from that point on, almost to the point of melancholy, that he could not tread on the international stage. With his background, and his international journalism, he believed he would have been a great success. So do I. During the years in his political wilderness, he continued to be interested in Germany. Erika apart, he had been passionately interested in the Weimar Republic of 1919–33. I think Crossman was drawn by political violence: Weimar; Palestine – he would say, 'I'm very much an internal Israeli,' or 'I was an internal German,' i.e. a Social Democrat, confronted by Fascists and Communists.

Crossman had a lot of comings-and-goings with the German Embassy in London. I once told him that my father and mother had met Ribbentrop and taken an instant dislike. 'So did I,' said Crossman. His main contact was Werner Kissling, a Second Secretary. Kissling, by chance, was the man who had given the immediate order for one of the arrests of Hitler in the 1920s. So as soon as Hitler came to power he sought asylum in London and went to Cambridge as an anthropologist. I knew him as a child when he came to stay at Finlay Mackenzie's fishing hotel at Lochboisdale, while he was studying the Black Houses of South Uist. Kissling warmly approved of Crossman, which would not have been the case if Crossman had ever been pro-Nazi. Crossman was a stirrer-upper by nature. Weimar, Palestine and Cultural-Revolution China suited him down to the ground as consuming interests.

After the war, Crossman was one of the moving spirits in initiating the Königswinter Conferences of the Deutsche-Englische Gesellschafft, and had a warm working friendship with Lilo Milchsack, organizer of these important annual spring Anglo-German get-togethers.

I noticed that when he was Minister of Housing and he might be forgiven for turning to the home news when the morning papers came through the door, he did nothing of the kind. He turned to the foreign news, to read about the internal troubles in Poland or Eastern Europe, or pieces on the cultural revolution in China.I think he was hooked on internal political violence in places which he knew personally. He actually liked, adored socially and politically turbulent situations.

I can just imagine Communist Premier Chou En-lai's intellectuals being entranced. I arranged a dinner for Crossman to meet Singapore Premier Lee Kuan Yew, with whom I had had a humdinger of an argument the previous year over a sixteen-course dinner in Singapore. Crossman, from the moment he sat down at table, thought Lee as a double-first Cambridge lawyer was fair game, and before the soup had arrived had burst out, 'I know I'm talking to Harold Wilson's favourite foreigner, but...' Until long after the coffee was cold, the argument went on, unabated. I reprint Lee's nice letter.* But, he went on BBC1's *Panorama* and said in the course of the interview: 'If I thought Britain was governed by men like Tam Dalyell, then Singapore would have no hope: but since I know that Britain is governed by better men, such as Harold Wilson ... all will be well between us!' My constituents were amusedly annoyed!

In August–September 1958, Crossman had gone on a private *Daily Mirror* visit to Russia and China. He got on well with the Chinese, he said, because he found them very serious people.

*   PRIME MINISTER,
                                                               SINGAPORE.
                                                               7th July, 1967.

Dear Tam,
        Thank you for arranging the dinner with such stimulating company.
        That we disagreed on the means of how Britain should achieve a credit balance in her East of Suez balance of payments is only natural.

But the fact that we can get on to the same wave length and use similar vocabulary makes things so much easier.

My best wishes to all our friends that evening. I shall read their contributions to the debate on East of Suez with great interest.

With all best wishes,
Yours sincerely
Harry

Mr. Tam Dalyell, M.P.,
House of Commons.
London, S.W.1.

NINETEEN
In Parliament

Looking back with the advantage of hindsight, Crossman's career as a pivotal figure in the government came to an end in July 1967 when he irrevocably made up his mind not to seek re-election as a member of the National Executive Committee (NEC) of the Labour party. It was a great political mistake for a man who wished to remain a central major minister. In a curious, idealistic spasm, he intended to set an example to his generation – but it was not followed by Barbara Castle or anyone else. All he achieved was to remove himself when his influence on events as an independent character could have been extremely important. His life had been more in Transport House than in the House of Commons. Labour Party policy-making was home ground for Crossman; handling the House of Commons was playing away matches.

The trouble is that in British politics, if an MP is seen no longer to be fighting for a political future, colleagues reckon that it is a sign of slipping back down the greasy pole. One never stays still in politics. If an MP has not got a future, that MP does not have much of a present either. Reducing one's ambition diminishes effectiveness.

Part of the trouble was that Wilson said he did not see any purpose in Crossman's remaining on the Executive. Crossman interpreted this in the summer of 1967 as evidence that Wilson had despaired of reorganizing the Labour Party. And that he deemed at the time to be the sole *raison d'être* of his remaining on the NEC. Membership of the National Executive increases the dimensions of any Labour Cabinet Minister, if only because the need for friends and supporters on the Executive makes them virtually unsackable and their own person.

215

Another part of the truth was that Crossman felt he had to be loyal to Wilson on the NEC, in the way that a courtier has to be loyal, an extension almost of Wilson's Kitchen Cabinet. He used to say that no self-respecting man could be as close as he was to Wilson without getting the itch to escape from a position of mere influence to a position of real power. His henchman-loyalty was being strained. Policy discussions at the NEC on subjects such as Vietnam were troubling his conscience and his whole inner being. Crossman was not an easily embarrassable man, but he was embarrassed by some of the policies he was being asked to support. And he told me frequently in the spring of 1968 that he was seeing too much of the Prime Minister, and the difficulty was that the more he saw of him at close quarters, the less he now liked him. In a confused way, Crossman imagined that returning to a large Government Department would make him a power in his own right. So it is to Parliament that we must now turn.

In Parliament, Crossman had some close and trusting relationships with certain Tories, in the coterie of his pair, Sir Alexander Spearman. Spearman was one of the leaders during Suez of the moves against attacking Egypt. He was in a position to say to Crossman, 'Country before Party, Dick. I beg you to stop the "Eden must go campaign", since this will make it impossible to get rid of him!' Crossman acted accordingly.

An element in his passionate belief in Select Committees was his equally passionate view that Parliament had allowed itself to be cheated of the truth about Suez. No Select Committee had ever raked over the ashes, as had a Select Committee on the Crimean War, which in 1854–5 chose the topic 'The Army before Sebastopol'. It was colloquially known as the 'Who shall we hang?' Committee! Nor was there the prospect of a successor to the Select British South African Committee which scrutinized the Jameson Raid in 1896. Exactly sixty years later, events were to be subject to no such scrutiny. By 1966, Crossman believed that Suez, exactly ten years earlier, had become ancient history.

In April 1967, when Anthony Nutting's devastating disclosures about Suez were being serialized in *The Times*, Crossman expressed sympathy for Selwyn Lloyd having to carry out Eden's policy. *Tempus fugit*! All through the aftermath of Suez, Crossman was a leading advocate of the exposure of Selwyn Lloyd. The sober reality was that the Crossman of 1967 was learning how he had to swallow Wilson's policies on Vietnam, and that the Crossman of 1957 did not understand the bitter pills that

Ministers may have to take, if they are to remain effective. Never did experience of high office so moderate a man's opinions of his opponents as occurred in the case of Crossman.

Other close Conservative friends were Quintin Hogg and David Ormsby-Gore. Among the younger Conservatives, Crossman was friendly with Sir Edward Boyle. Shortly after Crossman died, I stayed the night with Edward Boyle in his Vice-Chancellor's house at the University of Leeds. I put it to him that Crossman had been fascinated by a profile of Boyle by Peregrine Worsthorne in the *Spectator*. The future editor of the *Sunday Telegraph* pointed out that 'Boyle's real mistake was not to recognize that the strength of the Conservative Party is its vulgarity,' the part which Boyle found most distasteful. Boyle volunteered that he thought Worsthorne and Crossman very near to the mark! He added that he did not share Crossman's high regard for Mrs Thatcher, his successor in charge of education on the Opposition front bench! Yes, the former Joint Parliamentary Secretary at the Ministry of Pensions and National Insurance (1961–4) was described by Crossman in his diary for Sunday, 26 October 1969 as 'rather a pal of mine, I got on very well with her when she was at Pensions and she is one of the few Tories I greet in the lobby. She is tough, able and competent, and unlike Boyle, she will be a kind of professional Opposition Spokesman.' Both Crossman and Charles Pannell, the former Minister of Public Buildings and Works (1964–6), her pair, forecast that Mrs Thatcher would be a formidable member of any Tory government, and was as likely to lead the Conservative Party as Shirley Williams was to lead the Labour Party, but more likely to be the power equivalent of Barbara Castle. I too had a favourable view of Mrs Thatcher – until some months after she became Prime Minister!

Crossman cared very much what the Opposition thought. In particular, when he decided to depart from the job of Leader of the House, he was ultrasensitive on the question of the conclusions likely to be drawn by Selwyn Lloyd and Willie Whitelaw, who had worked so loyally with him on the Services Committee. Selwyn Lloyd recorded in his diary: 'My activities are as follows: House of Commons – leading our side on the Select Committee on Procedure – rather a bore – but helpful to Willie Whitelaw, and, with Crossman as Leader of the House, the consideration of the Reports is quite exciting.' (Quoted in D. R. Thorpe, *Selwyn Lloyd*, 1989, p. 408.) Crossman was touchingly concerned to have the good opinion of the leading Tories – or at least not to earn their justified bad opinion. Late in life he became acceptable among opponents as he had not been so much in his earlier career. And acceptability combined with respect among opponents is a great advantage, if not a *sine qua non* for being an effective minister.

In the middle 1950s Crossman's personal relations with many of his own Labour colleagues in Parliament ranged from the sad to the abysmal – and vestiges of the antagonism shown to him as Minister of Housing dated from this period. One reason was Crossman's dim view of the House of Commons. Though his opinions on this topic and some others see-sawed up and down, on the whole his settled opinion of the House as a collective entity was that it loved complaining about itself, but basically the MPs liked the House as it was, doing in his view very little work, having most of the debates on the floor, and resenting the harder work of committees. Unsurprisingly, the resentment was reciprocated by those who sweated their guts out doing the dogsbody but essential work of the Commons (for which we are paid by the taxpayer) rather than prancing around Transport House and the wider world.

Another reason was that Crossman pointed out in his columns the inanity of standing-committee procedure. Government backbenchers simply wasted their time, since they were hardly allowed to speak, because this would prolong the business and provoke another opposition speech. Opposition arguments were amateur and bogus, said Crossman, because Opposition MPs tended to have only the haziest notion of the details of the clauses under discussion. Crossman suggested that they should be given access to Government briefs as, to be fair to him, he was to suggest fifteen years later when he himself was in the Government as a senior Minister. The suggestion went down like lead – and so did the criticism of the hallowed committee system.

MPs resent messengers from among our own number who tell us that we are wasting our lives. The Commons tea-room fraternity of the day did not know Crossman. How could they? He never bothered to spend time with them. So he appeared to be a bully who rarely deigned to appear. Actually I don't share the widespread opinion that Crossman was a bully. He was a thug and a basher – but not quite a bully. He would bash colleagues when they offered dogmatic opinions on issues that he thought they knew little about. The offence threshold of MPs is not high; and like a basher-boy, he did not realize the power of his own punch.

Yet another reason was the growing and incessant argument about whether the Labour party could or should be run by the personal leadership of Hugh Gaitskell or a collective leadership. I believe, from what I was told by participants who were MPs when I was first elected in 1962, that this was a more profound issue than the arguments about defence. As Crossman, in his capacity of Party Chairman in 1960, was against Gaitskell's insinuations that the Party Conference was being brought into disrepute, it was understandable that he should side with the roundheads of the Executive against the cavaliers in Parliament, who wanted to concentrate power in the party leadership.

And yet herein lay a deep dilemma for Crossman. One of the real divisions in the Labour Party has always been that chasm between practical policy and emotional protest. Practical policy was usually represented by the parliamentary wing and emotional protest, not to be sniffed at, by the party. Yet Crossman did not see himself as an emotional protester. He lamented that it was all too rare for us to discuss alternative policies or indeed alternative attitudes. I found that Crossman's view of the Left was always ambivalent and complex. For example, the Left did not say, 'We have a different policy from support of the Americans in Vietnam.' According to Crossman, the Left said, 'That is the official line and we object to it!' Understandably, Crossman's ill-concealed view of the intellectual inadequacies of some left-wing MPs bred resentment.

So did his impatience with members of the Right. Crossman thought that milieu were spunkless. A particular *bête noire* was Patrick Gordon Walker, whom he blamed for losing the racially divided constituency of Smethwick in 1964 to a man whom Harold Wilson, in his opening speech as Prime Minister, described as a 'political leper', Peter Griffiths. What Crossman could not stand was dithering, and he was livid with Gordon Walker over the Education cuts of January 1968. 'Either a minister takes a decision,' he stormed, 'and does not resign, or he resigns, saying it is a heartbreak. What Gordon Walker and those of that ilk are doing is to stay put with heartbreak.' This revealed a pathetic weakness and earned Crossman's contempt.

The deepest reason of all for Crossman's difficult relations with Labour MPs can be explained in a short story. During my candidature in Roxburgh, Selkirk, and Peebles in 1958–9, one of the three Labour MPs who came to speak for me was the Rt Hon. John Edwards (he had been General Secretary of the Post Office Engineering Union, and one of my most prominent supporters in Galashiels was an old and valued member of that union, who had John Edwards to stay with him). In 1963, I said casually to Crossman that I was sad that John Edwards had died prematurely (at 55), and could not participate in the science policy discussions. Whereupon Crossman responded what Creevey-like I recorded: 'A few weeks before he died unexpectedly, and after fourteen years as parliamentary colleagues, I talked to John Edwards properly for the first time in the early summer of 1959. Previously I had regarded him as a self-important, ambitious, very narrow Christian careerist, who became Stafford Cripps's PPS as soon as he set foot in Westminster, and then went on to the front bench as a junior minister at Health, the Board of Trade and the Treasury. But I was sitting having a gin and tonic in the Smoking Room, and Edwards and I were the only Labour members there – it would have been offensive and embarrassing not to talk. To my astonishment, he poured out his heart to me. He told me that during the time of the Labour Government, it was true that he had been ambitious and must have appeared to people on the Left as a self-seeking type, intent on ascending the greasy pole. But he was also a man who, since he became General Secretary of the Post Office Engineering Union at the age of thirty-four, had needed to be busy doing something constructive. Rather pathetically, he complained that since 1951 he felt that he had little useful to do. So he decided that *faute de mieux* he would beaver away in the Council of Europe Assembly. As a result of his solid work and devotion to the ornamental trappings of the Strasbourg set-up, he had just been elected as chairman – he was the first man from Britain to get the job. And then, looking at me with a tear in his eye, Edwards muttered wistfully, "And, Dick, all I get is envy and unconcealed hatred from Labour MPs here, who expect you to sit in the House of Commons tea-room, and do nothing. It is futile to do nothing, when the Party is falling about our ears. MPs who cannot do anything outside Westminster, sit around and do nothing. But those of us who can do anything are driven to go out – and are hated for it!" I thought there was a great deal of truth in what John Edwards said. The Labour party was ideologically disintegrated by the fact that Keynesian welfare capitalism was seeming to prove an adequate substitute for Socialism.'

Crossman's relations with another Socialist intellectual of stature, John Strachey, were complex. They were friends – John and Celia Strachey stayed at Prescote on more than one weekend – and potential rivals for a Cabinet place in the late 1950s. Strachey, who was a fellow MP for Scotland (Dundee, 1945–63), told me that he thought the lectures Crossman gave on China in the autumn of 1958 were among the most brilliant he had ever heard. I thought it suited Strachey to portray Crossman as a racy lecturer rather than as a rival for Minister of Defence. He would praise Crossman for things that were not competitive politically. Crossman thought Strachey agreed with him on military strategy, culminating in the 1961 compromise on nuclear weapons. But he found that Strachey deferred to Gaitskell, and would not go along with any policy in which Frank Cousins acquiesced. When Strachey died unexpectedly in 1963, Crossman said to me '*De mortuis nil nisi bonum*; but I got so angry with him at the end of his life when this great pillar of the Left Book Club, faced with crunch issues on defence, would simply shrug his shoulders in the way I presume everyone does, if they have been cured by psychoanalysis of their convictions.' It might not be too harsh to reflect that the shade of Strachey, who was firm to his dying day against End-of-Empire commitments in the Far East, might have said the same of Crossman on Vietnam!

Crossman unfairly observed that the weakness of the Labour Party in Parliament had more to do with lethargy than with left-wing militancy. But then Crossman never did really understand the lives of MPs who did not have their main home in London. Of course, Labour MPs from the North of England, Scotland, and Wales wanted to get home on a Thursday night. So would Crossman have done, if he had a solid day's work to do in his bailiwick on Fridays and most probably on Saturdays and Sundays too. Crossman began to understand the feelings of his colleagues more sensitively when Ian Mikardo pointed out at the NEC in June 1967 that back-bench MPs were like workers excluded from managerial decision, and that they felt acutely a sense of exclusion because they had no opportunity to share in decision-making. I felt that in the early 1960s Crossman's own frustrations as a backbencher had rather receded into the background of his mind.

Crossman, who by that time (1963) had mentally recuperated and had a revived purpose in life, in the shape of the real prospect of a Wilson-led Labour Government, told me that he had become politically defeated. He was like many other Labour MPs of the time, a missionary without a mission, or at least a missionary ever more dubious about his mission.

Crossman explained that he himself had changed as a person. From

1954 he had taken to actually going home to dinner to see his new wife, and then dropping into the House to vote. Suddenly it dawned on him how most politicians since time immemorial had regarded politics: 'not as a mission or vocation but as a rather pleasant public service, which one takes on in addition to one's main interests and one's private life but without permitting it to tyrannize over the others.' In the mid-50s, Crossman felt himself becoming a private person again, in a way which he had not felt at any time that he could clearly remember in his adult life. From the moment he went to Oxford, he had been first and foremost a public person, in the sense that it had never occurred to him that the Goddess Politics should not be accorded pride of place. If he failed to give politics first place, he had had a bad conscience.

Crossman told me that, without becoming unduly introspective, he thought that one reason for going to join the *Mirror* was because of the 'Edwards effect'. He said he was not alone. Nye Bevan and Jennie Lee had become more interested in their farm, and Nye was a token member of the Shadow Cabinet. Ian Mikardo was immersing himself in relations between Britain and the German Democratic Republic, and developing his interests in the Leipzig Fair. Crossman told me that he thought Mikardo was doing more good for Britain in such activity than padding the corridors of the Commons.

There was, however, another side to the coin. Crossman was ruminating on the shortcomings of what he was later to describe as the dignified part of the Constitution, the formal, rather set-piece debates in the Commons. Unlike many of his colleagues, he never once put his hand to the essential work of trying to improve Bills in committee. Most MPs spend a sizeable proportion of our lives 'upstairs' in the committee rooms, listening to long speeches, often from front-benchers, arguing detailed amendments, hour after hour. It was not surprising that lawyers and journalists like Crossman, who were earning substantial sums of money and never turned up to do a share of the grind in the morning, were resented like hell.

Crossman's counter-punch to this also had uncomfortable force. In the nineteenth century, when the hold of Party was loose, committee stages of Bills were genuine committee stages, and MPs spoke – and voted! – as they believed right. With the coming of tighter party discipline, committee stages had become sheer pretence. If the object was to improve a Bill, it could almost always be done in one day. The only possible value that an Opposition could get out of a committee stage was propaganda value, so everything became a question of propaganda tactics. The respectable attitude of some of his parliamentary eminent colleagues became ridiculous. They were simply being taken in by their own myth that they were doing some good in committee, whereas in fact, they were making MPs and Ministers waste their time. Committee work was simply a forum for creating parliamentary reputations and indulging egos.

I do not think Crossman was right. Many people outside Parliament, who are going to be affected by new legislation, are interested in the despised committee work – and if a party displays sloppiness in committee, it gradually percolates through to the public that perhaps that party is not quite fit to form the government of Britain.

Crossman's position was chicken-and-egg. The ever more decrepit parliamentary oligarchy hated him. He wrote in the popular press articles to the effect that they were rusty, idle and disconsolate. They would not listen to his amply-offered advice. He saw little or no prospect of their being returned to power. And Oppositions who see little or no prospect of forming a Government tend to lose their appetite for doing so.

Crossman antagonized some of the MPs who did work exceedingly hard at the business of the Commons. One such was Willie Ross, Wilson's 'Basso Profundo', who represented Scotland in Cabinet over every Wilson change. In my opinion, it was his bad relations with Willie Ross that turned Crossman into a devolutionist, and not any deep constitutional analysis, which would have been characteristic of him. Crossman's pro-Scottish parliament views jelled on 6 May 1968. He told me that he was going to cancel his meetings that Monday afternoon and come to sit on the front bench to listen to the second reading of the Social Work (Scotland) Bill. The point was that this legislation was based on reports which were twelve months in advance of the committee under Sir Frederick Seebohm that was considering social work structures in England, for which delicate area Crossman was responsible. Crossman genuinely wanted to hear what was said about the Scottish solution, and indicated he would be present. As the debate was about to start, I was nabbed by the Government Whips and told to tell Crossman to keep out of the chamber, as his presence would be interpreted as a dark English conspiracy. Willie Ross did not want him appearing to meddle in Scottish business.

Crossman saw this incident as the ultimate symbol of separation between England and Scotland: 'You and Willie Ross – you're just as bad as he is, really, though in a less uncouth, smoother way! – go around shouting about the Scottish Nationalists wanting separation, but what both of you and your friends actually want is to keep your Scottish business absolutely privy from English business. You and Willie Ross want a system which gives you the worst of both worlds, and that's why I'm in favour of a Scottish parliament.' In vain did I try to point out to Crossman that he could not have a subordinate 'Parliament' in part, though only part, of a kingdom which above all else we wished to keep united. And how did he as a great constitutional pundit fancy me, as MP for West Lothian, being able to vote on the most delicate issues of housing, health, education and local government finance for the West Midlands, which he represented, but not for West Lothian, which I represented?

One of the reasons that I was so supremely confident about voting against my Party over a hundred times on three-line whips during the debates on Devolution in 1978–9 was that a decade earlier the whole issue had been hammered out on the anvil of argument with Crossman. If Crossman could be defeated by me in argument, I reckoned I could cope with such extremely able colleagues as Bruce Millan, Willie Ross's successor as Scottish Secretary, and John Smith, to whom James Callaghan had entrusted the devolution brief. Crossman's final riposte to what became known as the 'West Lothian Question', so christened by Enoch Powell, who heard me ask it *ad nauseam* during the forty-seven days on the floor of the House that we kept devolution going (with James Callaghan's benign acquiescence) confirmed me in my determination to oppose devolution at the 1979 referendum. 'Well,' said Crossman, 'there is no earthly reason why Scotland should not be like Northern Ireland!' This was a judgement about which he became increasingly uncomfortable in the 1970s, and for which he apologized to me shortly before he died.

As is its wont, devolution discussion ended in fiasco in September 1968, with James Callaghan suggesting to Crossman that a Royal Commission be set up under the chairmanship of Rab Butler or Lester Pearson, the former Canadian Prime Minister. Crossman told me that either of them would have been too musty. By that time Callaghan and Crossman wanted to wash their hands of the whole difficult subject. Crossman did have a low fed-upness threshold.

Crossman was the parliamentary godfather of specialist departmental

Select Committees. And I cannot think of any other Leader of the House, with the possible exception of Norman St John Stevas, who would have fought so hard. Apart from ministerial qualms from Cabinet colleagues, Tony Crosland at Education, and Tony Wedgwood Benn at Technology, Crossman faced furious hostility from Sir Solly Zuckerman, the recently appointed Scientific Adviser to the Prime Minister. Crossman was very angry indeed at Zuckerman's saying testily to him, 'What are your Specialist Select Committees, really? What are they for?' I asked Crossman what he said to him. 'Unlike Solly, I was patient and good-tempered!' Crossman had done what he often did to obstinate friends, for he admired Zuckerman. He sent him a recent book to read, in this particular case *The Member of Parliament and the Administration* (1966) by David Coombes, which considered very perceptively what the Select Committee on Nationalized Industries did. As one of the original members of the first Select Committee on Science and Technology, under the chairmanship of Arthur Palmer, I am sure we did excellent, serious, worthwhile work and Crossman was justified in his fight for the concept. Another of the original members, Dr David Owen, told me that he agreed with me in this.

Where Crossman was unique among senior Ministers was that he actually wanted the Select Committees to scrutinize Departments fairly. He told me that he thought John Silkin, the Chief Whip, was a bit two-faced about the 'Crossman–Silkin reforms' and particularly in relation to Select Committees. Silkin had told Crossman to stick to policy, and he would do the personal relations – at which, in my opinion, he did genuinely excel. Crossman discovered, or thought he discovered, that Silkin was not really concerned to re-establish Parliamentary authority *per se*. On the contrary, Silkin's prime concern was to select members of Specialist Committees on the basis that the MPs chosen by the Whips would prevent the committees from being the tough inquisitors of their own Labour ministers which Crossman desired. Crossman kicked himself for having allowed himself to get involved in a monumental row over the remit of the Select Committee on Agriculture with Professor John Mackintosh, who not only had written great books on government and parliamentary procedure, but whose constituency covered the famous potato-seed growing red soil of East Lothian.

The real cause of his wrath were the Government Whips for stultifying the Select Committees. I remember vividly a picturesque occasion, latish at night, after a good dinner – I never saw Crossman drunk or the worse for wear — when he barged into the Whips' Office and told John Silkin and some of his open-mouthed and ribald colleagues that they were all as bad as Polycrates. And, in a treasured moment, Joe Harper, miner from Pontefract, said, 'And who, Dick, might this Mr Polycrates have been when he was at home?' I waited agog to hear what Crossman would say to the pride of Whips who saw the possibility of late-night sport to pass the dreary hour until the vote.

Unabashed, Crossman explained that Mr Polycrates was the Tyrant of the sixth-century-BC Samos, who had great good fortune, took over neighbouring islands, and the coast of southern Turkey. According to Aristotle, said Crossman, he kept the people of Samos fully employed but executed any possible rivals or sent them off on suicide missions to help the Persians, under Cambyses, against the Egyptions. 'You just want Mackintosh off the committee, so you can cut off the most tall-growing corn, just like Polycrates. And the others you, like Polycrates, bribe with false coins. He won over the Spartans, and you win over the backbenchers with the promise of under-secretaryships which you know you cannot deliver to all to whom you've made promises!' Cleverly, Silkin, ever the adroit turner of a conversation, inquired what Herodotus had to say about Polycrates. The Whips had won. The following day they told me they had enjoyed the fracas greatly.

Later, in 1982, when I was causing great embarrassment over the Falklands War, the first move of the Chief Whip, Michael Cocks, was to offer me a glass of sherry, and a place on the Select Committee on Foreign Affairs. Having reduced him to giggles at so crude an attempt to gag me, I politely declined. Membership of a select committee has come to mean membership of a team — and serious critics find it difficult to keep within the unwritten code of conduct, of restraining individual criticism, if not going technically as far as breaking the rules.

Crossman got into even stormier water when he championed the Select Committee on the Ombudsman or Parliamentary Commissioner. To put it mildly, his ministerial colleagues were less than entranced by the prospect of Sir Edmund Compton, the formidably able Comptroller and Auditor General who tutored me in the ways of Whitehall when I was a thirty-year-old member of the Public Accounts Committee, as first Ombudsman delving into secret files in their Departments, discovering which civil servant was responsible for which mistake or controversial decision, and enjoying the capacity to get well behind the facade of ministerial responsibility to parliament, to see how decisions were really taken in a Department. Nor was the position made any easier by the story that went the rounds of nervous ministers that Edmund Compton, when asked whether he preferred being Ombudsman to a permanent secretaryship in the Treasury or Board of Trade, had replied good-naturedly by quoting Pope Leo x, 'Now that God has given us the papacy, let us enjoy it!'

No minister reflected the shudders of Whitehall more expressively than the reforming Home Secretary, Roy Jenkins. He thought Crossman was altering the entire constitution by jeopardizing the doctrine of ministerial responsibility. Crossman told me that Roy Jenkins was really alarmed that Sir Edmund Compton would be able to find out that a particular civil servant had taken a decision without the Minister being consulted. Crossman's comment in December 1966 was that he was sad that Roy Jenkins and senior civil servants should cavil at the whole idea of permitting the House of Commons – through its agent, the Ombudsman – to investigate the detailed workings of the Executive. With the hindsight of twenty years and more, the establishment of an Ombudsman did not lead to administrative Armageddon – nor did it lead to quite the number of injustices being dealt with which Crossman hoped and anticipated.

Most Ministers, by the time they reach senior level, display great skill in taking evasive action at the despatch box. Crossman got into difficulties precisely because he would insist on being candid about the difficulties of proposals such as those for an Ombudsman. He believed in meeting troubles head-on. It was simple: awkward issues should not be evaded. Crossman was in favour of a strong Parliamentary Committee, but he found it extraordinary that his colleagues should envisage themselves as a full-scale Shadow Cabinet. He thought that this was likely to inhibit opposition. And, a third of a century later, it is my view that the received wisdom of Oppositions having a Shadow Parliamentary Under-Secretary of State to the Ministry of Agriculture, Fisheries and Food is ridiculous – and not only ridiculous, but it weakens the Opposition in its role of criticism. Why? Because Shadows are human. They want to be seen to do well in relation to their parliamentary performance by their colleagues. With their opposite number in Government, they develop, if not an 'I'll scratch your back if you scratch mine' mentality, at least a restrained *modus vivendi*. Given the British adversarial system, this is simply not healthy. Crossman was right about the shortcomings of the full panoply of Shadow Government.

He also resented those who had been pillars of Shadow Cabinets while he had been out in the political cold. This was part of the reason for his unnecessarily edgy and poor relations with Michael Stewart. In April 1967, he and Anne came back from seeing the film version of *A Man For All Seasons*. He had enjoyed Paul Scofield in the title role in the play. Why had he not been stirred by the film? 'It's like this. I confess I am really on Henry VIII's side. This, as your Burns would say, "unco guid" pious man, Thomas More, who sticks to the oaths he's made, and goes on to disregard any practical political reason which crops up, makes me jolly angry, and Michael Stewart makes me angry in Cabinet, in just the same prim way.' Crossman's siding with Henry VIII reveals a lot about the realpolitik aspect of Crossman.

More than any other senior Minister, Crossman, having languished for nineteen years on the back benches, understood the extent to which the whole of the parliamentary system is geared, not to help backbenchers criticize Ministers, but to help Ministers overcome backbenchers. Life was too easy for Ministers. And with the speeding up of questions by the Speaker, Dr Horace King, the last anxiety was removed. As questions rattled on, scrutiny became cursory: there was no proper investigation.

He believed that the American government faced a level of critique that our much-vaunted Mother of Parliaments did not offer. In Washington in 1952, Mr Justice Frankfurter had explained to him how the decisions of the Supreme Court mattered. Senator Robert A. Taft of Ohio had demonstrated to him the power of Senators in a long interview. And John Foster Dulles himself had acknowledged the power of Congress.

Frequent reference by Crossman to long meetings, *tête-à-tête, à deux*, with American heavyweights, did not endear Crossman to parliamentary colleagues who would not be afforded such treatment by American heavyweights. It was not questions in the House of Commons which bothered Crossman, but the hostile letter to him as Minister. The reply was something in black and white which could be quoted against him if it were not carefully phrased. The consequence was that he would worry away at letters of response which most ministers would have signed with little more than a glance as they were submitted by Civil Servants. As a journalist, Crossman was more conscious than most how replies to letters by ministers could be published in the press with commentary.

Very unusually among holders of senior ministerial office, and uniquely among a dozen Leaders of the House whom I have known, Crossman disliked the Commons as a place. At the time of the death in October 1969 of Emrys Hughes (Keir Hardie's son-in-law), for twenty-three years MP for South Ayrshire, and previously editor of *Forward* for 15 years, Crossman pinpointed why he often loathed the Commons: 'Look at what the place does to people.' Take Emrys Hughes. When he was elected he was a fine editor and a talented journalist. When Crossman visited South Ayrshire in 1946, he thought the younger Emrys and his wife Nan reflected the serious political mood of the area. Yet, over the years, Crossman watched Emrys Hughes running down and running to seed as a serious politician (though not physically). Hughes allowed himself to become a sort of professional funny man at Prime Minister's Questions. He introduced a bill to abolish the monarchy, and when the Speaker asked formally, 'Who will sponsor the bill?' Hughes replied with a poker face, 'Mr Macmillan, Mr Butler and myself!' (It was not the Prime Minister and 'Rab', but Mr Malcolm Macmillan, MP for the Western Isles, and Mr Herbert Butler, MP for Hackney, left-wing chums of Emrys Hughes.) Part of the trouble with the Commons, as Crossman saw it, was that MPs tend to self-parody and caricaturing themselves which leads to political destruction.

On the other hand, Crossman thought that the atmosphere of the House of Commons did matter to a Government. So long as Government back-bench MPs estimated there was a decent chance of actually winning the next election, or at least winning in their own constituencies, they were tied to the Government by a string of loyalty. But if the Commons atmosphere went sour, and a lot of Government MPs discerned that they had little or no future in the Commons, then like a flight of starlings, they would hop on to the perch of saying in unison: 'I may as well stand up and be defeated for my Socialist principles rather than be defeated for supporting a government which is sacrificing them. Anyway, rebellion in these circumstances will make it easier than loyalty to return to the Commons, given the likely attitudes of delegates to Constituency Labour Party selection conferences!'

In this Crossman was right! Rebels of the late 1960s found it significantly easier to return as 'retread' MPs than loyalists. But one could only get things done by being part of a group such as Keep Left or the

Bevanites. It was uncongenial to him just being an atomized MP, fighting for himself, and to get his name in the papers. Yet it was all very well for Crossman – he was a political journalist who got his name in the papers anyway!

He believed that too many parliamentarians developed a liking for Parliament for its own sake: he thought the purpose of being in Parliament was to get things done. Crossman perceived Parliament as an institution which had developed a life of its own, unhealthily remote from Whitehall. This was epitomized for him and me one November late afternoon in 1967. Crossman was late for a meeting which he had arranged in his Leader of the House's room. He told me to go and keep his two guests happy with sherry from the cupboard. Enter first guest: Sir Barnett Cocks, Clerk of the House of Commons, head of the Clerks Department, who as a group were unhappy about aspects of the Specialist Select Committees. I poured out sherry. Enter second guest: Sir Burke Trend, Secretary of the Cabinet, later to be Lord Trend, Rector of Lincoln College, Oxford. I poured out more sherry. Embarrassed silence. 'I don't think we've met, they said to each other in unison. It spoke volumes to Crossman that his PPS had to introduce the 'Pope and the Patriarch!'

TWENTY
Diarist

As a young MP, like my friend and contemporary John Morris, QC, erstwhile Secretary of State for Wales, I was befriended by Megan Lloyd George. And it was she who pointed out to me a very formative experience in Crossman's life, which led forty years later to the *Diaries*.

When Crossman arrived in Oxford, the Warden of New College was H. A. L. Fisher – Herbert Fisher, former President of the Board of Education, and later (in January 1936) to publish his 1200-page *History of Europe*, putting him in the class of his brother-in-law F. W. Maitland, Bryce, Morley and Gibbon as a great historian. Crossman indeed compared Fisher with Thucydides, who lost a battle in the Peloponnesiam War and was dismissed from his command. He consoled himself in exile by writing the greatest history of war. Fisher, an MP only from 1916–19, put through a major Education Act (1918), went down in 1922 with Lloyd George, but turned defeat into victory by producing the *History of Europe*.

Late on Sunday evenings, Fisher would invite some undergraduates to his study in the Warden's Lodging, to be in the company of Gilbert Murray or Hilaire Belloc, Graham Wallas or General Smuts. There Fisher would recapture the ecstasy of public life which he had tasted, all too briefly, and he would live himself back to his seat at the Cabinet table in Downing Street or to the Council of the League of Nations at Geneva or to the smoking room of the House of Commons. But it was not only the Sunday evenings. A few – very few – undergraduates were invited by Fisher to his country cottage. At the close of the weekend, Fisher and his guests would walk up to Churt for dinner with Lloyd

231

George. 'There, at either end of the table,' Crossman recalled, 'sat thesis and antithesis, the well-born academic and the self-made Welshman, united by their passion for the game of politics from which both had been forcibly retired.'

Megan (having made it clear that *she* and not Lloyd George's friend, Frances Stevenson, did the arranging of the meals, as the daughter of the house!) told me that her father was enormously impressed by this strikingly handsome blond boy with a quicksilver mind. She thought that it was not only on those Sunday evenings that Crossman acquired a taste for politics,but that he was entranced by 'thesis' and 'antithesis' and their talk of great events.

Several years later, when Crossman was a young don at New College, and wondering whether to stay in Oxford or take the plunge into politics, Fisher sent for him to tell him that he would recommend that his fellowship be renewed for seven years. Crossman recalls Fisher as saying, 'Now let me talk to you, not as warden, but as a personal friend. I stayed in Oxford too long, and I went into politics at the top. That was the cause of my failure. Go in now while you are young. I can see that you have the desire for it which I had at your age. Whether you succeed or fail does not matter. It is the life which matters. I would like you to avoid my mistakes.'

Crossman took Fisher's advice. He was eternally grateful.

Now, a poignant personal memory. On a November night in 1973, I had ambled back from the House after a 10 p.m. vote to 9 Vincent Square. I went along to say goodnight to Dick, and found him, not in the sitting room or the bedroom upstairs, but in his study downstairs, which really had not been used much since October 1964 and which was a huge clutter. 'I'd better talk to you,' he said quietly. 'You ought to know that today it has been confirmed that I have a malignant tumour which cannot be reversed.' I was stunned. 'So I'd better get on with organizing the Diaries!' He was breathtakingly matter of fact. Herbert Fisher had left a great book, and he wanted to try to make sure that he did the same. For a man who had been told that day that he had at best a very few months of life with full mental powers left to him, his self-control was mind-boggling. To the Diaries he then returned. His behaviour that night simply confirmed my long-held opinion that the writing of the Diaries was the main *raison d'être* of his wanting to be a member of the Cabinet. As far back as 2 February 1959, he had written of his strengthening feeling 'that it is very much more useful my writing about politics than being a mediocre politician. I do happen to feel at the moment that I am capable of investigating well and writing well, but on the other hand I must be in the Cabinet if I am going to write the book I want, which is not a repetition of Bagehot (Bagehot was never in Government) but something of my own, even more from inside...'

Writing the 1963 introduction to Walter Bagehot's *The English Constitution* (1867) he developed the ideas that came out of those discussions between H. A. L. Fisher and Lloyd George. (Ever since as an undergraduate I attended a lecture in Cambridge in 1955 by my then supervisor, Noel Annan, I had been interested in Bagehot, who was editor of the *Economist* between 1861 and 1877. Annan praised him as an essayist and subsequently made me read Bagehot's *Essays* and *The English Constitution*.) When Fontana decided to reprint the classic in paperback, Crossman added a powerful fifty-page foreword. What, he asked, was the timeless quality of the book that Bagehot had dashed off as a serial? Quoting the former prime minister, Arthur Balfour, Crossman emphasized that Bagehot did look closely and for himself at real political life. He ceaselessly endeavoured to discover how public business was in fact transacted, as distinct from the way its transaction was officially described. Bagehot, like Balfour, had a contempt for what they regarded as the 'literary' view of constitutional procedure. Crossman saw Bagehot as one of the greatest political journalists of his or any other age, equally skilled in the crafts of reporter, leader writer and editor. Crossman ascribed his pre-eminence to the fact that Bagehot eschewed 'literary' pretensions, and stuck to his trade. It was this that made him immortal.

It was in the course of describing the contemporary political scene as he actually saw it that Bagehot hit upon the secret of British politics – the difference between the myth and reality, and also between the dignified and the efficient exercise of power. And there was a resemblance for Crossman between Bagehot's theory of class politics, and Marx's theory of class war. Crossman opined that we should not be surprised that Bagehot, the liberal reactionary, and Marx, the Communist revolutionary, were in such cynical agreement about the differences between appearance and reality in British politics, and the ingenious contrivances by which the real power of the business community is concealed from the public eye. Herbert Morrison and Harold Laski have subsequently given detailed descriptions of how Cabinet and Parliament have operated since the war, showing that appearances no longer bore much relation to fact. Party loyalty had become the prime political virtue of an MP, and the test of that loyalty was his willingness to support the official leadership when he knew it to be wrong. A result of the virtual disappearance of an MP's independence was that the point of decision had been removed from the division lobby to the Party meeting upstairs. The debate on the floor of the House of Commons had become a formality, and the division which followed a foregone conclusion. It was what was said and done in the secrecy of the party meeting which was now really important – though the public could only hear about it through leaks to the press. Groups had to be formed. The struggle for power which gave any real meaning to democratic politics had become hidden from the public eye. The struggle for real power took place behind closed doors inside the Government party, and for Shadow power inside the Opposition party. Crossman perceived that, driven underground by the requirements of party discipline, cliques and cabals emerged to fight for causes or uphold principles, only to be disintegrated from above by threats of expulsion and offers of preferment.

By the 1950s, there was no 'loyal' way either of removing a disastrous leader, or of promoting to power a saviour at loggerheads with the machine. Under prime-ministerial government, secondary decisions were normally taken either by the department concerned or in Cabinet committee. In 1963, Crossman already had come to perceive the Cabinet as a place where busy executives seek formal sanction for their actions from colleagues usually too busy – even if they do disagree – to do more than protest. It was seen by Crossman, after Macmillan's 'little local difficulty' and the resignation of Peter Thorneycroft as Chancellor of the Exchequer in January 1958, that each of these executives owes his allegiance not to the Cabinet collectively, but to the prime minister who gave him his job and could easily take it away.

Cabinet ministers had gradually become little more than glorified agents of the prime minister. (Ironically, this was much less true of the Wilson government, but has reached its apogee in the subsequent Thatcher governments.) The choice had become one between collective obedience and the political wilderness. Crossman believed he had a mission to illuminate these developments and that no one else could do it better than he. By becoming a member of a Cabinet like H. A. L. Fisher, he would have the advantage over diarists like Samuel Pepys and John Evelyn as well as constitutional theorists like Walter Bagehot.

From an academic view, it was rewarding that Crossman did become a member of Cabinet. He had failed to notice a new development, and so had the academic community until that time. In addition to the Cabinet committees which only ministers normally attended, there was a whole network of civil-service committees. What ministers did was therefore strictly and completely paralleled at the official level. This is not in dispute. What is in dispute was Crossman's conclusion from his discovery. He jumped to the conclusion that the decisions were often precooked in the official committee, up to a point at which it was well-nigh impossible to arrive at any conclusion other than that already decided upon by the civil-service officials in advance. Worse still from Crossman's point of view was the fact that if agreement was reached at the intermediate level of a Cabinet committee, only formal approval was required from the full Cabinet. This was the device, Crossman surmised, by which Whitehall ensured that the Cabinet system was relatively innocuous, and that Downing Street got its way.

My opinion is that it was not just the search for academic truth that infuriated Crossman, and roused him against the system of precooking. He was piqued or justifiably angry at being excluded from the Overseas Policy and Defence Committee, and being relegated, as a second-division home front Minister, to the Home Affairs Committee, the Economic Development Committee, the Immigration Committee, the Broadcasting Committee, and the Legislation Committee. All I can say is that when I first worked for him in 1963, Crossman was firmly under the impression that as a prospective Secretary of State for Education he could look forward to a major Cabinet finger in the pie of defence and foreign affairs.

There was another delicate matter, a supremely delicate matter, which caused Crossman a kind of sotto-voce deep-felt concern that is unusual in Ministers, who have so many worries that they do not want gratuitous trouble. This was the accuracy of the Cabinet minutes. Crossman used the word 'travesty' about them. They did not, according to him, even attempt to be an account of what actually took place in Cabinet. I was not in Cabinet, but from March 1965 until the fall of the Labour Government in 1970, I saw a great many, though not all, Cabinet minutes. From what other members of the Cabinet said to me and to other members of the PLP, the minutes did not tally with what had taken place in the Labour Cabinet. The minutes, submitted by the Cabinet Secretary, the late Lord Trend, were an amalgam of the official brief which a minister took along to Cabinet, the official papers on the original policy, and the official conclusions. The minutes failed to described the real struggle which, according to Callaghan, Barbara Castle and George Brown off the record, had in fact taken place. The abstracts anaesthetized the ministers' contributions and usually did not identify who had said what. This had the effect of enormously strengthening the Civil Service against the politicians. Though Crossman was to make little progress against an increasingly Burke Trend/ Civil-Service-orientated Prime Minister, the *Diaries* did expose this situation. I believe that after the *Diaries* were published, the Conservative opposition studied what Crossman had said, and vowed to take action against the civil service. The Crossman *Diaries* proved to be a valuable ammunition dump for the incoming Thatcher government.

Crossman's was not literally a daily diary, written up each night. Had it been, many judgements might have been different. As Michael Foot pointed out, an MP or Minister will become increasingly sharp-tempered as the week 'in this place' (i.e. Westminster) progresses, and return refreshed after a weekend at home or in the constituency; therefore attitudes at the beginning of the week are likely to be more charitable than those prevailing at the end of the week. Denis Healey had the impression that many of the Monday and Tuesday events which Crossman wrote were coloured by the benefit of hindsight of what happened on Wednesday, Thursday and Friday. Crossman was fond of saying that memory is a terrible improver. His friends have to concede that Harold Wilson's week could indeed be a long time in politics, and that hindsight from the rural weekend could be an improver.

It is worthwhile describing the sheer mechanics of how Crossman went about his task. Normally, he would have been back at Prescote at teatime on a Saturday, if not earlier. After supper, he would spend about three hours, putting his thoughts down on separate pieces of paper under headings in his Greek-influence ballpoint handwriting. He would then slot into the roughly ordered pieces of paper some of the official documents that his department had sent to Prescote, check through his ministerial engagements diary for each day of the week (giving his official and unofficial appointments), look at the Cabinet minutes, and flick through the Cabinet sub-committee minutes. He would then glance at the daily press-cuttings files which his civil servants' press office had prepared each day, on the criterion of being worthy of ministerial attention, and flick through Hansard, looking at the topics raised on Tuesdays and Thursdays at Prime Minister's Questions, and at any debate which either impinged on his ministerial actions or he otherwise found interesting. At that point, he picked out those incidents or events which he thought worth recording; he scribbled notes on them in the margins of the papers he had arranged, and married them up to source material. Having done this, he would talk to Anne and Patrick and Virginia, if it was not ridiculously late, and go to bed. He kept to the same routine if there were weekend guests.

After a prompt breakfast on Sunday morning, he would go to his study, overlooking the Oxfordshire countryside, and dictate for up to a couple of hours. Later in the week, the diary was typed out by Jenny Hall, his excellent secretary and archivist.

The differences between a daily diarist and a weekend diarist must therefore be taken into account. Especially during the period 1966–8 when he was Leader of the House, his conversations, his talks and his reactions tended to be mushed up in a general impression. A great deal of flesh and blood, he told me before Christmas 1967, in the shape of chats over meals and whispered conversations on the Government front bench was being boiled up together. He was spending a great deal of time with Harold Wilson, and tended to remember only the impression which was left after each meeting, or those nuggets of discussion which actually resulted in something being done. He was, on his own admission, not very good at remembering what Wilson actually said; on the other hand, he could repeat almost verbatim his conversations with Callaghan and Jenkins. (I thought this told us more about his colleagues than about Crossman.)

There is another mechanical but consequential point to take into account. For some months, Crossman found that it was much more difficult to dictate to a machine than to a secretary. 'I am far more considerate,' he told me one Sunday when my wife Kathleen and I were guests at Prescote, 'to these frightful wheels turning in front of me than I ever was to poor Ruth!' Ruth Cohen was his secretary of the 1950s, when he was dictating the diaries which the indefatigable and scholarly Janet Morgan miraculously rescued from a score of musty files, rusting at the hinges, of close type on heavy foolscap, and edited into *The Backbench Diaries of Richard Crossman* (1981).

After a few months he got over his inhibitions, and anyone who listens to the tapes will detect an enormous improvement in fluency between November 1964 and the summer of 1965. A more serious difficulty about the tapes is that Crossman depended on tone of voice, emphasis, nuance, and inflection, even more than most of us politicians to convey our meaning. A tape recorder cannot even query, let alone object. And that makes reliance on tone and inflection the greater. Do you speak into a telephone answering machine as you would speak to a friend in person on the end of a telephone? Probably not. *The Backbench Diaries* were dictated, but with the written, not the spoken word in mind. This may partly explain why Denis Healey finds them, content apart, so much more satisfactory than *The Diaries of a Cabinet Minister*.

There is yet another difficulty. It was brought home to me by an outspoken, charitable and exceedingly able Clerk of the House of Commons, the late Sir Richard Barlas. He pointed out the occurrence of Crossmanese, where words were used in an unusual sense. For example, Crossman's 'You puzzle me' should be interpreted 'I understand perfectly well what you are trying to say, but I disagree profoundly.' He also reintroduced words such as 'odious' (to describe self-seeking political behaviour) to the contemporary vocabulary of public life. In cold print, even those of his ministerial, as opposed to his backbench, Commons speeches which linger indelibly in the memory of those who heard them, such as his wind-up to the Queen's Speech, demolishing Iain Macleod, on Tuesday 7 November 1967, arguably the greatest Parliamentary *tour de force* of the 1960s, tend to look flat in Hansard. Nonetheless, I quote one short section which, to my mind, has not dated at all:

> When I listened to the right hon. Member for Enfield, West (Mr. Iain Macleod) I was back in Oxford common rooms; I was almost a member of a seminar and listening to a brilliant academic lecture, listening to the right hon. Gentleman dazzling and pirouetting on the point of a needle, thinking aloud – something I have often been accused of doing – thinking aloud and at one terrible point saying, 'But I am talking seriously here to serious people, but outside, there we have selective quotation.'
>
> I thought that I would just have a look. Let us look at the difference between the right hon. Gentleman here addressing the Chancellor as a fellow expert and what he says to the poor boobs at Brighton. I shall return the compliment. I shall address the House in an academic fashion on the seven-point Brighton programme, the programme the right hon. Gentleman did not dare to put here to the Chancellor, but the programme which he put to the Tories and to the country.
>
> Let us go through it rapidly. I will not take long on each point because

they are simple points. They are points which I can understand as a non-economist. Point No. 1 was

'policies of lower personal taxation'.

That is simple, direct, in staid responsible terms. I do not know quite what it meant, so I looked up with interest – I think I have it here – the interview which the Leader of the Opposition gave to Ronald Butt, of the *Sunday Times*. the right hon. Gentleman put it rather more clearly. He said this:

'Conservatives believe in reducing the burden of direct taxation, in moving over to indirect taxation . . .'

Let me translate that into simple English. This is what it really means: Conservatives believe in reducing the burden of taxation on the wealthier classes by using taxation to raise the price of things which loom heaviest in working-class budgets. Here, in modern form, is the old traditional theory that the upper classes need the incentive of lower direct taxation and the lower classes need the incentive of higher prices. What is a bit surprising to me is to hear this 19th century nostrum of Dickens's 'Hard Times' enunciated as 'with-it' 1967 Conservative policy.

(*Hansard*, 7 November 1967, p, 970)

Perhaps fortunately, Crossman's memory for anecdotes – I am the same – was like a sieve. Thought he could be extremely amusing, he was simply incapable of repeating a funny story. On the other hand, his practical memory was very good indeed at recalling key chunks of conversation verbatim, or anecdotes with a significant political moral to be drawn. His diary was very much that of the practitioner or doer, in contradistinction to the diary of the observer or pundit. Crossman's diaries are different from those of other MPs, such as Harold Nicolson, who sat for West Leicester in the 1935–45 Parliament, and Paul 'Chips' Channon, in that they were on the periphery of power, while Crossman was sweating away in the wrestling match that is the British Cabinet, trying to get his way. It was almost incidental that he had been an academic student of British politics, writing the diary with a special interest in how decisions were taken.

Where Crossman does succeed brilliantly is in his stated aim of keeping a record of the transient impressions of politics as they occurred to him. A great value of the *Diaries* is that there is a record, before they were forgotten, of opinions which were proved wrong and judgements which one would rather not have made. Most politicians who write succumb to the temptation to telescope events into conformity with their present interests and so distort or improve the path.

This curious sense of being an inside observer rather than a participator never really left him. Coupled with the fact that he had felt he was living on borrowed time ever since he nearly died on the way home from Algiers in 1944, from a dangerous burst ulcer, he was more detached than most of his Cabinet colleagues. As early as the summer of June 1965, he told me he would regard it as a bonus if Harold Wilson kept him on after the long recess: 'Well, you know I've had my nine months as a minister, which is almost long enough for my purposes.' Since, as he candidly and disarmingly admitted, there was a touch of affectation in the remark and he did want to stay on, I thought he was indiscreet in airing this view to colleagues. But I genuinely believe that Crossman thought that he had reached the top and was having his chance, and that at first he did not expect to be a Minister for very long. Beyond question, the bulk of the Parliamentary Labour Party did not anticipate 'Dick staying the course'. Indeed, had there been a sweepstake on the first Cabinet minister to quit the government on some pretext or another, Crossman would have been the clear favourite. My colleagues would rib me with the joke: whose PPS are you going to be when Crossman departs in smoke?

In August 1965, Crossman told me on the phone that the novelist and journalist Hugh Massingham, on behalf of the *Sunday Telegraph*, had asked him to lunch at the Savoy, and made a cash offer for extracts from the *Diary* as soon as the Labour Government collapsed. Crossman said that he was not writing for sale in that way, and he certainly would not want to write the kind of article for which Massingham and the *Sunday Telegraph* would want to pay a great deal of money.

The diary was, at that time, possibly the basis for 'a serious book on the inside view of politics', but was more likely, Crossman hoped, to be published in the raw state, provided he remained in office long enough. He made it clear to Massingham that in no way was it 'designed as a sensational effort to cash in on topicality'.

It was a relaxation of tension to know that the moment Harold Wilson said that his life at the ministry had to end, there was an alternative life ready in Oxfordshire. He had the strength that comes to a politician who knows that all the eggs of his life are not in the political basket. (If all my own eggs had been in the political basket, I fear I might not have campaigned so relentlessly myself, risking the fury of my party colleagues on certain issues.)

A year later, in July 1966, Crossman told me that Anne would like him to retire and prolong his life, and that he had enough on tape to write the kind of book he wanted. By November of that year, his literary agent, Helga Greene, former wife of Sir Hugh Carleton Greene of the BBC, was completing a contract with the publisher Hamish Hamilton and the *Sunday Times*. He reckoned he had three to four years' work after he had left the Cabinet, and retired from politics. He also realized that his ability to write a major book and his blissfully happy home life with Anne gave him the strength of detachment.

In the spring of 1967, Kathleen and I stayed at Prescote for the third weekend in February. We told Crossman that we wondered if the Diary was not becoming an addiction. To our surprise, he admitted it. We also mentioned Churchill's view that keeping a diary was dangerous for a minister since it could become an end in itself, causing unwise action. He concurred – it was a danger. That weekend I also realized the extent to which wounding statements were going into the tapes. When I queried this, Crossman quietly retorted that diaries were no good unless they were candid – to which there is no convincing reply.

Equally, if Crossman puts in print that a Senior Permanent Secretary is incredibly obtuse, has no ability in handling politicians, and has been a complete flop; or, that a distinguished press peer, created by the Labour Government, is a 'complacent sod', no one should be surprised if they hit back during posthumous reassessments of Crossman. Had Crossman lived, writs would have been flying in all directions after publication. Not that the harsh things he said at the time pretend to be considered judgements.

The row over the publication of the *Diaries* took place after Crossman was dead, and has been well covered in an excellent book, *The Crossman Affair* by Hugo Young. However, I quote without comment two laconic conversations which might have given Crossman a foretaste of the difficulties which sadly he did not live to see developing.

In April 1967, Crossman was to give the annual Granada lecture on the media, which commanded a fee of £750. Crossman, unable as a Cabinet Minister to accept this himself, wanted to give the money to an amateur mill-repairing organization in Warwickshire, near his constituency. The Cabinet Secretary, Sir Burke Trend, when asked about the propriety of such payment, pretended to know little about it.

Crossman: What are the precedents?
Trend: There are no precedents, because no Tory was silly enough to ask us.
Crossman: Well, I'm the kind of person who would ask, because I don't like hypocrisy.
Trend: I know. I think that's just what you are – the kind of person who asks that kind of question.

After he had retired and become Rector of Lincoln College, Oxford, I asked Lord Trend about his assessment of Crossman. He was, rather to my surprise, exceedingly warm in his praise, using the word 'honourable' about his conduct, and 'pertinent' about his contributions. Above all, he singled out 'good judgement', which was the last thing Crossman's popular image would have suggested.

In September 1967, there was a Cabinet wrangle over the publication of memoirs.

Wilson: Can't we agree that the Leader of the Party should informally read all manuscripts written by members of his ex-Cabinet before publication?
Voices: Harold, would you have permitted Hugh Gaitskell to vet your own autobiography?

And, why if the diaries were the *raison d'être* of being in the Cabinet, did Crossman not give up as soon as he thought he had enough material? I believe there were three reasons which combined to keep him going to 1970. First he wanted more and different material from different ministries. Secondly, he did not want to end up as Leader of the House, and desperately wanted to introduce his pension plan. But, thirdly and most potent of all, he recollected those two men, pining at Churt for the game that had brought them together, thesis and antithesis, David Lloyd George and H. A. L. Fisher.

Epilogue

The greatest disservice I rendered Crossman, apart possibly from being in Indonesia in May 1969, when the teeth-and-specs calamity befell him, was my acquiescent demeanour in the spring and summer of 1970 about his going to the *New Statesman*. My gut instinct was that it was a terrible mistake to go to a job that he had longed to get some fifteen years before. Times had changed. The staff had changed. The circulation had dropped. The influence of the *New Statesman* on the Left had plummeted. And Crossman had his books to write, which were surely more important than ephemeral journalism. On the other hand, he was determined to accept the invitation from Jock Campbell, the chairman of the *New Statesman*. And I thought I knew him so well by that time that there was, on this issue, no point in arguing.

Why did he insist? It was not money. It was not vanity. It was not even that he dreaded, as many prominent politicians do, being a 'has-been'. It was partly that he genuinely supposed he could revamp the *New Statesman*, and make it once again a paper of influence. It was partly that, having been denied the opportunity so long, he wanted the experience of actually managing and running an organization. It was partly that, though he was forever telling his close friends that he was living on borrowed time, he was in fact counting on another ten years, leaving him seven to do his book writing while fully *compos mentis*. But in my opinion there was one reason above all others why Crossman arranged to go to the *New Statesman*: to cock a snook at the shade of the late editor, Kingsley Martin. It was the only way of exorcising the

243

bitter memories of being denied by Kingsley what he believed was his journalistic birthright, having worked for him as assistant editor from 1938 to 1955.

Crossman, on taking the editor's chair, suggested to me that I should transfer my *New Scientist* weekly column, then three years old, to the *New Statesman*. I flatly refusd on the grounds that I was incapable of doing a *New Statesman* snide-type column, but was at ease on home ground in *New Scientist*. I don't think Crossman thought for a moment that I would make a *New Statesman* columnist; I think he just wanted friends around him in the office.

I look forward to reading what his assistant and successor, Anthony Howard, has to say about Crossman's period at the *New Statesman*; he was in the office in the same way I was with Crossman for six years in his minister's offices. I can only comment that Crossman dragged me along to Great Turnstile, the *New Statesman* office, on three or four occasions. I sensed hostility to him from the journalists and most of the staff. I wasn't surprised. To all intents and purposes, he was an outsider, imposed on them from on high. He seemed to me to be moody, bossy, and generally the ex-minister at his worst. He was very hurt when I told him that he was treating the journalists as if they were junior civil servants. He retorted that since I had been so little in Great Turnstile, I was not in a position to make any such judgement. For my part, I never set foot over the *New Statesman* doorstep again during the time he was editor.

I had the impression that most of the staff and journalists were being rotten to the long-serving old boy, and this had the effect of bringing out his abominable, bullying worst. I just wanted no part of the whole sultry scene. But Tony Howard may have a different perspective. He was there, and I wasn't.

Though I continued to stay in Vincent Square and personal relations with Crossman and Anne Crossman continued to be excellent, the *New Statesman* was tacitly a non-subject. I think he knew he'd made a mistake ever going near Great Turnstile. Confusion followed upon confusion. Crossman felt it demeaning. He revealed all to me in one throwaway comment, just before Christmas 1970, 'Kingsley is having the last laugh now!'

Where Crossman was back in his element was as a twice-weekly *Times* columnist. He used it partly to further the causes which arose out of unfinished business at the Department of Health and Social

Security. I quote a section from Crossman's contribution on the plight of one-parent families

> But disablement is not the only gap in our 'cradle to grave' social security. In 1969 the Labour Government set up the Finer Committee to investigate the problems of one-parent families. Nearly four years later the report is still unpublished and the problems are getting steadily worse. The one that worries me most is that of the deserted mother. Usually she has to rely on alimony. If her husband behaves decently or alternatively if he can be traced by the court she gets the money and she can make do. If, as happens constantly, the husband disappears without trace, she is left without any means of support and is driven to ask for supplementary benefit on which she may have to live for years. Even if she does get the alimony for a month or two she is always under the constant anxiety that suddenly one week it will not be paid.
>
> Why should the deserted mother be denied what the widowed mother receives as of right? When we appointed the Finer Committee I assumed that it would make the obvious recommendation. In future the deserted mother would not have to depend on alimony but would draw the same benefit as the widow which she would receive as of right from the DHS (sic). Having taken responsibility for her maintenance the State would have the job of collecting the cash from the husband.
>
> Unfortunately the Finer Committee has dallied and nothing has been done ... The Secretary of State is a humane minister and I hope he will deal with this one outstanding anomaly while he is waiting for Finer. He has been given an ideal Parliamentary opportunity since the 10-minute rule Bill presented by Tam Dalyell got its first reading with the approval of the whole House of Commons last week. A private bill of this kind, whatever its merits, stands no chance unless the Secretary of State gets it into Committee and persuades his colleagues to give it some government time. Sir Keith won a great deal of good will when he first took office by repairing an omission of mind. He gave pensions to the over eighties as of right without waiting for his major Social Security Bill. He could maintain his reputation by doing the same for the deserted.
>
> ('Personal view', *The Times*, Wednesday, 20 December 1972)

Let the last word rest with a lifelong sparring partner of Crossman's, John Boyd Carpenter (for whom I campaigned as Speaker of the House of Commons when Selwyn Lloyd was elected).

Boyd Carpenter had known Crossman as a young don at Oxford,

when he was an undergraduate. Crossman was the Labour speaker when Boyd Carpenter made his first broadcast on the BBC. Crossman shadowed Boyd Carpenter from 1957 to 1959 when he was Macmillan's Minister of Pensions and National Insurance, and the role was reversed when Crossman was Minister of Housing and Local Government. Boyd Carpenter writes:

'And Crossman had taste and courage. When he underwent a serious internal operation I wrote to him with good wishes, and expressed the hope that he would soon recover. He wrote back. "You know me, I always do things in a big way." This told me in the most tactful way and without self-pity that he was dying.'

Crossman had style.

Index